Arabian
Time Machine

Helga Graham

Arabian
Time Machine

Self-Portrait
of an Oil State

HM HOLMES & MEIER PUBLISHERS, INC.
IMPORT DIVISION
IUB Building
30 Irving Place, New York, N.Y. 10003

William Heinemann Ltd
15 Queen Street, Mayfair, London W1X 8BE

LONDON   MELBOURNE   TORONTO
JOHANNESBURG   AUCKLAND

First published 1978

© Helga Graham 1978

SBN 434 30350 x

Printed and bound in Great Britain by
Morrison & Gibb Ltd, London and Edinburgh

THIS BOOK IS *the result of the work of a small cottage industry and I should like to thank the workers: Mohammed Said who interpreted where necessary; Said, my driver; Heather Addison and Siham Sawan who provided vital assistance and back-up; my two translators James Budd and Abdullah al-Ud hari; and Nadia Hijab, just for being around.*

THIS BOOK IS *dedicated to a pretty, blonde, enterprising (and perceptive) English secretary who took off from England to work abroad and see the world. After a number of years in South Africa, she decided it was time to move on; she contemplated living in the Gulf. Despite dire warning of the barbaric habits of Arabs, she bravely decided to take the risk and went to work there. After some time, she concluded that the people were hospitable, considerate, humorous and intelligent. 'They don't,' she said, 'seem like Arabs at all. They seem quite normal.'*

Contents

Illustrations

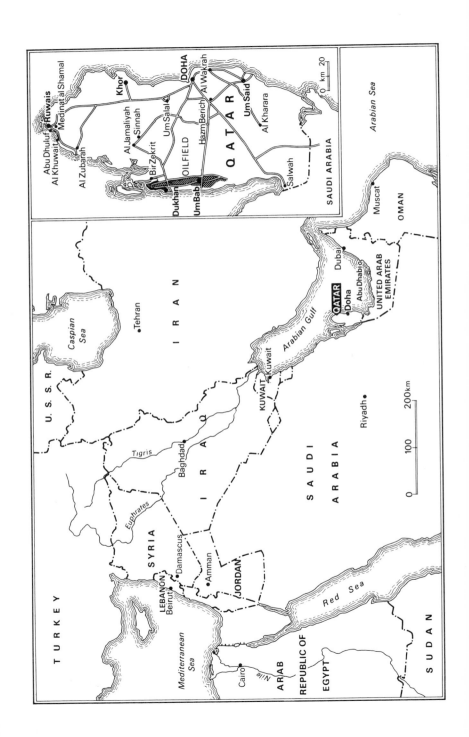

Introduction

The Challenge

Nowhere in the world are conditions more challenging to the survival of life in any form than in Arabia and the Gulf: it would seem as if God were using this desert to test the powers of endurance of the creatures he created.

The summer climate is among the worst to be found anywhere. For many months of the year the temperature is over 100 degrees fahrenheit (37 centigrade). But heat can be borne; humidity is worse. In the summer the level of humidity rises sometimes to 90 degrees and remains high even during the reasonably mild winter months. The Gulf, in mid-summer, is like a sauna. Stepping out of an air-conditioned room into the heat and humidity has the same impact, dizzying and slightly sickening, as an unexpected blow on the head. Further away from the Gulf, in the interior of the Peninsula, the humidity lessens; on the other hand, the desert in winter can be bitterly cold and the temperature below freezing point. Rainfall is scant anywhere and at any time: it is around 75 mm per year generally. Hence the desert. The deserts of Arabia cover more than a million square miles, and nearly half of that area is covered by the great southern desert, so vast, trackless and arid that even the Arabs call it the Empty Quarter. Parts of it are unforgettably beautiful: the endless mass of the dunes, monumental and ever moving, like some very slow⁄

motion film of the sea. The colours are the more remarkable for being unexpected: brick red, russet, peach and pure gold, running into each other anarchically like dodgem cars at a funfair. The Empty Quarter is the back-garden, so to speak, of the lower Gulf. Dunes stray like outposts over the Saudi Arabian border into some of the Gulf States including Qatar, but most of the desert in this coastal area is altogether duller and flatter and dustier. It is generally earth-coloured and made up of salt flats, cobble conglomerate and limestone plateaux.

Through this desolate peninsula nomadic tribes known collectively as bedu (or desert people) have roamed since the earliest times in search of the sparse grasslands, or vegetation in any form, to feed their camels, sheep and goats; their lives a pawn to passing showers and infrequent water-holes. They depended mainly on milk and dates to stay alive; meat was a rare luxury. They lived in goat or camel hair tents, enduring the cold of the winter and the heat of the summer with equally little protection. The only way out of the particular 'poverty trap' they were caught in, to use the terms of modern sociological jargon, was to raid and loot other tribes or else to exact a levy on passing camel trains of traders. Niebuhr, an eighteenth-century traveller who had great affection for the bedu but was unusually unsentimental about them, admitted that the accusation of robbery 'was not altogether unfounded'. Raiding was the only way in the anarchic desert to redistribute the cake, or more aptly, the crumbs. Sometimes it was simply the only way to survive.

On the eastern sea-board of the peninsula there were few trading caravans passing through, so here the bedu turned their raiding attention to the sea. Throughout the nineteenth century the eastern coast of the Gulf was known as the Pirate Coast and greatly dreaded. The British, ever anxious to safeguard their trade routes to India, did their best to stamp out the piracy but it continued spasmodically into the early years of the twentieth century. Some-times the bedu ventured quite far afield on their raiding expedi-tions and returned with slaves from Africa or Oman. Slavery, albeit on a more limited scale and in a seemingly milder, more paternalistic form than elsewhere, was ended in the Arabian Peninsula only after the Second World War.

On the shores of the Gulf the bedu sometimes led a settled, or semi-settled, existence as fishermen or pearl-divers. This was the case in Qatar, in particular, which was surrounded by rich pearl banks, though the existence as fishermen or pearl-divers was quite as precarious and virtually as poor as the life of the bedu. But though a few of the bigger pearl traders made a better living, pearling gradually died out from the nineteen thirties, when Japanese cultured pearls began to kill the trade in natural pearls. Like the Great Depression in Europe, this was a terrible time in the Gulf. During the Second World War, when rice supplies were sometimes cut off, people died of starvation.

The life of the bedu, then, was harsh and it was uncertain, but it was not uncivilised. As if to compensate for the inhumanity of their surroundings the bedu have traditionally aspired to some of the highest human values. They admired some of the more obvious qualities that enable human beings to survive in the desert, such as bravery, endurance, prudence and solidarity. But they also prized others that are less than essential to survival: hospitality, generosity, forgiveness, justice and equality. The hospitality of the desert Arab is legendary. Yet when a very poor man killed his last animal to feed a guest who might be a total stranger—which he was bound to do according to the strict code of the desert—he might well be endangering his own livelihood and survival. One of the last of European travellers in the desert, Wilfred Thesiger, relates a story in one of his travel books which neatly illustrates the vital importance of hospitality in the desert: 'I glanced back and was relieved to see that it was only a small boy, hurrying along to catch up with us. We waited for him. He was dressed in a white shirt and head-cloth, and wore a dagger; he was little more than four feet high and perhaps eleven years old. After we had formally exchanged the news, he stopped in front of our camels, held out an arm and said, "You may not go on." I thought, "Damn, are we really to be stopped by this child?" The others waited in silence. The boy repeated, "You may not go on"; and then, pointing to some dunes five or six miles away, added, "You must come to my tents. I will kill a camel for your lunch. I will give you fat and meat." We protested, saying that we had far to go before sunset, but the child insisted. Finally, however, he gave way, saying "It is all wrong but what more can I do?" '

It may well be that bedu hospitality and generosity are in equal part legend and legendary. Certainly English and American puritans were rarely as thrifty, hard-working and God-fearing as they liked to think or wanted others to believe. Equally, the bedu were probably not always as generous, brave and enduring as they might have wished to be. As illiterate men, they were also in some ways narrow-minded and bigoted. But the dominant values of a society, even when not always observed, tell a great deal about it. And from this point of view the bedu society of the desert which is fast disappearing was in many respects a remarkable triumph of spirit over matter.

Because of their desert environment, the social creativity of the bedu, which was considerable, was never institutionalised. The spirit of democracy might exist in the desert (if the other person did not come from a tribe you very greatly disliked); the form of democracy inevitably did not. Equally, the aesthetic inventiveness of the bedu found its outlet not in objects, but in words. There were not many pots in a bedu encampment or village, but never any shortage of poets. The arts of poetry and story-telling were highly prized in the desert and the poet had a prestigious position in society. Even a great warrior like the founder of the State of Qatar, Sheikh Jassim, could add im-measurably to his prestige by turning his hand to poetry; he wrote a moving elegy to his wife Nura. Today the bedu, or those who hold with bedu values even if they no longer live a bedu way of life, are adapting with great alacrity to the modern world and addressing their poems to the Chevrolet and the MIG rather than the camel. In sum, life in the desert may have been poor, but primitive it was not.

Still, it is not easy to assess what, in the final analysis, bedu life was really like, or how it was seen by those who experienced it. Virtually all we know of it has been passed on by Western travellers whose baggage, unlike that of the bedu, was very heavy, especially in cultural prejudice. As it happens, Western prejudices were usually favourable rather than the opposite as far as the bedu are concerned, but this does not unfortunately make their writing much more helpful in achieving any real understanding of the people. For it was often heavily romanticised. And a romantic gloss is no more helpful than any other kind of gloss.

Arabs, in general, were bad news in Europe from very early on. For one thing the Arabs almost conquered Western Europe, and for another Christian writers heavily distorted the teachings of Islam. Muslims were people who ate live babies etc. When Europeans actually came to visit the Arab world, many of them very quickly warmed to the bedu, and one can very well see why. The combination of 'nobility', extreme poverty and the desert holds obvious attraction to the romantic mind. So while the urban Arab, under the corrupt rule of the Turks, remained pigeon-holed in the 'baddy' compartment, a special niche was found for the bedu under the heading of 'noble savage', it being understood that the bedu was noble because he was poor. As soon as he was no longer poor he was also no longer noble. But this is to anticipate history.

Another category of person who was naturally drawn to the desert were neurotics, masochistic characters like T. E. Lawrence. One feels that Arabia, for them, was one vast public school playing-field without the grass or the half-term or the showers when the game was over, the ideal outlet for their neurotic need to test their powers of endurance to the limit.

Yet for the bedu enduring was not a masochistic exercise, a spiritual luxury or indulgence, however one chooses to see it. Enduring was simply the only alternative to going under. There was nothing romantic about it. This was once pointed out quite forcibly to Thesiger by some bedu who accompanied him on his travels through the Empty Quarter. They were either arguing, for the fourth day running, over the price someone's grandfather had paid for a headdress twenty years previously, or meditating on the possibility of discovering hidden treasure—anyway talking about money, and passing the long hours of forced march in the desert. Finally, this began to prey on Thesiger's nerves and he scolded them for their money-mindedness. To which they answered, quite justifiably, that it was all very well for him since he had plenty; but for them a very few *riyals* meant the difference between starving and not starving. They might have added that while he could—and did—leave the desert, they could not.

Thesiger was unquestionably attached to the bedu, and he knew them well. But it is difficult to avoid the conclusion that he, like many other Westerners, was guilty of over-romanticism. While the bedu may well have possessed remarkable human qualities, he was also a ragged, half-starved, illiterate human being. Their assumption that the bedu character they admired was entirely the product of desert life led the romantics both to cover up the unpleasant sides of his life and to conclude that prosperity would doom the people. This may or may not turn out to be the case. But one feels that such dogmatic judgements from people with well-padded pocket books and full bellies who were free to return to hot baths and prosperity when they chose to do so, are a little insensitive. They seem never to have asked themselves whether there might not be a case for the bedu to trade in some of the noble qualities of endurance and bravery against a little of the material prosperity they took for granted, or to have asked the bedu what they would themselves choose.

In the event, when prosperity did finally come the bedu, understandably enough, were not in the least disposed to think of themselves as doomed by it. God, so to speak, relented and, as the old people in Qatar solemnly express it, He opened the gates of prosperity. Or, to put it more prosaically, oil was discovered; it was discovered, moreover, in the poorest, most backward and least populated of the Arab States. The general impression conveyed by the citizens thereof—the older people who are more disposed to meditate on such things—is that the oil is no more than their due, a very timely compensation for the harshness of the lives they had led hitherto, Praise be to Allah.

For Westerners, oil is obviously not the rich source of philo sophy, religion and poetry it is for the Gulf Arabs. They see no poetry in the black gold of the desert, as the bedu call it, and they certainly discern no hint of God's grace in its location. All of which is understandable, but not very imaginative.

For several thousand years life in the desert continued at the same even rhythm, until suddenly in the 1930s oil was discovered in the Gulf, first in Bahrain and then in Saudi Arabia. Saudi Arabia began to receive some small income from the oil before the Second World War, but, except for Bahrain, small Gulf States only began to benefit very recently, within the past couple of decades or so. What this oil money has meant to the peoples of the Gulf is not hard to put into words, but very difficult to convey through words. In practice, oil means cold water in the summer and air conditioners; warm clothes in the winter. It means having enough to eat rather than starving. It means hos pitals where there was disease and knowledge where there was ignorance. It means the traffic roundabout with the rosebush, unfailingly present in every Gulf Government publication—and no doubt equally unfailingly ignored by the Westerner in earnest quest of the picture of the camel. People who have lived with roundabouts all their lives cannot possibly be expected to know that a roundabout means that there are roads and roads mean there are cars and cars mean that instead of three days enforced march on camel back without shade, one can drive to see one's relations in a couple of hours. If the rosebush stands for anything, it stands for the capacity to achieve, to explore beyond the narrow limits of mere survival. This feeling is expressed by the Qatari girl who said—speaking of the rather fine old restored palace which is now the museum in Doha—'I didn't know we could produce something as good as that.'

To understand the real impact of oil in Arabia requires not simply a grand totalling of all the air conditioners, roundabouts, and roses, but a leap of the imagination. While material things count for much, they don't count for everything. What people in the Gulf feel has happened to them is best expressed by the metaphor used by the old people, of the gates opening. They feel that they have been somehow let in after being locked out—a sense of release. Of course prosperity breeds its own problems, as people in the Gulf have already discovered. But among the old, there are few if any who would be prepared to go back. Certainly they raise their hats to the greater human qualities people had in the past, but they feel mainly relief to be living in the present.

However, this is not a modern fairy tale where everybody lives happily ever after. In this particular story the coach turns into a pumpkin, not exactly at midnight, but certainly sooner or later. In other words, oil is a wasting and limited resource which will one day run out. When is not quite clear and varies from country to country. In Qatar the present limit for oil seems to be some-where around the year 2000. After that there will still be gas. But here again resources are not unlimited and the yield from them is smaller. The area has no other resources.

It is as if the people of the Gulf have been let into a kind of Garden of Eden. Only, unlike Adam and Eve, they have no real choice in the matter of staying or leaving. Expulsion being certain, the only choice the Gulf people have is whether simply to enjoy themselves while they can or whether to work at preparing the wilderness for their return. Practically speaking, they can either return to a bedu way of life or else use the present oil money to develop economically and socially and create an economic framework for the future without oil.

But development is never a simple process. The business of creating schools and hospitals and roads and ports and airfields and making them work is a highly complex operation even today in the industrial West which has had several hundred years to master the techniques and adapt to the values of a totally new system. In the countries of the Gulf, development is even further complicated by two factors. One is the scale of their wealth; the Gulf States came into a great deal of money very quickly, within just a decade or two. This means that however hard the authorities struggle to keep the development process under control, it will inevitably proceed at a very rapid pace indeed. It is simply not realistic to expect anyone with a very fast sports car to run it at forty miles per hour as if it were a family saloon, even if this is the fastest speed warranted by the state of the roads. In other words, people need time to adjust mentally to a vastly different social and economic system compared with the one they were used to, but the imperatives of the situation are such that they are having and will have very little time indeed.

The second complicating factor, paradoxically, is the relatively small indigenous population of the area. The whole Arabian Peninsula has probably no more than twelve million people and over half of these live in countries like the Yemen, without oil. Given time it is possible to create the educated elite and the skilled manpower to run hospitals, schools, ports and airports that had to be run originally by foreigners—Westerners or other Arabs. To a large extent this is already happening. Foreigners are moved either out or sideways as local people come back from universities and technical colleges abroad to take over their own countries. But foreigners will still be needed to work in the labouring jobs in the manufacturing and other industries being created in the area by Governments that are only too well aware that they cannot, in the long run, rely on oil-based industries. Foreign labour is there to stay.

Development, then, is no soft option. It means the influx of many foreigners into tightly-knit traditional communities—one of the most difficult problems for any human society to face, as the phenomenon of foreign workers in Europe amply illustrates. It means drastic changes in and challenges to present values if only as a result of the extraordinary pace of change. So is development really the only alternative to going backwards? The people of the Gulf, helpful outsiders have suggested, could very well live happily ever after on the interest from foreign investment of their oil income and, as a further refinement of the argument, live anywhere in the world they choose. They could all even move to a deserted Pacific island—or even buy one—so that nobody need live in the unhealthy and unpleasant climate of the Gulf.

The fact that these are not serious options underlines some of the dilemmas of the area. The notion of a collective move need hardly be dwelt on: it is not realistic. All human beings, however irrationally, are attached to their land, the present author no less to her soggy Scottish peatbogs than the Gulf Arabs to their impossible desert. As for the other notion—living off oil money without undergoing the traumas of rapid development—this has two snags. Unfortunately, they are major ones. In the first place, this would make the Gulf Arabs totally dependent on outsiders, whether other Arabs or Westerners, who would be running the schools and hospitals that would have to be created anyway. Historically, this has meant one thing: the eventual supremacy of those who run everything. It has happened before in Arab history, as when the Seljuks began to dominate their Arab master in Iraq in the eleventh century. Secondly, by just living off their wealth, the Gulf Arabs would all too easily lose their rights to it. They are very small States surrounded by greedy neighbours who would welcome an excuse to plunder their wealth. So development in Arabia and the Gulf is really inevitable as well as inevitably fast and problematic.

It is not the purpose here to argue that the so-called oil rich Arabs of the Gulf and Arabia are burdened by their wealth or weighed down by social and moral dilemmas. Money is a useful commodity. It enables people, Arabs among others, to enjoy some of the best things in life and this is precisely what they are doing. So far as the social dilemmas are concerned, most people in the Gulf are normal, moderately short-sighted human beings who just get on with the business of living without spending too much time on analysis, and are not over-concerned about the distant future so long as their own and their children's future is guaranteed. Some are more altruistic, others less, as in the West.

Figures produced by Dr Hassan Abbas Zaki, who is head of the Abu Dhabi Development Fund, help to put oil wealth in some perspective. He points out that the oil revenue of the United Arab Emirates in 1974 was less than the amount Americans spent in the same year on salad dressing, cooking oil, and similar products. The oil revenues of all the Gulf countries together were less than the amount Americans spent on pet food and outdoor recreation goods, and the oil revenues of *all* Arab oil-producing countries was less than the combined sales of the Ford Motor Company and General Motors.

The purpose here is really to try to introduce a measure of balance in the picture Westerners have of the Gulf Arabs and their countries, a picture that is heavily lop-sided. The whole weight of the western media comes down squarely on the Arabs' money to the exclusion of all other considerations. The picture sways wildly to one side, weighed down by a pot-bellied Arab worth his weight in gold. All other facts about him—that he might have children, a country, values, interests, a profession or skill, are ignored. The ironical thing is that this caricatural post-oil bedu is the exact reverse of the romantic pre-oil bedu. The noble bedu of former times, of not so very long ago, was as totally unmaterialistic, supposedly, as the present day Arab is exclusively materialistic. The pendulum has swung with a vengeance.

To see the present day Gulf Arab into perspective it is necessary to understand that behind this Arab world of newspaper headlines with its flavour of exotic wealth, there is another Arab world the West knows very little about, as Robert Stephens writes in *The Arabs' New Frontier*. It is the bread-and-butter, everyday world where people have to earn their living, the world of farmers, factory workers, business men, civil servants, engineers, where tractors and trucks have long been replacing camels, where giant dams and diesel pumps are taking over from water wheels, where more and more villages rely on power stations instead of kerosene lamps, where thousands of students go to modern universities instead of Koranic schools, where more and more girls work computers and run clinics instead of staying behind veils and shutters at home.

It is this aspect that makes the Arab oil States interesting, not simply their wealth. Many peoples in history have made and spent money. But no other people have been propelled, as if in a time machine, through so many hundred years of history so rapidly.

It is a unique human experience which, in all fairness, deserves to be acknowledged as such. Individuals have moved from fairly simple tribal or agrarian communities into the highly complex modern industrial society we now live in. But never a whole society. The people of Arabia have had, on average, between ten and twenty years to adapt to a form of society whose structures have evolved in the West over nearly a thousand years from the feudal, pre-scientific society of the middle ages. These are people who have already met the challenge of adapting to some of the harshest conditions in the world; whether they can now meet the challenge of adapting to the twenty-first century, while skipping about nine centuries in between, remains to be seen. Certainly, the small size of the populations involved lessens the scale of the adventure—but it is still an adventure for all that.

City State

Qatar is one of the oil States of the Gulf (traditionally known as the Persian Gulf in Iran and the West but by the Arabs as the Arabian Gulf) and like most of the other Gulf oil States it is small in size and population. It is a peninsula which projects, like a splayed thumb, due north from the Arabian shore into the Gulf for a hundred miles; at its widest point is measures about fifty miles and it covers approximately 4,000 square miles. Qatar's landward frontiers are with Saudi Arabia and Abu Dhabi. Saudi Arabia is the largest State in the Arabian Peninsula with its million square miles of deserts. Qatar's nearest seaward neighbour, twenty miles away across the Gulf, is the island State of Bahrain; beyond Bahrain, on the other side of the Gulf, lies Iran.

In 1949 when oil exports from Qatar began, the local population consisted of nomadic tribesmen, pearl divers, fishermen and a few traders—in all no more than 20,000 souls. Nowadays the total population is moving upwards towards the 200,000 mark, of which perhaps 50,000 are Qataris. Most of the population lives in Doha, the capital.

Qatar officially became an independent State on September 3 1971. Two days later the treaty arrangements that gave Britain special powers over Qatar's foreign and defence affairs were abrogated. So ended a very long relationship derived originally from Britain's nineteenth-century preoccupation to safeguard the sea-route to and from India. It was on account of her Indian empire that Britain in the nineteenth century moved into the Gulf where her main interests were to contain Ottoman influence and curb local piracy. But Bahrain, not Qatar, was the real centre of British operations, and Britain's treaty with Qatar dates only from 1916.

The States on the Arabian coast of the Gulf (including Saudi Arabia) share a common religion, language and culture, but there are regional differences between them as between one English county and another. A Yorkshireman feels different to someone who comes from the south coast and a Qatari feels distinguished from a Kuwaiti or Saudi or Bahraini. Bahrain has the longest experience of modern social and educational development of any of the Arab Gulf States, largely because oil was discovered there in 1932, earlier than elsewhere on the Arabian side of the Gulf. But Bahrain never had much oil and today is able to export very little. It is a relatively poor State though much better off since the 1973 oil price rises, and even receives aid from its oil-rich neighbours, a kind of blue-stockinged Cinderella of the Gulf. Saudi Arabia, on the other hand, is everybody's big brother. Like the elder brother in an Arab family, Saudi Arabia feels overall responsibility for all the other members. As the largest State of the Arabian Peninsula, it offers a military umbrella to all the others, though some, like Kuwait and Abu Dhabi, also have umbrellas of their own. Moreover, the holy places of Islam, Mecca and Medina, are in Saudi Arabia and this further reinforces her influence although it also means that her own social development proceeds at a more conservative pace. As Saudi Arabia began to benefit from oil money, many Qataris emigrated there or else to

Bahrain, when the pearl trade was dying and there was hunger in many parts of the Gulf. Kuwait began to develop with its oil money in the 1950s, later than Bahrain or Saudi Arabia, but before that it had been a small but important port. Kuwaitis are now the sophisticates of the Gulf, the big city relatives so to speak of their Qatari country cousins. Dubai, now a leading member of the United Arab Emirates, was a busy port, a relatively prosperous centre before oil was found there in the late 1960s. Abu Dhabi, now the biggest and richest member of the UAE, was, like Doha, never an important port; as in Doha the local community was until fairly recently small and isolated. But as soon as the country had a secure income from oil, from 1970 on, Abu Dhabi began to develop very rapidly indeed.

Qatar's first oil exports left the country in 1949. But both development and real oil wealth were slow in coming. The former Emir was conservative and it took time fully to exploit the country's resources. The construction boom began in the mid-sixties, but development took off seriously only after the present Emir took power in 1972. A lot of people have become really rich, as distinct from comfortably wealthy, within the past three or four years.

In the 'league' of Gulf oil States, Qatar rates as one of the late developers and so is relatively less advanced socially, economically and politically than some of the others, for example, Kuwait or Bahrain. But their own more controlled pace of growth, as they see it, is a source of pride to Qataris rather than the reverse. *We* don't, they often insinuate and sometimes say, rush headlong at modernisation the way some people do. . . ! This caution seems to result from three different influences. First is the equable temperament of the people. Second is Wahabism, a strict puritan and fundamentalist form of Islam which demands exact obedience to the maxims of the Koran and considers such obedience as sufficient guide for the moral conduct of both the individual and society. Wahabism has been powerful in the Nejd region of central Arabia from the eighteenth century, but it spread to Qatar in a less austere form: for example, cinemas are permitted in

Qatar but not in Saudi Arabia. Finally, the personal impact of the present Emir is very important.

Qatar is ruled—and very actively ruled—by the Emir, Sheikh Khalifa bin Hamad al-Thani, who came to power after a bloodless coup in 1972. He had previously been Prime Minister under the old Emir, his cousin, who was a religious conservative. Unlike his cousin, Sheikh Khalifa is a moderniser and an able administrator; by temperament, he is a man who likes to take the steering wheel himself and who drives with his hand on the gears. The Hollywood image of the oriental despot lolling idly on silken cushions which colours Western ideas of Gulf rulers could hardly be more inappropriate—besides being geographically misplaced. Much nearer the truth would be the Hollywood image of the big business tycoon to whom work is an all-consuming occupation, who maintains close and constant control over his affairs (in this case Qatar's), to whom time is money and every minute precious, who rarely takes time off to enjoy his private life.

Even on the historical count, the oriental despot notion is very wide of the mark. Traditionally, the Sheikh, as the Emir used to be called in the old days, was not a hereditary leader but one emerging from and depending on a consensus. Arab tribal leaders held the same position *vis-à-vis* the elders of the tribe as the British Prime Minister is supposed, theoretically, to have within the Cabinet; they were no more than *primus inter pares*. Since the end of the last century when Sheikh Jassim turned Qatar into a single entity, the very numerous al-Thani family have ruled the country. But even then tradition prevailed and the most able rather than the first-born was chosen by the family as ruler. Today, the still small number of educated people, and the need for rapid decisions entailed by economic development and the vastly increased amount of wealth controlled by the ruling family, has put much more power on the hands of rulers like Sheikh Khalifa. But he would never think of riding rough-shod over the tribal loyalties and rivalries which still exist. And the older people, while they admire and respect him, call him Khalifa without any further ado and are not afraid to tell him exactly what they think.

Constitutionally, Qatar is in a transitional phase. The old *majlis* where any citizen could come and present his or her grievances and complaints to the Ruler still exists; it takes place early every morning. At the same time, there is an Advisory Council which remains a consultative rather than a representative body.

The social changes which have modified the position of the Emir have also affected the extended al-Thani family (there are at least a couple of thousand members of the family). Nowadays they are all called sheikhs, while in the past only the Ruler was so called. In the old days, they found whatever work they could, like everybody else. It was only with the discovery of oil that they became a class apart. It was only then that they began to receive a guaranteed State income like European royal families. At the beginning of Qatar's development most of the money was in their hands. But now the big trading families, which have emerged within the past ten years or so, have as much and usually a great deal more money than the sheikhs. The average Qatari sheikh receives about £2000 a month which makes him comfortably off but not, in today's terms, really rich. To become really rich a sheikh has to work like everybody else. Most of the ministers still come from the al-Thani family. But power is bound to become more evenly distributed in the future. At the beginning of Kuwait's development, all the ministers there came from the ruling al-Sabah family; now only a few do (though they hold most of the key posts). It is a question of time.

Qatar's oil wealth is spent, as in every other Gulf country, on massive economic development programmes and on the social services. Little, sensibly enough, is devoted to military expenditure. A sizeable percentage is reserved for aid to developing countries, mainly but not exclusively Arab countries. In recent years Qatar has spent between 11 and 20 per cent of her GNP annually on foreign aid.

During the first stage of the country's development, the accent was inevitably on creating an infrastructure: roads, hospitals, schools, ports. Now the emphasis is on industrial projects. Economic diversification is the key concept behind the development programme; even primary school children know what it means. Broadly, it means, of course, that countries like Qatar must lay an economic foundation which will not depend entirely on oil exports. Qatar plans to provide 30 to 40 per cent of its GNP from sources other than oil sales within the next five to ten years.

This production is expected to come largely from industrial projects on which Qatar may spend $1.5 billion before 1980. These projects include petrochemical and expanded fertiliser plants, a gas liquefication plant, and a steel complex using local gas. Most of this industrial activity is confined to Umm Said, a growing industrial town twenty-five miles south of Doha. The city itself will be centred on the port and behind it will be the heavy industrial area, the steel plant, the fertiliser works and the accompanying housing. Beyond this heavy industrial core there will be an outer ring of light industry and more housing.

Qatar's social services are very extensive. A house is the birth-right of every Qatari. Senior officials and employees are given a large sum, part loan and part gift, to build their own houses. But the Government also builds houses which are given free to citizens with lower incomes. Both categories are given an extra allowance for furniture and receive free gas and electricity. Education is free and anyone with reasonable academic qualifica-tions can study either at home or abroad at the State's expense. The health service provides free treatment at home or if necessary abroad. This is why so many Qataris travel abroad for medical treatment, especially in June and July. The apparent sudden serious deterioration in so many people's health during the hot summer months doesn't fool the authorities, of course. It seems to be official policy to turn a blind eye to the extension of the activities of the Ministry of Health into the field of tourism, on the sensible grounds that if this is the only way some people can afford to travel, then they shouldn't be stopped, since travel is culturally beneficial and broadens the mind.

Some of these privileges, however, are reserved for Qatar nationals. Foreigners have access to the free primary and secondary education and to the health service, but they cannot own property and they obviously don't qualify for a free or subsidised Government house.

The foreigners working in Qatar may be divided into two broad categories. There are the labourers, small shopkeepers and the domestic and hotel servants: these are mainly Baluchis, Indians and Pakistanis. The foreigners in the middle and upper managerial and technical class are sometimes Western (often British) but predominantly northern Arabs: Palestinians, Egyptians, Jordanians. Mixing people with such different cultural backgrounds obviously creates problems. Foreigners don't always like it when they are displaced by a newly-trained Qatari, while the Qataris object when they are forced, as they occasionally are, to struggle to assert themselves in their own country against foreigners in entrenched positions of power. But, by and large, the system operates remarkably smoothly compared with the considerable social and political conflict created by the presence of foreign workers in Europe in recent years. There are some inevitable resentments, but so far there has been no actual friction. In the short term, the main reason for this harmony is simply that people earn much more in Qatar than they do in their own country and so are particularly anxious to avoid trouble. This is particularly true of the better qualified people who can often save more in a couple of years or so in Qatar than they can in a lifetime at home; the labourers are comparatively less well rewarded. But, in the long-term, the situation may become more complex because foreigners outnumber the Qataris, and the children of those who settle in Qatar will want more equal rights as citizens. Sometime in the future other Arabs may be given a special status in all the Gulf States. But to open up a community in this way is always an extremely delicate political operation. So time, plenty of time, will be needed to give the Qataris and other Gulf Arabs a chance to adjust.

Hardly Exotic

Doha, the capital of Qatar, is by no means the exotic Eastern city of Western imagination. It is no more exotic than an average Western semi-administrative, semi-market seaboard city with a population of around one hundred thousand. There are regular traffic jams between five and seven o'clock in the evening. The construction cranes outnumber the mosque towers in the ratio of at least four to one. The ocean-going freighters that wait to be unloaded in the congested port are electronically controlled and disgorge cars, steel and washing-powder. Most of the buildings are modern and international–Western in style and, like most modern urban architecture anywhere, some of it is nice and some of it is nasty.

As a city Doha is, in fact, a very recent creation. Most of it was built within the past ten years and almost all the rest had been constructed in the previous ten years. Before that Doha was a very small fishing village made up of mainly mud-brick houses which were cool and well suited to the climate but tended not to last for very long. If today Doha is not yet the bustling metropolis that the Qataris hope it will one day become, this is because all throttles have not been opened as elsewhere in the Gulf, this not being the Qatari way. But the pace of growth is still fairly brisk by any Western standards. One imagines that the ranch towns in the United States must have grown like this when the railways opened up the West Coast. Streets have sprung up so fast that half of them have not yet been named. Trying to locate a house in Doha is wellnigh impossible, like fitting together the pieces of a jigsaw puzzle which represents an unfinished picture.

All this is very trying for the foreign television crews who come in quest of 'Arab' local colour. Fortunately some refined instinct peculiar to television crews enables them to track down the camel market, the sheep market and the seasonal falcon market—all unknown to many people in Doha—and so to survive in modern urban Arabia.

Except in the extreme south, there have never been cities before in the Arabian desert. So many of the modern ones look a little out of place, lacking in self-confidence, as awkward as an uninvited guest at a party. This is hardly surprising when one considers that desert Arabs have generally been nomads, living in tents. Still, it is not true to say as one European traveller has that the desert produces much that is noble but nothing that is gracious. The desert—or rather its oases—can give rise to a distinctive style of architecture that is both attuned to the environment and also elegant. In the narrow, partly green Hadhramaut valley of South Yemen there are cities of grand seigneurial mansions made mainly of mud brick, finely decorated with massive wooden doors, trellised windows and jutting covered balconies. These houses tower above the highest palm trees and in the case of Shibam, an astounding mud Manhattan, challenge the very cliffs that enclose the *wadi* or valley. But then the extreme south of the Peninsula, especially the Yemen, has been known throughout history as *Arabia Felix*, fortunate for being relatively fertile, for being the source of the prosperous incense trade and close to some of the world's main sea-trading routes.

The Arabs of the Gulf never knew this kind of prosperity or settled ease. Most of them were nomads, living at subsistence level, forever on the move. Even the semi-settled pearl divers and traders seldom had sufficient surplus income to spend on embellishing their houses. In Qatar almost every plank of wood had to be imported. Stone was scarce. Sand, admittedly, has always been plentiful. But the psychological ease and aesthetic inventiveness that wealth permits were largely lacking, at least where material objects were concerned. The arts of story-telling and poetry, as already mentioned, were another matter. To this general rule there are a few exceptions. There are the vivid but harmoniously coloured rugs and saddle bags of the bedu which are still to be seen at the Doha museum, and a very few buildings, including the museum itself. Most of these houses are at al Wakrah, a ruined coastal village where the most prosperous citizens, the pearl traders, lived during the hey-day of the trade. Here, amid the rubble, there are the remains of some interesting decorative work: ornamental arches, wall recesses and geometric designs carved into the gypsum and plaster which covered the walls.

But Qatar's real showpiece is the museum. Once the palace of former al-Thani rulers, it was allowed to decay but has been sensitively restored, with the help of early photographs and the memories of older members of the family. The palace is in reality a collection of separate buildings included within a single com-pound; most were constructed around the turn of the century, except for the two-storey central *majlis* which was built only in 1918. This is how people then lived, in compounds which might include up to fifty or even sixty people. The structure is composed of much the same elements as al Wakrah, although the overall scale is much grander. The basic plan consists of one or two rooms at ground level, fronted by a verandah or porch. Those rooms are entered from the long side and are known as 'broad rooms'. One such room may be partitioned off by a screen which does not rise to the full height of the room, making a private alcove. An external staircase leads up to a balustraded roof which sometimes includes an upper-storey room. The walls are broken open by numerous windows, often set at ground level, and other devices for controlling the admission of air and light. The roofs are made of painted timber. Decoration is provided by elaborate arch-headed windows surmounted by stucco panels, by cornices, recesses, balustrades and terraces. The materials used for con-struction were gypsum, plaster, rubble and wood. All the build-ings are washed white and grouped asymmetrically around the central chamber; the overall effect is one of simplicity and elegance.

The architect, Abdullah el Mail, is reputed to have possessed a kind of demonic virtuosity. He was never seen to make plans or to calculate dimensions. He just produced his instructions, like a conjuror produces a rabbit from a hat, seemingly out of nowhere. But he was always right, even as far as predicting when the building would need attention, i.e. in forty years' time. Today the gardens within the walls are planted with flowers and lawns and the rooms furnished in traditional style, mainly with rugs and cushions placed against the wall. The best time to visit the museum—which includes other local items of interest—is during the hour before nightfall, when the sun is sinking. At that time the light in the Gulf is as pure as the light in Greece and the dazzling daytime whiteness fades as the palace walls take on the opalescent shine of the sky, as if trying to retain the light.

Like most modern cities in developing countries Doha began by turning its back on traditional architectural styles; and, like most modern cities anywhere, it grew at first in a fairly haphazard fashion. Fortunately, the authorities woke up sooner than in many other places and both trends are now being reversed. The new city to be built just across the bay from the old one has been carefully planned, and there is a gradual awakening of interest in traditional Arab architecture. Moreover, when the great building boom began in the mid-sixties, there was less money available than there is now. For this reason and also because, contrary to Western ideas, Qataris do not throw their money around, a lot of the first buildings were constructed cheaply by poor architects. There are still some fairly hideous concrete blocks left from that time, but, compared with some other places in the Gulf, most changes in Qatar tend to proceed at a fairly sedate pace and therefore the damage done has not been irreparable. Luckily, many of the roads were built as fairly broad boulevards and lined with trees, so Doha has at least managed to avoid that pinched and cramped look, like a child in clothes it has outgrown, that over-rapid growth leaves imprinted on many cities. Although the roads are broad, many are still bumpy: but then, as the municipality quite justifiably claims, it would be pointless to surface the roads properly while the city is still growing at such a pace that they would have to be dug up again in no time for more water pipes and underground cables to be laid.

Doha is only at the beginning of its development; the next ten years could change it out of all recognition, but in what way it is impossible to tell as yet. It is an ideal size for planning. For the time being it is still a relatively small place, but at least it is a place with a recognisable identity of its own. In atmosphere it is not unlike a large English market town where people will say they are busy but still stop to talk, and where everybody knows every-body. As an international architect who came to Doha said: 'What I like about this place is that it's so small you can put your arms round it.'

In fact the sea has its arms round Doha, or almost—the sea and the gently curving lines of the shore that meander on for some kilometres, half-encircling it. Like the vines that ramble over old houses, the straggling sea-line both softens Doha and prettifies it. For most of the year the Gulf is an iridescent turquoise green, slightly unreal like a colour in a child's drawing, blotted with patches of pale pastel greens and blues where the sea bottom is shallower. When there is a breeze the sea is pocked with feathery wavelets, on which the traditional dhows with their high stern and aft beams gently rock. Even when the winds become very violent, the Gulf never seems to react like the North Sea, with high, heaving, free rolling breakers. Instead it seethes and boils like a cauldron and turns very dark blue. Beyond the dhows which are never anchored very far from the shore are the ocean freighters waiting to be unloaded. The Gulf—with its boats, its sparkle, its changing moods and impertinent colour—lends the town vigour and gaiety and provides a sense of continuity, a link with the past.

Apart from the sea, Doha's second great asset is the fact that it has a town centre. Unlike many modern cities in the Gulf and elsewhere that ramble on like a tedious argument without theme or conclusion, Doha has a heart. Sometimes it beats a bit wildly, but it's there. This core comprises mainly the palace that houses the Emir's office—the *diwan*—and the long avenue of new buildings leading up to it, mainly government ministries. Some of the very recent ones have real style, like the new Foreign Ministry which is built in yellow sandstone and is predominately traditional in conception, while the Monetary Agency is an example of what is best in modern architecture. The older ministries, like the Education Ministry or the Ministry of Finance and Petroleum are simply nondescript modern blocks—happily not too tall—functional and set back in greenery, but undis-tinguished.

The Emir's working palace is a very large Indian-style building set on slightly rising ground overlooking the Gulf and separated from it by the sea road and by green lawns which, like a society hostess's hair-do, seem somehow to require constant attention. One or two Baluchi gardeners are forever on their knees there, weeding or watering, or whatever it is they do. The *diwan* is simpler than most Indian-style buildings: there are fewer columns, onion-shaped arches and windows, and the predominant white, backed by blue, tunes in well enough with the natural colour scheme of Doha. Even so, the sight of it takes one aback at first, as when a friend appears in a totally new style of clothing. One may decide that while it suits him for a change, it wouldn't do for him to dress like that always. Equally, a large number of Indian-style buildings in Doha would look out of place, but just the one harmonises quite happily with its surroundings. It's a cheerful building and recalls Qatar's long-standing association with India.

If every city has its eccentricity, Doha's is quite indisputably the sugar-pink and white-and-blue clock tower on the roundabout in front of the *diwan*. It looks decidedly Alice-in-Wonderlandish, as if a white rabbit were at any moment to appear and stare at it muttering, 'It's later than you think' which, anyway, would be a pretty apt comment on Doha where it's always rather later than people think. Still, as with the remarkable pieces of Victorian extravaganza that decorate English towns, one gets used to it, and even grows perversely fond of it, it's so integrally part of the place and so utterly individual. On a sunny day, the clock tower, the *diwan* and the turquoise sparkle of the Gulf all seem of a piece and if it were suddenly to be replaced by a Henry Moore one would feel (secretly) aggrieved and bereaved.

This view of the *diwan* as the centre of town, it should be said, is the view of an outsider. For the Qataris the *souk*—the market—is the real heart of Doha. Most of the shops are glass-fronted. Wares do tend to spill over on to the pavement and there is an open market which sells clothes, vegetables, meat and Persian carpets. All in all it's not unlike Petticoat Lane except that there are no antiques or *bric-à-brac* worth mentioning in Doha, while in London it's not usual to see a boy buy a live hen and ride off on his bicycle, holding it by the legs.

Nowadays the *souk* sells more or less anything that can be bought in the West. In the old days the shops were very basic in their wares and run either by Iranians from the other side of the Gulf or by Arabs who had lived in Iran and come back, the so-called Howla Arabs. The local tribes scorned any form of commerce except for the pearl trade. Now things have changed, of course, and Qataris have caught on to commerce very speedily. But generally they are involved in big business or else in the administration of an enterprise. The small shops and the day-to-day operations of bigger stores are still in the hands of Iranians and Howla Arabs who have been joined in recent years by Indians and Pakistanis.

Where window-dressing is concerned, most shop-holders seem to work on the principle of the more the merrier. Shop windows are habitually choked with goods; every square inch filled as if free space were taxed. The shop names, written in English and Arabic, are worth reading. The words 'new' and 'modern' appear in almost every shop name: the Modern Gulf Grocery; the Modern Dress Shop; the Modern Pharmacy; the Modern Man; Modern Constructions; the New Friends Tea Stall; the New Cloth Shop; the New Care Pharmacy. The word 'national' comes up too, but more sparingly: the National Pharmacy; the National Laundry. There is a touch of Indian inappropriateness here and there: Fancy Suitings; the Snow-White Laundry; the Universal Hair Cutting Saloon. The City Hotel, it should be said, is merely a restaurant. It is quite common here to call a restaurant a hotel. Most of those in the *souk* are frequented by Indians or Baluchis. The Europeans go to the three or four main Western-style hotels and sometimes to an Indian restaurant which may well have the distinction of being the only place in the world to serve curried spaghetti bolognaise. Qatari youths sit in the Kentucky Chicken House or Juice stalls, for alcohol is officially banned here. Some of the Qataris go to the luxury Gulf Hotel,

or to the other Western hotels. But, in general, expatriates and
Qataris entertain at home. There are very few places for them to
go for outside entertainment, except the new cinema and the
bowling alley in the Gulf Hotel.

Finally, there are the trees. They are not unusual or interesting
in any way, just ordinary evergreens with nice glossy leaves that
shine in the sunlight. The only thing notable about them is that
they are there at all—both inside the city and out in the desert. But
this really is notable, although it is probably necessary to have seen
trees in desert places to understand why. With trees, as with pain,
to observe is not necessarily to understand; both have to be
experienced. Trees in the desert, even when they are only those
low thorny trees which, like Victorian sideboards, seem positively
to attract the dust, are infinitely precious: they give shade, even if
only a little; they break the tedium of the long straight lines and
flat planes; they allow the eye to rest momentarily from the
blinding white glare of the sun; they reassert life in an environment
which can seem as silent and immutable as death.

In the past there were few trees in Qatar. Although the national
emblem consists of crossed swords and a palm tree, palm trees
were in fact rare. People might have just one at home in their
courtyard, or there might be a dozen or so together in the desert.
Even today Qataris use the Arabic word for forest to describe
what in most Western countries would hardly qualify as a copse.
The word *Doha* itself is said to mean 'the place of the big tree', as
eloquent a comment as any on the sparsity of the vegetation in
Qatar, indeed throughout the Gulf generally, in former times.

Nowadays, thousands of trees have been planted. As saplings,
both inside Doha and out in the desert, they are surrounded by
sturdy wooden fencing; like the heavy bars outside a jeweller's
shop they are evidence of the value of the commodity within. Not
only is it expensive to plant the trees (often in rock) and to keep
them constantly watered, but the trees in Arabia are subject to
many hazards: the desert wind; the roaming animals; the small
boys; the careless car drivers. Admittedly these hazards are not
exclusive to Arabia, but if a driver knocks down a tree in a

country where trees are an accepted part of the scenery, the gap would never be noticed. In Doha such a gap is as glaring as a missing front tooth.

Doha, and Qatar generally, is somewhere one remembers for the people rather than for the place itself. The country lacks the grandeur of the Empty Quarter or of the great deserts of central Arabia or of the mountains of Yemen and Oman. The colours are monotonous; blues and yellows that shade into white and whites that contain yellow and blue. The land is flat and glides undramatically into the shallow sea. It is a compact, low-key domestic place which leaves blurred rather than vivid impressions on the mind. One that persists with unusual clarity is of a Qatari in his long white *thaub* or a Baluchi worker in his baggy working clothes lying stretched, in the fierce heat of the middle of the day, in the scanty shade of a five- or six-year-old tree. It is a touching sight.

Qataris at Home

Just as Doha is now a modern city much like any other of comparable size in the West, so most Qataris live fairly average workaday urban lives by any Western standards. They live at home with parents, and brothers and sisters, sons and daughters—rather more of them, admittedly, than most people in the West have. They go to school and have to pass examinations. They work in Government departments and business offices (rather harder in the latter), but rarely in factories or at labouring jobs. Apart from some of the older men, most married Qatari men have one wife who seems to require as much information on their comings and goings as any Western woman. In the evenings, they watch television or visit their friends; those over thirty discuss land prices and inflation, those under thirty talk about the latest television film and who won the last Grand Prix. At week-ends—Thursday and Friday—they go fishing, play or watch football, or go out into the country. They rarely go to public places like cinemas and restaurants and, if they do, they will almost certainly go without their wives. Most people, including even some of the millionaires, live in comfortable but not particularly glamorous villas. They tend to have very large, air-conditioned American cars, not because they are status symbols but because they are suited to the climate in the Gulf and, anyway, are no more expensive than other cars. Gold wrist watches, on the other hand, are as common and pass as unremarked as a brolly in England on a rainy day. Quite a high proportion of people can afford to go abroad to avoid the scorching summer heat, to rent expensive cars and stay in expensive hotels. When they can't (and sometimes even when they can), the State pays. What Qataris want from life is in most respects similar to what Westerners want from life. They want their children to get on, they want better houses, cars, clothes, furniture and they want to travel. There is certainly a great deal more opportunity to make money in Qatar than in the West, but everything is dearer there also.

Twenty years ago, it was all very different; but nowadays most people in Qatar and in Arabia live in much the same way as people do in the West. Certainly, very considerable differences in values remain under a surface that grows daily more Western— for example there are now buses but women still hesitate to take them. Between the social traditions of a semi-bedu society which Qatar was until very recently, and the economic structures of the modern industrial society it is trying to become, the gap is, understandably, still far from being bridged. So people in general, and women in particular, live under considerable strain.

But although East and West still differ in some of their values, this does not justify the underlying assumption current in the West that the values of the Gulf Arabs are alien or bizarre. Different they certainly are, alien they are not. The differences that exist are relative and historical, they are not absolute. Take the segregation of the sexes and the closeting of women behind veils and shutters. This tradition still continues to some extent and it is unquestionably out of step with present-day practice in the

West. However, the concept on which this segregation and sequestration are based—that women should be protected—is by no means alien to the West. And the idea of family honour and the need to safeguard it—another reason why women's liberty is curtailed—was a principle firmly upheld in many parts of Europe, especially in the south, until relatively recently. Most of what remains of traditional behaviour in modern Arabia was also prevalent at one time in the West.

Take the relationship of the individual to the family or community which today is one of the major social differences between Eastern and Western society. In the West, individualism emerged as a principle at the end of the Middle Ages; in practice the individual, particularly the female individual, remained dominated by the family and the community until well into Victorian times. In the Arab world, the individual is still subordinate to the family or the community, particularly the female individual, but with the break-up of traditional communities and the increase of education this situation is changing rapidly.

Arab and European values have developed on a different time-scale, but their origins and ethical basis are similar. Religion —Islam and Christianity—has been a dominant influence on the cultures of East and West alike. And Islam and Christianity are both monotheistic religions linked to Judaism. They differ basically only on the means God has chosen to reveal himself, and about the nature of the revelation which they agree was made by Christ and the revelation which only Muslims believe was made by Mohammed. But while Muslims, in the main, respect Christians as people of the Book (i.e. believers in One God), acknowledge Christ as a prophet and the kinship of the two religions, Christian writers down the centuries have often vilified Muslims as infidels, labelled Mohammed as a 'false' prophet and misrepresented Muslim beliefs. (Their hostility owes much to the Arab invasion of Europe in the Middle Ages.) And yet, the ethical codes of Islam and Christianity have much in common although Islam is more specific about its application to society as well as the individual. Apart from these social regulations and differences in the detail of religious practice, the moral code by which a good Muslim lives is similar to that followed by a good Christian.

Misconceptions in the relations between Arabs and the West change only slowly. A good Muslim, down the ages, would never have recognised himself or his beliefs in most popular Christian writings about Islam. Equally, Gulf Arabs today are far removed from the caricatural oil-rich Arabs portrayed in the Western media. Their character, and that of the Qataris in particular, is in fact not unlike that usually ascribed to the English, except that the English are possibly more imaginative and certainly a good deal more eccentric. Temperamentally, Qataris are practical and level-headed. But like the English they are matter-of-fact on the surface and often sensitive and highly strung underneath. (They show it in different ways: since Qataris, when seated, can't swing their foot like the English do in moments of stress because it is not polite in Arabia to cross your legs and show your soles, they twitch their whole leg instead.) Both peoples are pragmatic, fundamentally honest and inclined to see the funny side of life. Like the English, Qataris often give the impression of taking nothing in, but are very observant. An English lady with many years' experience of Qatar and the Gulf once commented of Qataris that they react so little when you talk to them that you assume that they're either not listening or not quite understanding —until suddenly they make a remark which indicates that they have sized up the situation very accurately. Even the local form of Islamic puritanism is very like the Victorian puritanism that lingers on in England: strict about religious observance, moralistic, prudish in sexual matters, disapproving of pleasure. The only mysterious thing about Qataris is how they manage to remain sane amidst such rapid social change.

It is easy to overestimate the effect of money, on some levels at least. The effect of oil money on the economy and society of Qatar is clearly enormous. But its impact on the character of the people is less dramatic and harder to measure, at least in the short term. Qataris are a semi-bedu people who have lived by a simple, strict code for centuries; it will take more than one generation of wealth to change them. Oil money in Qatar is still a very recent phenomenon and while it is impossible to prejudge the future, so far there is remarkably little evidence of the arrogance and wild extravagance one might expect from newly-rich.

There is a local millionaire who is reputedly building himself a villa with gold-plated door handles. But this is not specially outlandish. The English aristocracy in its time owned enough silver plate to sink several fleets. There is another millionaire whose son reacts to the word 'Europe' as automatically as a Pavlovian dog, bursting into a rather astounding eulogy on the joys of Vienna. Everybody has been to London, so he evidently thinks Vienna is more distinguished. Although this young man's fulsome speeches are treated as rather a joke, it is the young men in Qatar of school and university age who are most vulnerable to the more harmful effects of wealth. The young women have to struggle to prove themselves and their abilities—and such struggle rules out complacency or arrogance. Those men and women who are over thirty, or even over twenty-five, have often known poverty as children and so have some idea of the value of wealth. But by the generation now growing to manhood, money is taken for granted. The effect, if any, of this change can only be measured in the long term.

At least a century ago, a romantic Western traveller in Arabia was disappointed to find that the Sultan or Emir who was entertaining him was seated on a divan covered not with cloth of gold and precious jewels, but with honest Manchester cotton. Today, when Western consumer goods and technology are even more in evidence, the differences between the material equipment —houses, furniture, etc. of societies of the Gulf and the West are usually only in detail or style. They point, like half-concealed clues, to society as it once was.

There is, for example, a distinct difference in style between the average Qatari house and the average Western house. In the past Qataris had few possessions and little or no furniture—it is said that the owner of the four-poster bed in the museum slept under it and used the canopy to store his goods. Today Qatari houses amply fulfil every Western expectation of what a house should have: bathroom fittings in pink or blue, sofas, armchairs and bedroom suites. And yet. . . . Even some of the richest houses, even though perfectly tidy and clean, often have an air of being unloved. The Qatari and his or her house, one sometimes feels, are like a couple who are a couple in name only, they have no intimate relations. When Qataris really want to relax, they take off if they are men to the sea or to the desert; the women settle down in their courtyard. But neither men nor women are given to pottering around their houses fixing shelves or sewing curtains.

Household fittings seem, at first sight, to be ill-attuned to the climate. Despite the heat and the humidity, carpets are usually very thick, curtains very heavy and drawn tight from morning to night, so that the electric light—and, of course, the air condition-ing—is always on. Gradually, as one learns to live with the climate it becomes clear that it is precisely *because* of the weather that houses are fitted like this, i.e. to keep the heat and sunlight out. It is as if people were insulating themselves in a cocoon from their harsh environment. This is exactly what many desert creatures do: they dig a deep burrow in the sand and hide in it during the daytime heat.

Traditional social customs account for some of the more obvious differences between Qatari and Western houses: the way that the furniture is arranged, for example. In many houses the chairs in the sitting-room—or room for receiving guests—the *diwan* it is called—are ranged round the walls facing inwards in a solemn row, leaving a great space in the middle of the room which either remains empty or, more usually, is occupied by a few low tables. This is simply because it is a social misdemeanour, in Arab eyes, to turn one's back on another person.

Qatari houses often contain a great number of chairs and sofas mainly because there are a large number of people in a Qatari family and people are still very family-minded. Twelve sofas and chairs are fairly normal, up to twenty-five not unusual. As a result *diwans* tend to look a little bleak and impersonal, like a hotel lounge. Moreover, the type of furniture generally favoured—roomy, old-fashioned, heavily upholstered arm-chairs rather than the more streamlined modern type—reinforce this impression. Sometimes an ultra-modern lamp strikes a different note, but generally Qatari *diwans* are as conservative in style as gentlemen's clubs in England. Experiments in interior decoration are usually confined to the more private sector of the house.

The size and location of the *diwan* is an interesting social indicator. If it is very large, this usually means that the family is traditional in outlook. Most traditional families, moreover, position their *diwan* slightly apart from the rest of the house so as to segregate the men from the women more completely; in such houses the *diwan* either has its own outside entrance next to the main door, or it may be a separate building altogether just within or just outside the big wall which, to ensure privacy, surrounds every Qatari house or villa. But usually only the most conservative families go as far as building a separate outside *diwan*. On the other hand, paradoxically, only the most modern-minded families would have a really traditional Arab *diwan* with cushions on the floor instead of sofas and chairs, but they would always have a Western-style sitting-room, too (with chairs).

Some features of Qatari houses may be explained by tradition. Others seem so alien to local tradition and to the environment that it is tempting to see them as a form of psychological compensation. Under this heading might be listed: violent colours, the large quantity of ornaments and knick-knacks; the number of bathrooms and boxes of Kleenex; the prevalence on the walls of paintings of European pastoral subjects, and Alpine scenes in particular. The absence of anything eastern or old is striking.

There are (usually) few colours in the desert. In the past, the bedu seemed to compensate for this absence by weaving brilliantly coloured camel-bags, rugs and cloth for their clothes. Their colours were vivid but harmonious. Today Qataris still like bright colours. Only now they no longer weave themselves but buy ready-made clothes and furnishings. It is true that many of the Western-style fittings, furnishings and clothes on the market are often less than tasteful; all the same, one still gets the impression that Qataris have been slightly disoriented by adopting Western styles and decorations and have lost some of their innate sense of colour—hopefully only momentarily. The cloth shops in Doha, for instance, stock dress materials in violent colours that are not available in any Western store—colours that are both lurid and astonishing like the jelly at children's birthday parties. Sophisticated Qataris like sophisticated Westerners choose cream for their carpets and black for their wives' party dresses. But average Qataris like their colours as the English like their tea—strong and sweet.

The bedu's lack of material possessions in the past no doubt explains why Qataris today accumulate so many objects. In the bedrooms and the dining-rooms—for the *diwans* have their own particular style of sobriety—there are often dozens of gilded and painted vases, lining the tops of the wardrobes, filling the sideboards both inside and outside, arrayed along every shelf in sight. There are also massive wooden elephants from India as lamps or tables or just as ornaments. Animal carvings of every description and size are immensely popular—for evident reasons. Then there are the knick-knacks and gadgets, no matter whether the house belongs to a cabinet minister or to a taxi driver. The cigarette boxes like a fire engine or a submarine, or the Taj Mahal. The lamps that light and change colour all the time, like a continuous firework display. The cigarette box with a bird on it; you press, the cigarette is released, the bird with a long beak bends down, picks up the cigarette—and promptly breaks it in half. (The owner is happy, living in Doha and still throwing away three cigarettes out of five.)

Once, it was not easy to get water to wash well. In the desert the bedu often had to perform the ritual ablutions before prayer with sand or with a stone because there was either no water or only enough for drinking. Nowadays even medium-sized villas have two to three bathrooms; everybody must have their own bathroom.

Then Kleenex. Cartons of Kleenex lie everywhere: in offices, in cars, in the bedroom, in the bathroom. One Qatari with two children once owned to using twenty boxes a week. Now that people are able to keep themselves clean, they are meticulous about doing so. Only they have not quite got round to organising adequate supplies of towels and napkins. Besides, Kleenex is labour-saving in these days when servants are harder and harder to come by. Kleenex is a good deal more important in modern Arabia than the camel; when the West begins to grasp such humdrum realities as this it will have made some progress at last in understanding the East as it is today.

There was no tradition of painting in the desert for practical and religious reasons. The bedu found an outlet for their creative impulses mainly in poetry and language, but also in weaving. Even today Qataris often have no pictures on their walls and this is one reason why the *diwans* look bare. Sometimes they hang up texts from the Koran, which might be embroidered, or photo-graphic calendars issued by the ministries. In the wealthier houses there are modern Persian rugs on the walls, often depicting demure young women dancing or holding bouquets of flowers or fruit or musical instruments. Actual paintings are rare and they tend to be of two kinds. There is the picture picked up while travelling —a flowering cherry-tree from Japan or the cheeky children painted by the artists of Place Pigalle. But the most popular type of painting by far is the Alpine scene with high green hills and trees and waterfalls—treasures for a desert people.

There is rarely anything eastern or old in a Qatari house. Just as young Westerners fill their houses with incense burners and camel-bags and other eastern and pseudo-eastern traditional objects, so Qataris want nothing but what is modern and conse-quently Western. Occasionally they may have an old Kuwaiti chest—these are big old wooden boxes, very splendidly decorated with brass studs, where the pearls were often stored in the old days. Persian rugs are common, but only modern ones. If you ask Qataris why they don't like old things, they will just say that they have had enough of them.

There are houses in Qatar which contain the best of everything the West has to offer. David Hicks, the British interior decorator, has designed the interiors of several houses here. But such houses are not typical. Compared with some other Gulf countries, the average Qatari is wary of too much change at once and this attitude is reflected in the type of house and furnishing he chooses. Even so it is arguable that the Qataris have already abandoned too much of their own tradition; but in time a new balance will probably emerge.

What the Struggle to Survive Did

To survive in hot deserts is a struggle for any living thing whether plant, animal or man. So they adapt themselves. The acacia which is fairly common in Qatar developed long taproots which go deep enough to reach a permanent source of moisture in the water table. Where mammals are concerned, scarcity of food means that they have to be able to locate members of their own species over long distances; this accounts for the long ears of many of them. The ears of the desert hare, for instance, are quite out of proportion with the rest of its body. The camel has double eyelashes to keep the sand out of its eyes and re-cycles its urea.

Human beings, too, have adapted to the desert, not physically but mentally and psychologically. Qataris don't have specially large ears or eyes, but they have almost uncanny powers of observation and a sensitivity to people and their surroundings. It is not difficult to imagine how these powers were acquired. To survive in the desert it was essential to store away every scrap of information: to observe every camel track which might bring friends or foes, any gesture that could presage treachery, any animal movement in the direction of water. There is a bedu story which illustrates this heightened awareness of the desert nomads. Among bedu, who were only rarely able to eat their fill, greediness was a trait greatly despised. One day a young boy said to his mother that he preferred to eat when there was no moon, because then people could not see how much he took. His mother listened and said to him: 'The next time there is no moon, take a piece of rope and try cutting it with the blunt side of your knife.' One night when there was no moon he remembered his mother's words and did what she told him to do. From all around, out of the dark, voices cried: 'Can't you see! You are using the blunt side of your knife.'

Even now Qataris will notice, unobtrusively but unfailingly, whether their guest is sitting in a draught, would like more food, needs a cushion, feels bored or hungry or angry. They often hear a noise, like a car approaching, well before anyone else. And even if absorbed in conversation with one person, they seem to be able to take in what is happening around them as if, like flies, they could see out of the back of their heads. The old life seems also to have made them suspicious, a little mistrustful. It is as if they still feel they cannot afford to drop their guard.

This kind of sensitivity gives desert bedu with no education a facility in handling unforeseen or potentially awkward situations which a trained diplomat might envy. One of the great rituals in Arabia has always been coffee-making. In the old days the bedu would start to prepare the beans as soon as he saw a friend or stranger in the distance. And even now it is essential to accept coffee and to sip at least one cup even if the taste does not appeal— for the Arab coffee has cardamom in it which is an acquired taste. Among the bedu it was and still is normal to serve men before women. If a foreign woman goes out to a bedu encamp-ment and sits with the men any acompanying male guest will be served first, but he will signal that the woman should have priority and from then on the woman will unfailingly be served first. No one says anything, but everyone takes note.

Sensitivity to and consideration for the feelings of others is one of the most attractive characteristics of the bedu and the Qataris have not lost these qualities. But hyper-sensitivity of this kind also has drawbacks. People are so anxious to please a stranger or guest that they may over-react if the latter shows signs of displeasure or boredom. So it is essential for the guests to be equally sensitive towards their hosts if misunderstandings are to be avoided.

There is one subject about which Qataris display little of their habitual flexibility. This is the crucial question of who is and who is not a Qatari. The more educated are less excitable on the subject (usually but not always) but the uneducated and, in particular, the bedu or people of bedu origin are as obsessed with genealogy as the dukes of France at the court of Louis XIV to whom one-sixteenth of the wrong kind of blood spelled instant shame and ruin. But at least the dukes of France applied themselves to the issue methodically. Equally, the Qatari Government has formal rules governing the application for Qatari citizenship. But public opinion is much more erratic. Someone will assert dogmatically that so-and-so is not a Qatari; while someone else will assert the opposite with equal vehemence. No one will ever explain how they came to their conclusion. Like a bloodhound's sense of smell, the ability to distinguish between fellow nationals and those of foreign origin seems to be an inborn instinct. As far as the bedu are concerned, their deep interest in the subject may be explained in terms of still surviving tribal feeling. Small communities who take in large numbers of outsiders also often feel the need to reassert their identity. Then, the less educated also have some very understandable grievances. They see outsiders coming into Qatar and becoming wealthier than many of the Qataris. Like Europeans *vis-à-vis* their foreign workers, they are not always prepared to admit that if these people are there it is because they are needed and the work they perform could not get done without them. The issue is a delicate one. In view of the complications involved and despite all the lists of 'genuine' Qatari families thoughtfully provided by bedu friends, the present author intends to make the unpopular assumption that anyone who says they are Qatari *is* Qatari.

Speaking for Themselves

Qatar is a small Arab society in the throes of very great change. But this book does not set out to analyse either the society or its transformation. Arabia and its people have been described and judged all too often by outsiders. The purpose here is simply to provide the people with the opportunity to speak for themselves, about the past, the present, the future as they appear to them, about anything they choose to discuss. This introduction is intended to give the general reader with no knowledge of Qatar or the Arabian Peninsula some basic background information and a frame of reference to allow the reader to assess the people and their ideas, within their own historical and cultural context, rather than from a purely Western viewpoint. Anyone entering into a foreign culture is inevitably blinkered to some extent by their own assumptions but they need not be blinded by them.

The series of interviews recorded here with people from Qatar do not claim to present the truth about Qatar society in any scientific or academic historical sense. People in Qatar, as elsewhere, have widely divergent views on every aspect and problem of their society; each also has his or her own set of value judgements. One woman is perfectly contented with her life; the next is frustrated. Their own personal situation will inevitably affect their view of society as a whole. People also have very different attitudes towards the past. Everybody can speak only for him or herself.

There are many contradictions in what people say and there is no attempt here to correct them. A bedu says he would do away with his wife if she were to abandon her face-mask (the Qatari equivalent of the veil). In the next breath he claims he wouldn't actually mind himself, but that his wife's family would object. In a society which is changing so fast, opinions are inevitably in a state of flux and confusion.

There are also many factual contradictions. One old woman says that there were celebrations when the pearling boats came back at the end of the summer; somebody else says that there were no celebrations. Perhaps one has a faulty memory. Perhaps what they both say is true: there were celebrations in some places and not in others.

The most glaring inconsistencies generally concern age, the age people attribute to themselves and to their parents. One man of sixty, for instance, claims that his father is one hundred and twenty. This may be so, but it's highly unlikely. In the course of a two-hour talk the oldest man in Qatar, reputedly one hundred and twenty-five years old, aged by fifteen years; at the end of the visit he was one hundred and forty. The truth is that most people simply don't know their ages accurately. Birth records are a recent innovation. Most people know about their age only what their mothers or fathers tell them: that they were born during the great rains, or the year the pearling fleet was shipwrecked, or when their uncle was eaten by a shark, or when he built his house or married his wife—or during the Zubara War. The Zubara War was a local conflict which has gripped the imagination of the Qataris in much the same way as the Battle of Bannockburn has indelibly marked the Scots and one of the curiosities of Qatar is how many people claim to have been born at that time, perhaps just a case of retroactive patriotism. One very unwarlike gentleman claimed to have fought in the Zubara War.

Some people, when offered an audience, cannot ever resist trying to gain reflected glory from history. That there have been few such people among those interviewed is much to the credit of the Qataris. For Qatar is a small developing community with all the virtues and failings of such places: human warmth but also eternal gossip and hyper-sensitivity to criticism. For this reason also, most names in the book have been disguised and social distinctions between sheikhs and non-sheikhs have been dropped.

The author was not subject to any official restrictions or any directions as to whom to see or to avoid. There has never been the slightest interference with the choice of interviewees. However, this free access to people was given on the basic understanding that the book would not touch on formal politics nor offend religious sensibilities, which in Qatar are still very strong. But since the author's choice cannot help influencing the resulting picture, I should perhaps say something of my own assumptions.

Of course, from a world viewpoint it would have been more 'just' if so much of the world's oil had been discovered not in the sparsely populated Arabian desert but in heavily populated but poor countries such as India or Egypt. But then when has there ever been a just distribution of the world's resources? If there were, then the abundant resources of the USA should be distributed more evenly, say, throughout Africa and South Asia. The Qataris and the Gulf Arabs have as much and as little right to their oil and to their wealth as other people have to their national resources. In the absence of a just global distribution of wealth it seems particularly unmagnanimous to begrudge wealth to people like the Gulf Arabs who have lived for centuries not far above starva/tion level and who, to avoid going backwards, are forced to adapt to changed circumstances more rapidly and more com/pletely than perhaps any other human group in history.

Finally, since economic circumstances have dictated that Arabs and Westerners must be in close contact from now onwards, it is perhaps an opportune moment for the West to break with its age/old habit of either romanticising or vilifying Arabs. If they did, then they might conclude like the secretary to whom this book is dedicated, that Arabs are not like 'Arabs' at all. They are quite normal.

PART ONE

The Old World

I. PEARLS

'We are all from the highest to the lowest slaves of one
master, Pearl.'   *Mohammed al-Thani*

Said, Old Diver and Sea Captain

Said, now in his sixties, is one of the generation of Qataris who went to sea
as a child and spent at least thirty years pearling before the trade finally
collapsed: a quiet elderly man with a kindly manner and an air of authority
held in reserve. His skin is very brown and sun-creased, his features well
defined and still handsome and when he is amused his face lights up with a
most infectious smile. People say of him that he can't refuse anyone anything,
admiringly, for generosity is the greatest of the virtues in the Arabian world.
He sits daily in the museum, just a stone's throw from the Gulf, patiently
providing information on ships and pearling (and answering the dumbest
questions with courtesy) for radio and television, local and foreign, and for
anyone who asks, his only protest an occasional sideways glance, as if to
locate the exit. The younger generation of Qataris like to hear about the age
of pearling and woollen bedouin tents, although it is slightly startling to find
that they regard it already with the detached interest and awe reserved for the
most distant of historical phenomena.

In the evenings the former pearling crews often gather around Said to beat
their drums and sing the old sea-shanties. There are powerfully rhythmic, if a
little repetitive. But to attend one of their sessions in person is a real

experience while, when broadcast on television, Gulf sea-songs are oddly insipid, as uninspiring as a print compared with the original painting.

Like almost all of the older people, Said is disinclined to be romantic about the past. Life was hard then, he insists, and anyone who claims the contrary is fooling himself. But he still loves the sea: 'When I look at the sea I feel a great yearning for it. We have lived with the sea from childhood until old age, so it is natural we should feel this way.' Some of the older people share his nostalgia. Others remember their time at sea with undisguised aversion: the eternal wetness, the discomfort, the hunger, the thirst. But there is one sentiment that appears to be common to all who have ever been involved in pearling in the Gulf: a deep affinity for pearls, a kind of bond akin to what peasants feel for their land. Those affected are quite blinded to the possibility that others might not share their feelings: a former pearler simply does not grasp that the sight of a pearl does not automatically entrance the beholder. Said voices the inner conviction of his generation—and of countless generations in the Gulf no doubt—when he says: 'I feel comforted when I look at pearls. Everybody *must* feel like this—happy—when they look at pearls, whether or not they understand them.'

Diving for pearls started at sunrise and ended at sunset. In Qatar or Bahrain and Kuwait, the oyster is called the pearl's mother. When I was a diver, I would go down into the sea with two ropes; a string with a lead object attached to it would drag me down to the sea bed—all this was done without the aid of breathing tubes, of course, in those days. A second rope would be tied round a bag, a bag made of string, like a fishing net. I would pick up the oysters and put them in the bag until I felt short of breath. I would then pull on the rope which was attached to my toes. A man above would be holding onto the rope; when I pulled, the man above hoisted me up. When I got on to the deck I took off the bag with the oysters in it and tipped them onto the deck. Then I took the line, tied it round my foot, and on my other foot there's the weight. I took a few breaths until I felt there was enough breath in my lungs, then I dived in for a second time and so on for the whole day until sunset.

On the following morning, we would begin to open the shells. The day started joyfully if a big pearl was found. The crew would sing and dance if they discovered even just one good pearl. All shells were piled together, so no one would know who brought it up. The man who found it would take it to the captain. I remember once there was an Iranian *nokhatha* (captain) who borrowed money for his voyage from a merchant named Jaber Musallam. Fifteen days before the end of the season he went to Bahrain to ask Musallam to take his boat and settle his debt because he hadn't been able to find any thing. Musallam gave him an additional loan and refused to end his contract. In the remaining period of the season, the Iranian found two big pearls. He didn't know their value, and brought them to Musallam saying he couldn't find any more. Musallam was pleased and offered him sixty thousand *riyals*. The Iranian couldn't believe his ears, because sixty thousand in those days was equivalent to sixty million today.

One job I never had was that of the *nahham*. This was the member of the crew whose special job it was to inspire the others. He worked like the rest with the difference that he sang to encourage everyone. He worked as *seib* or *gheiss* but his colleagues gave him time off to sing which meant he had more rest than other workers. If he was a *gheiss* he didn't work hard, so as to be able to perfect his art. The *nahham* was like a human mechanic. He was as necessary to the crew as a mechanical engineer is to a machine. He began his day by chanting the morning hymn:

> *Oh Blessed Morning*
> *May we be fortunate today.*

This is the first song of the morning. Later he sings:

> *Oh pardoner of our sins*
> *May we ask you to forgive us.*
> *Your mercy is unlimited.*
> *We therefore appeal to you*
> *To bless and forgive us.*
> *Oh God I repent and turn from my sins*
> *To your love.*
> *It is you who grants us pardon. . . .*

At sunset, after praying in the name of the Prophet: 'God bless him and give him peace', the *nahham* sings:

Oh God, make our lives easy.
May riches come to us from God.
So that we may announce the good tidings to our families and
  neighbours
And anger the envious.

Most of the *nahhams* 'songs were religious, pleas to God. They composed no poetry. They learned all their songs by heart: other people wrote the poetry and the *nahham* learned it. Religious hymns were sung twice a day, in the morning and after the evening prayers. The *nahhams* sang poems on other subjects during the day. If the *nahham* went sick, there were always others to take over his job. Each ship had at least two, and usually three or four *nahhams*. Diving for pearls is hard enough; without the *nahham* it would have been even harder.

I went to sea at the age of six, but I did not work. I was a boy or a *tabbab* as we were called until the age of ten. When I was eleven I became a *gheiss* or diver, and continued as one for twenty-three years. Then I bought this ship with my own money and with the help of a loan from Abdullah Darwish. When we came back from the sea we used to sell the pearls to him. He would deduct the amount of the loan and give us our share, if there was any left.

I knew by experience where pearls were to be found. Good quality pearls are usually found in deep water. Of course, most of the Gulf is not very deep, but in some places the water may range from fifty to seventy feet. The island mountain of Halul for instance is surrounded by deep water where excellent pearls are to be had; it lies east of Qatar in the direction of Iran. Abu Ghaha, near Halul, is the deepest place in the Gulf.

National pearling rights were unknown in the old days: anyone could dive anywhere. Bahrainis came to search round Qatar, while the Qataris went off to Bahrain. There were never any restrictions or even difficulties.

Before we started diving we had some idea as to what we might find. We knew which 'pearl fields' as we used to call them would yield the best pearls: Halul, Abu Masan, Abu Graiha, Id El Gibli and a dozen others. All the fields were named by divers long dead. The first recorded divers—the first we know of—were called Ghilan and Mai. Mai was a woman but not Ghilan's wife. I suppose they might have lived four to five hundred years ago.

When the crew had opened them with a knife as I said, any pearls we found were handed over to the captain. He then sold them to a *tawash*, as the dealers or merchants were called. As soon as the captain received his money, he paid a share of it to each member of the crew.

In the Gulf these merchants were all local and Arab. They bought the pearls, then sold them in India. Sheikh Jasim, the grandfather of the present ruler, was a leading merchant. The pearls were sent with a messenger who was given a part of the price paid. From the boats we used to sell the pearls to the small *tawashs*. Every five or six days, a *tawash* came to the boat to buy pearls. These pearls bought at sea were sold to the big merchants, either here or in Bahrain. Each season leading Indian merchants would go to Bahrain to buy the pearls. These merchants paid for them only a fraction of what they later resold them for. You know, Arabs call pearls 'the stone of many surprises'—that is to say it is a source of income to many people.

A pearl is top grade if it is flawless, if it has no defect. Such a pearl is so fine that you can see your face reflected in it. It is sometimes called the changing jewel stone. You see, it turns a different colour each time you look at it; it attracts the eye. A good *tawash* who is an expert on the quality of pearls may buy one jewel stone for twenty thousand *riyals*. A pearl of the second grade is called 'the unknown'. An ordinary diver would not recognise it because it lies under a cover which, when peeled off, reveals a good quality jewel underneath. But the specialised *tawash* knows it at once. He may buy it at ten thousand and when he peels it, he finds a special jewel we call *zaini* which he sells for thirty thousand.

The next grade is called *batun* or 'Bombay belly': a round pearl with a flat bottom. It would remain steady if stood up on its flat side. It is used to decorate gold. The *gallah*—changing pearl—is better. The Bombay belly is also used to make necklaces for rich women. It is better than the 'unknown' because it requires no effort to peel it. It is a pure pearl. But the *zaini* is better than the Bombay belly.

Another kind is the *tambula*. It is oval. If two similar jewels of this kind are found they are immediately made into ear-rings; merchants would pay any price for an identical pair. But they would have to be identical in size, colour etc. . . . Such pearls are rarely found.

The rare stones we used to sell separately and immediately after they were discovered. In the course of a season, each big boat used to earn something around twenty thousand *riyals*. This was a large sum of money in the past. The divers were never promoted: they remained divers. But the *tawash*, who sometimes made a hundred per cent profit, could become a bigger merchant by increasing the number of his boats. The captain, after paying his crew their share, had little left for himself. Sometimes he had to buy a new boat or repair his old one after settling his debts to the big merchants such as al Darwish or al Manaa. These merchants used to lend money to see the men through the winter season. They waited for the end of the summer to get their money back from the returning pearlers. It was on account of these loans that the divers and those who pulled them up could never become rich: they were forever having to settle debts. Those whom God blessed made good money; others were unable to do so.

I myself was a *tabbab*, then a *gheiss* and then a *nokhatha* with a crew of sixty-one. Others, too, could get on like this: they could become a *nokhatha* with one or two boats. But they could not become merchants.

Even when I became a *nokhatha*, still I used to dive sometimes. Once when I was on the sea-bed searching for shells, a shark attacked me. When I saw it, I pulled the rope: while I was being pulled up, the shark snatched the basket which the *gheiss* used for keeping the shell he picks.

Sometimes a shark will pass by without attacking. At other times it severs a limb. But you would not feel the pain immediately. It takes at least a quarter of an hour before you realise that a limb has been amputated. A shark has four teeth on top, four below. They are only about two centimetres long but they are sharp and fit together, like the teeth of two saws: this is why they are able to snap off limbs.

Sometimes sharks will snap off legs or arms and then go away. At other times, when they see blood, they come back to eat a man up.

Some fishermen use big hooks which are called *midar* to catch sharks. Bigger sharks are caught by big hooks called *mormos*. As a bait we use the hind leg of a lamb. The hook is tied to a strong rope. When a shark bites, many men pull it to the shore. Some- times we find half a shark; the other half is usually eaten by a bigger shark. A big shark could weigh two or two and a half tons. They are not very tasty; only the small ones are good to eat.

There is another dangerous fish, we call it the wolf. If the shark finds fish to eat, it seldom attacks men, if it does not find fish— then it will attack men. If the wolf fish sees blood it gets more savage and does not leave a wounded person until it devours him. It looks like a shark but its mouth is different; the wolf has eight teeth on top and eight in the bottom. Once on the Omani coast a wolf devoured seven people. There is another dangerous fish covered with sharp pointed prickles. It is not a man-eater but if any of these prickles dig into your flesh you are immediately poisoned and will die within four days—unless of course a holy person saves you by reading special verses over you. In such cases a doctor is of no use. A holy man reads an incantation like this: 'God is your saviour. He protects you without mediation. He removes your hardship. . . .'

Big jelly fish are a menace, too. They look as if they were made of nylon . . . and have threads. While I was working on a boat at Umm Said, a sailor caught one thinking it was a fish. It touched him on his side and burned him. We took him to the doctor who thought he had been in a fire. He treated the sailor but never believed that a sea creature could burn like that.

We have dolphins, too, in the Gulf. A dolphin looks some-thing like a human being. It lays eggs on shore: some four to five hundred eggs at a time. It tries to hide these eggs and checks every three or four days to see if they are still there. The eggs that are buried do hatch and dolphins are incubated. Others, which drift out to sea, do not hatch and those that are not buried are eaten by birds.

Big dolphins are found off the Oman Coast and we call them *homers*. Once I was at Halul island. While I was walking near the shore, I saw a male and female dolphin mating. They were very close to the sea. When I came closer, another male dolphin jostled the first male and tried to take his place. I soon called the other men and eight of us carried the three dolphins to an English-man's car and took them to his house. But he refused to eat them; he thought it was cruel. He had his wife with him. We would have eaten them because their meat is good. But instead we put them in his swimming pool for the night. The following morning the Englishman called us, asked us to load them on the car, and drove to the seashore. We threw one of the males into the water first. It remained very close to the shore. Then we threw in the female. As soon as she was in the water the male went on with his mating. Then we threw the second male which again started to push the first male and try to take its place!

In our time we did not fear the sea because our livelihood depended on diving. Nowadays people are afraid to swim two metres away from the shore. One reason is that there are more sharks now than there used to be. Garbage and food remains are thrown into the sea from the ships that anchor there; fish follow this garbage and the sharks follow the fish.

I gave up diving eighteen years ago. When the pearling business died, I ran a taxi boat. In fact, I owned my own boat and trans-ported goods and passengers between Qatar, Dubai, Bahrain and Kuwait. When the museum opened here in Doha a few years ago, I joined its staff. I am responsible for the boats there. Today when a sheikh sails, he asks me to go with him. I do this because people no longer know the old names and the old places I used to visit, so I go along to guide them.

My wife died and I married again only a short time ago. My new wife is twenty-nine years old; she is a widow with a daughter and son, both of them small. Married life is the same as it ever was. But an old companion is more precious than a new one: I hold the person who lived with me from the days when I was young until now very dear. Though I live the same kind of life at home.

In the past we had to endure many difficulties and hardships. Now we lead a more comfortable life. People get salaries even when they stay at home. Especially here, the Government takes good care of the people. In the past, people were attached to the sea, but they had to toil from sunrise to sunset to earn a living. During the day, they ate dates and drank water. Their first meal was dinner. Divers used to go for five days without eating bread; they ate only dates and fish and only on every fifth night would they be given bread. Still, young men then were stronger and healthier than the youth of today. We could dive and work hard for long hours. Today's young men can no longer do this. The older generation were better people. They were more manly, more courageous, more hospitable. Now people are too money-minded. The old were different. They cared for honour, for generosity. Now people have grown selfish: whether they have one *riyal* or one million, they are equally ungenerous.

The past was better because I was young then. But in other ways the present is better. Life is easier now. We move around by car. We have air conditioners, refrigerators, cold water. In the past we used to fast during the month of Ramadan for seventeen hours in the summer, then drink hot water at sunset. Now, thank God, when we break the fast water is cold, air is cold and meat always available. To claim that the past was better is simply not true.

When I first heard that oil had been discovered here I felt happy and optimistic—I knew that oil brings wealth. But I did not really believe we would become rich until it actually happened. God mentioned in the Koran that there is wealth under the ground and that this black gold is one of the earth's riches. Thanks be to God (*he kisses his hand*). Before oil, we had a hard life.

Ahmed, Pearl Expert, Jeweller and Multi-Millionaire

Ahmed is one of the notables in Doha—one of the richest men in the country and in all the Gulf: a banker, with a major influence on the foreign exchange rate in Qatar; jeweller with a string of prestigious shops throughout the Gulf. When the pearl trade collapsed in the immediate post-war period, he and his family, who had been pearl traders for generations, were forced, like so many others, to look elsewhere for a livelihood. He opened a small jewellery shop in Doha and with it he laid the foundations of his fortune. Nowadays he runs a vast business empire and selling pearls accounts for no more than a very small proportion of his total turnover. But pearls remain the speciality of his jewellery shops as well as an enduring personal passion.

Ahmed was born and brought up in Bahrain. Temperamentally as well as physically, he is quite unlike most Qataris, although the distinction is no doubt merely personal rather than regional. Despite his relative youth—he is only in his late thirties—Ahmed is a weighty individual in every sense: tall and heavily built, formal and formidable in appearance, with heavy, brooding eyelids which emphasise the overall image of a man preoccupied with important matters. Firmly established in his position, he does not feel the need to win people over. But when he chooses to display it, he has a great deal of charm. At the same time, there is a melancholy strain in his character, unusual in Qataris. Again in contrast to Qataris who, once they have decided to trust someone, are generally astonishingly direct and open, Ahmed will answer professional questions carefully and concisely, but he reveals nothing of his own accord. And where the details of his personal life are concerned he stalls completely. Beyond the fact that he has a 'good' boat and goes fishing on Fridays, he will divulge very little about himself, his opinions or feelings.

His house confirms the impression of a man not given to self-indulgence. The villa is reasonably large and comfortably furnished, but it is by no means

Said, old diver and sea captain

Ahmed, pearl expert, jeweller and multi-millionaire

luxurious. The small entrance hall with its lapis lazuli coloured wallpaper and large painted porcelain Italian chandelier is the showiest part of it. The Western-style sitting room is fitted with a thick turquoise carpet. The wallpaper is printed with a zig-zag design in turquoise, brown and white. The chairs are low, modern and comfortable and contrast interestingly with the overall colour scheme. And all of it points to an interior decorator with a brief to be modern, but not too fanciful. There is nothing Eastern in the room but for two modern Iranian rugs, depicting a couple of demure ladies, spot-lighted and hanging on the wall. There is nothing antique anywhere except a Kuwaiti chest. There is nothing personal at all, at least not in the public rooms.

In the Arab *diwan*, a small cosy room with cushions round the wall, Ahmed sits on the floor with a large cloth spread in front of him. This is how pearls were sorted, weighed and assessed in the past. The combined value of all the pearls on display is close to one million pounds, yet they are carried around not in cast-iron coffers but in squares of red material, tied at the top like a gypsy bundle. When untied, they reveal two great mounds of pearls of varying sizes, some of them quite small. The special pearls are wrapped in much smaller bundles and are placed in front of the larger mounds. There are very small black pearls which look like extra-large caviar eggs. There are grey pearls which are even rarer than the black ones. The best kind of pearl is the *dana*. They are large, perfectly round and pure in colour. They can be picked out very quickly, even by an untrained eye, by their rosy inner light.

To measure the pearls, Ahmed uses his father's old sieves; these are the size of breakfast coffee cups—they are made of brass and have holes of differing sizes, from quite large to small. A handful of pearls is passed through the appropriate sieve, leaving pearls of roughly equal size. A small scale suspended on a green string is taken from its metal box and the pearls are weighed against different sizes of Cornelian stone which have been brought from India. This procedure is more cumbersome than modern computer-controlled methods, but the results are virtually identical. Once they have been weighed, the pearls are sub-divided again. In general, the larger the pearl, the more expensive it is—but this depends on quality, too, of course. One pearl, found just three years ago off the coast of Qatar, is the size of a small pigeon's egg. Ahmed bought it for 350,000 *riyals* but wouldn't sell it for less than half a million *riyals*.

Dealing in pearls is a profession we have inherited from our fathers and grandfathers. Many generations of dealers in Doha specialised in natural pearls. After the decline of the natural pearl business as a result of the introduction of cultured pearls by the Japanese, we gradually switched to jewellery in general.

There were no government schools then, so we children studied in private schools in which we learnt to read the Koran. Later we learnt to write in the traditional Islamic school. We learnt a bit. But in time, while we were still children, we went to sea with our father to learn the trade. The divers, and the owners of the pearls brought from the sea, would come to our house to sell the pearls to my father. We were always present, watching how they operated, the way they sold and weighed the pearls, and traded both ways among each other. Sometimes they treated us to a special present, I mean, they would buy great quantities and then give us one or two rupees as a bonus, which encouraged us to be there. We enjoyed watching the business deals: they taught us the art of buying and selling. We began to recognise all the different kinds of pearl which they examined; to note which sort they were, their colour and their shape. That's what got us interested in pearls. That's how we learnt. From the age of seven or eight onwards a child begins to have a feeling for work. He instinctively feels he should carry on his father's trade. We never thought that one day the pearl business would come to an end, so we expected to follow the same trade.

But what encouraged us most were the presents. This was a great incentive. In the morning we would go out with our father or with our elder brothers so that when they bought anything we would be there. When a group of traders was buying pearls they would sit around after they had paid the vendors and they would start an auction. When a certain price had been reached it was the custom to give the children a rupee or two rupees or even ten rupees. To be given ten rupees was obviously a fantastic event. The present was rarely more than one or two rupees but it encouraged us to go into business. We were so happy with the money. Some tried to save it. I, myself, used to spend it because I got even more than that from my father. But I saw how the others often needed it. Usually they would take the money back to their families. Or sometimes they just bought sweets in the market to take home to their brothers.

There was also another very effective way of learning. Sometimes a pearl would stray onto the carpet from the cloth on which my father was sorting his collection. My brothers and I would pick these up and sell them back to him. In time we began to realise when we were being underpaid and, if not offered the correct price, we would sell to someone else.

The actual trading of the pearls did not take place at sea, but at home or in the market. The dealer or diver would come and offer his goods to, say, three of us sitting here. Each of us would try hard to convince the seller to sell to oneself rather than to the others. I would agree to buy the pearls for, say, 1000 rupees. Then after I've paid the price and the dealer or diver has gone, a group of people who are all our partners join us. One of us puts in a bid for the pearls and the auction starts. The original bidder has the right to change his mind twice about the deal. That is to say, if the offer rests with him and he doesn't like the deal, he has the right to withdraw and make another offer. But no other bidder has the right to ask for the price to be reduced once the offer falls on him. He must buy the goods, pay the fixed price and give a bonus to the children.

The profit the traders made depended on luck. Sometimes we made 10 per cent, sometimes 20 per cent or even up to 300 per cent. Some of the best quality pearls were covered by a thin skin. When you removed it you might find a big *dana*. It was luck; usually it was luck. The same was true for the divers. They chose a spot, dived in, and came up with large quantities of shells in which they might find only a few pearls of poor quality. There are thousands of different kinds of pearls; only one *dana* might be found for every one to two thousand pearls collected. The divers might be lucky and discover pearls of excellent quality, or they might not. The best spots for pearls lie between Bahrain and the coast of Qatar and near the islands close to Qatar.

We changed from pearl dealers into jewellery dealers thirty years ago. We went through a very difficult period when the pearl trade came to an end, we had no other choice. Some people had to sell their homes and others tried to work in different fields. The whole area went through a period of terrible poverty. Very few people managed to carry on the trade. The fact is, about thirty-five years ago the pearl trade died.

Some people in the Gulf turned to gold smuggling, although gold was never smuggled from Doha. The contraband trade started in Dubai and Kuwait, and went mostly to India. The reason for this trade was that the price of gold in the Gulf was much lower than it was in India. The price of a gold ingot in the Gulf was 63 rupees, while in India it sold for 264 rupees. Even allowing for the smuggling costs involved, the profit was high. After the increase in the value of gold, smuggling it began to die out.

In about 1950-2 we started to trade in jewellery on a very modest scale. Because we were so inexperienced we used just to mount pearls in rings, necklaces and other pieces. Then, as money began to flow into the area, we gradually developed and expanded. Now we produce jewellery of the highest quality, on a par with the most famous companies in the world. We also import precious stones and artificial jewellery, from Switzerland, England, Italy, China, India—from everywhere.

In the past, pearls were not much in demand by the local women because they were too expensive. Most families collected gold and gold jewellery—21 carat gold is what they prefer—which accorded with their taste. As for silver jewellery, it is not very popular. The Bedu sometimes like it, but people in the town rarely do. Most favoured are the large pieces like the *morta'isha*; this sometimes weighs up to one hundred and fifty and two hundred *lira*. It is even possible for it to be as heavy as three hundred *lira*. It is a big necklace, a kind of choker with pendants which sometimes hang down practically to knee level. Another big necklace is the *moa'ra*; this has a sizeable centre-piece. Generally speaking it is true to say that the bigger and more striking a necklace, the more highly it is prized here. That's the difference between the Gulf and other places. Elsewhere, particularly in the

West, large items may be appreciated, but smaller pieces—smaller than in Qatar anyway—are preferred.

But, of course, taste has evolved here a good deal. Qatari women—and a good many of them, not just a small minority—follow jewellery fashions closely. I'll give you an example. Yesterday I had a watch set in a piece of jewellery in the shop. A woman came in. When she saw the watch she said immediately, 'It's made by Pod.' Then another woman interrupted and argued, 'No. It's Piaget.' They've got to know what the top international jewellers are producing. They know how the fashions change: what was in fashion last year, what's happening this year, and they can guess what will happen next year. The women's desire to develop is greater than one imagines. They read the foreign press; they see television; they travel everywhere. Gradually they have been influenced by European taste and have come to like it.

Moreover, when men bought jewellery for women in the past they looked on it as a useful investment. Jewellery was regarded both as an ornament and as a guarantee against hard times. The potential material gain was an important element. But nowadays there are many people who are not concerned with the value of their jewellery, nor does it enter their minds that they might one day have to sell it. Still . . . it's human nature for people to want value for money, so that if they do have to sell their jewellery one day, they will not only get back what they paid but even make a profit on the deal. . . .

Qataris used to buy jewellery mainly during the various feasts, such as Eid and Ramadan, and also on the occasion of weddings. But these days what people see, they want to buy. The women are no different in this respect. If they see something they like they will buy it just like that, rather than wait for some important occasion. This applies not just to the Qatari women, but also to the foreigners. There are some women who have their own income and buy with their own money. But often it's the man who pays for the jewellery, while the woman chooses what she wants to buy.

Nowadays the Qatari women can and do buy the pearls that

few of them were able to afford in the past. Gulf people go abroad
—to India, to the United States—to buy back the pearls they were
once forced to sell. But they are also able to buy here as well as
abroad because the pearl trade has begun to revive. Imagine! It
began to revive here again. Around fifteen years ago a demand for
pearls appeared throughout the Gulf: in Bahrain, Qatar, Abu
Dhabi.

The main reason for buying natural pearls is investment. Last
summer I bought three natural pearls in London for £4,500. The
three pearls have a certificate from the man I bought them from,
certifying that they were sold one hundred and thirty years ago.
Although they are one hundred and thirty years old, these pearls
are in excellent condition. They look as if they had been fished up
today. The man who bought them over a century ago probably
paid £2,000 or less. Of course, there is a difference when you
compare the value of the pound today and then. But at least they
have kept their value or doubled their value from £2,000 to
£4,500. The Chamber of Commerce in England has a laboratory
for examining pearls so as to determine their age and their value.
They will do a test for you and give you certificates. These pearls
have certificates of purchase from an institution and valuation and
test certificates from the British Chamber of Commerce.

Japanese cultured pearls have a life span of twenty years. After
twenty years you see cracks in them and their colour turns salt-like.
You would find no sign of such change in natural pearls. It is
like buying diamonds, rubies, emeralds or any other precious
stone. There is demand abroad, especially in Paris and in New
York, for a certain kind of pearl. This particular kind of pearl is
smooth and very small. These pearls are used for making necklaces and bracelets. The quality is not all that delicate, but if you
saw what jewellers were doing with them you would understand
why they are in such demand. This pearl has a special name: in
our dialect we describe it as being between a *buka* and a large
buka. Any quantity of pearls available in these sizes goes immediately to Europe. I bought the three pearls in England from a very
big broker. He told me that he would buy any quantity of pearls

like these, any quantity, because there is a demand for them. Natural pearls are especially wanted because they are not affected by age. When the cultured pearl is large is takes time before it shows any signs of change. But when it is small it is easily affected by lips, perfume and skin, which make it crack and change colour.

If a natural pearl is exposed to a strong perfume, it will break. On the other hand, if a natural pearl is pierced, then the pressure is released and the air penetrates and the pearl will not break. But if, after an evening out, a lady were to put a necklace of natural pearls in a jewel box which retained the scent of perfume, the perfume would affect the pearls and break them. The fact that the pearls had been pierced would not save them. The reason is that the natural pearl is porous and is affected by pressure generated by strong perfumes. Rosewood and aloe-wood are some of the perfumes we use. If the pearl absorbs them for some time it forms hair lines. This is because pressure builds up in the pearl and eventually it explodes. After they used cultured pearls and saw that they were affected by time, they went back to natural pearls because time does not affect them. Moreover, people like to buy something natural. They have that instinct. For example, why should you buy diamonds or emeralds when jade is cheaper than emeralds and zircons are like diamonds but cheaper? Because diamonds and emeralds are natural. Buyers of jewellery with that psychology feel satisfied by such stones because they are natural and not artificial. And cultured pearls do not have the same reflections as the natural pearls. But who buys cultured pearls?

Gulf people buy pearls now, they know what natural pearls are, and what they mean. It is all psychological. The cultured pearls which were introduced to the Gulf and ruined the Gulf, were not genuine. They were cultivated and artificial. Now people have the means to buy pearls, to buy emeralds and diamonds in any quantity they like. If God has endowed you with wealth and you feel like buying something, you buy it just as you would buy an antique or anything else you may fancy. They look for rare pearls, they buy a beautiful pearl necklace, a beautiful string of pearls. It all depends on the taste and desire of the buyer, whether he is a Qatari or a non-Qatari. As a jeweller, most of the customers I get now in Doha are from the West and they buy pearls especially of the middling kind.

In my opinion the pearl trade will come to an end. It will end. Because people will lose interest in pearls. The sea will be poisoned like the sea of Japan was poisoned. But there will still be scope for pearls in some areas, that is if those areas remain free from pollution. Of course, pollution kills everything. In our region all the fish are gradually being affected. Tomorrow big ships will come to the harbours and there will be dry docks on our coastline and in my opinion the sea will suffer. Look at Japan. The artificial pearl trade there has already been affected: after all, they come out of oysters too. I think the pearl trade will end even if pollution does not affect the sea and the pearls at the bottom of the sea. For people will lose interest in pearls. No one will be prepared to bring workers, train them and send them to fish out pearls on pure chance. Our area is moving towards industrialisation, towards progress. Affluence obliges us to develop our country and our area so as to reach the stage attained by other countries. When we have the capability we will begin to build factories and start developing and thinking about the future. Our position will be better than in the past. We shall not go back to the past, because the past was based on pearls. No matter how great the quantity of pearls there might be now, they wouldn't provide us with sufficient income. Pearls can no longer be our principal trade. But we can say we will keep the pearls on which our trade was once based, as part of our history.

When I opened this jewellery business in 1952, incomes were low and our trade correspondingly modest. But we progressed. We didn't progress very fast for the first ten years, although our profit increased from year to year. The breakthrough came in 1973–4 and now trade is flourishing. Every year I make a few trips around the world to look for new designs and discuss jewellery business with other dealers. I go to Canton twice a year because China organises exhibitions and I also buy precious stones there. I also go to Nationalist China, Hong Kong and Bombay and to Europe.

My favourite cities in Europe are London and Geneva. I spent a lot of time in London and I would very much like to live there. I feel at ease in Geneva. Most of my business is connected with Milan and Switzerland. We sell watches; I am the agent of a number of international companies. The jewellery side of our business is connected principally with Milan: there is a permanent exhibition in Milan. In Europe I also go sight-seeing. I go to the theatre and cinema. I'm not keen on night clubs but I do go to very good restaurants. I try to enjoy myself as much as possible while I'm there.

People normally work eight hours per day. But we work ten hours or more because we must cover all the various aspects of our business. Beside jewellery, we run all sorts of business enterprises, including construction companies and banking. We have jewellery branches all over the Gulf. We work from ten to fourteen hours a day. Work starts at 8 a.m.; I go home at 1.30 or 2 p.m.; I go back to the office at 4 p.m. and stay there until 8 or 9 p.m. It's hard work but I enjoy it. I didn't go to university to learn this profession. If I had the opportunity to go and study I would be inclined to take up business studies with an emphasis on banking. I am very keen on banking. I started from scratch and gradually built up my business. I have appointed managing directors for all sections of my business but I control everything. I like work. I feel I could work harder than I actually do. Though God has endowed me with wealth and I don't need to work, if I were to stop working I think I would be finished. If I don't work hard enough I get restless and bored. I like my work very much, especially the jewellery side. Jewellery is in my blood; pearls are in my blood.

Personally I have a feeling for pearls and a wish to buy them. I sell natural pearls because I feel that they are part of my life. I started my life with pearls and grew up with them, and they mean something to me. I have my own private collection which is not for sale. And I have quantities of pearls for trade. When I am sad or tired I take the pearls out and look at them and lose myself dreaming of the past and singing the old pearling songs. And I feel happy; I become happy just by looking at the pearls. Naturally, the agony of the diver who brought up the pearls is present, too, but after the hardship he came up with something worthwhile. What you see in my hand now, he got only through hard work. I mean, pearls are very precious to me, and no matter how valuable they may be they are still more precious to me than their commercial value. This special feeling I have for pearls is what draws me to them.

2. THE BEDU

—the disappearing way of life of the desert nomad

The Radio Producer and Poet

Fahad the Poet produces the Bedu Corner, a weekly radio programme on bedu life and traditions. He is by origin a bedu himself, a blunt-faced man in his thirties who speaks his mind plainly—until it comes to saying what he thinks of the West which he has visited. Bedus are traditionally courteous to strangers and according to this code it would not be right to criticise the West in front of a Westerner. So he goes on evading questions on the subject for as long as he can:

'I have travelled abroad: to America, to London and France, By Allah, may you live long, my opinion is—I have no opinion, in fact. They're good, clean countries with cold air. I don't, may your life be long, have opinions on the subject. Not about the countries I visit. No, I restrict my opinions to the bedu. And when I went, my heart was with the bedu. By Allah, there is some difference between us and the European states, and especially between them and our bedu traditions. I don't need to speak on the subject. What I like in Europe is the fresh air. The weather and the lack of noise. It's not noisy there. It's true that it's not noisy here, but there are towns where there is noise. What I don't like in Europe? The snow.'

Eventually, under the pressure of insistent questioning and the assurance, frequently repeated, that criticism will not be taken as an insult, he gives in. One of his objections—against people with long hair—is rather startling considering that it comes from a bedu, for the bedu have always worn their hair long, and usually still do; but one sees what he means.

By Allah, the bedouin—long may you live—the bedouin are different: their values are different. There are two categories of bedu. There are the people of the sheep, they call them *ash-shuwwan*. Then there are the people of the camels—those are the true bedu. They are also known as the travelling bedu because they don't restrict themselves to one country, but go from place to place. They move until they come to a country where there's rain and greenery and they stay there and rest and when the grass is finished, they go in search of a colder climate or trees and forests for their animals.

The bedu, long may you live, is self-reliant. First, because he spends his childhood in the desert. At the age of seven or eight he sleeps in the desert by himself. So he learns to face wild animals with courage—that is to say he's not afraid of anything. For his livelihood, he depends upon camel's milk or meat he has hunted —gazelles, bustards, hares, such things. Now there are few bedu, but in their time the bedu lived a harsh life. They lived by looting and robbing. They were hungry.

When he grew up, the bedu youth was given weapons. His father would give him a gun, a horse, a sword and a spear. He wore these weapons and forged his own character with them: in this way he became a man. Once he had weapons, his next step was to get married and found a family. To pay the bride-price he went raiding with his tribe to capture camels or other animals. He would marry from his own tribe. And then, after he was married, he had to make a home, raise children and rear camels. After he had done all this he was a man in the eyes of the tribe; before, he was considered as nothing.

A bedu's only capital was what he could obtain by raiding others. What he took from another tribe in this way would become his by right. That was in times of hardship. There's been a lot of change now in this age of prosperity, of petroleum. If you go to a bedu settlement now, you can no longer say 'This man is a bedouin.' You will find that the bedouin have everything that can be had in the towns. He has many things now and no longer needs to raid. He eats the same food as they eat in towns. He has a car—he has everything that is available. He has a salary from the State. So now I don't think you could call him a bedu, but he still sets off and travels with the camels because he loves this way of life. He comes and goes, but the old times are over and finished.

When he travels now, the bedu lives a way of life that is close to the old way, except that he no longer has to face the hardship that people had to accept in former times. He lives in comfort.

The old-style bedu life existed until oil was discovered. But not the raids. The raids stopped when the State came into being, at the time of Hamad bin Abdullah, may God have mercy on him, and Abdullah bin Jassim. They took over from their father, the founder of the State, Sheikh Jassim bin Mohammed. When Jassim took control of the country, the raids, the looting and robbery stopped. There was no more raiding here. If anyone wanted to loot, they had to go further afield. But people still had to live. And they had no other source of livelihood than the sea.

When I was young I lived in Dukhan—Dukhan is in the west of the country, west of Doha. I used to herd sheep and goats. I used to come and go with the sheep and my father taught me the Koran. In the spring we went off into the desert and in the summer we came and settled in the town—here in Rayyan. I studied the Koran with a special Koranic teacher. Of course, I studied no other subjects with him except the Koran. At this time, I went out to the desert with my father. We stayed there for a while and then moved on to Saudi Arabia. There was poverty here; no rain and no life. So we went to Saudi Arabia with our animals and spent two years there. I came back here when I was fourteen years old.

When we came back the oil had begun to flow. Petroleum was found in the very place where we had been living and where there had previously been nothing. I saw installations and vehicles. I knew nothing about such things and was terrified of them. I asked myself 'Why have these cars come here?' Then I began to mix with drivers from my tribe and I went with them so as to learn to drive. I spent time with different drivers, then I came to Doha, took out a licence, and got a job as a driver. I worked for two months as a taxi driver. Then I went to the al-Thani family; I would go hunting with them—that sort of thing. From then on I found that each year was better, more prosperous, than the one before.

But life in Dukkan before oil, by Allah, that life was hard—anyway, that's what I think. We had nothing to eat but dates—dates and milk. Nothing else at all. Also I remember that while I was herding the sheep as a young boy I was stung by a scorpion. I was alone in the desert. My only companions were the sheep and a donkey which carried the water. I had heard that if you are stung by a scorpion, you must bury the affected limb in the ground. It was a bad night: from sunset until morning I had to remain in the same place with my knee buried in the ground. When I got up in the morning I found that I had no sheep. Nothing. I started to walk, feeling terrible, and somebody found me, half dead from thirst and from the pain in my leg. He took me to our tribe. The next night, while I was still in a bad condition, my mother died. That was a terrible time for me. It was then, after she died, that we went off to Saudi Arabia.

As far as my education goes, my father taught me much. He taught me how to write poetry, how the couplet ought to be formed, its principle and origin; also how to write satirical poetry. Then, when the schools started, I continued my studies in the new Rayyan school until I got my primary school certificate. After that, I started to recite poetry a lot. I would satirise poets and attend poetry reading and meetings. So people started to call me Abdullah ash-Shaa'ir, Abdullah the poet. Wherever I went I would be called by this name.

I was soon in the first rank of *nabati* poets—*nabati* is the name given to the poetic form favoured by the bedu. Whenever a wedding or party was held, I would be invited together with another poet and there would be an exchange between us. Each one would satirise the other. Each poet attacks the other, but when it's all over they greet each other. It's not serious. We always did this kind of thing on special occasions, such as Independence Day or Accession Day. From the day I began to become known as a poet, my prospects brightened. When radio and television started, the authorities said: 'This poet Abdullah must supervise the bedu programme.'

My upbringing and the fact of having talked with poets all my life served me well at this stage. I learnt by listening to someone reading an old poem while the others commented on it. They would observe that a word was not right here, and that the metre was faulty there and discuss the authorship of the poem. And so, gradually, I improved.

The subject matter of *nabati* or colloquial poetry is the same as in classical Arabic poetry: love, camels, horses, special occasions etc. Nowadays, the bedu even write poetry about cars: about the Mercedes Benz, the Ford and the Chevrolet:

> *The Benz of this new model and type*
> *We buy with the labour of our forearms,*
> *It is not a gift!*

They write about aeroplanes too. For example, if someone wants to send a letter or message—an imaginary one—he sends it via an imaginary poetic aeroplane:

> *I am a passenger on a plane*
> *Flown by a pilot who disregards his life.*

I have heard some bedu poetry about the MIG plane. But I don't write poetry of that kind. I write didactic and love poetry. Nothing else. The last poem I wrote was a piece of advice to my son:

Sahman, get a pen and paper,
My heart is bursting out.
Take down these lines, whoever listens to them
Will find a way through the closed door:
I advise you, my son, to avoid dishonourable people,
Keep away from them even if they are friendly;
Men who unfold in your heart a paper
On which they help you write doubts and suspicion;
Be careful and protect yourself from their evil,
And greet the men of the night who will return your greetings;
Whoever tries to exploit you, generous youth,
Leave him, let him go hunting, for the road is wide open;
Don't let down the kind man who honours you,
And greet the men of the night who wll return your greetings;
His tongue may steal what you hear at night,
What scoundrel brings this to the meeting?
He wants you to follow his path,
He is misfortune chained with hate.

I was taught by my father to be silent when I went into a *majlis*, to be sparing with words. My father also taught me to greet guests when they visit the house and to give them every assistance. He taught me good neighbourliness: to be modest before one's neighbour and friendly to him until he leaves. He taught me loyalty to my comrade. Suppose we set out together and the water supply runs low, if there is just one drink left then I should let my friend have it; or if there isn't much food I should leave it for the other. My father had faced this kind of situation himself, but I only lived this type of life for a few years, say three or four years. When I was grown up, companions of the road didn't— we praise Allah—have to choose who would have the last of the water.

But there is still humility. Humility is a virtue that I think I have retained in common with many other Qataris who also have inherited it from their grandfathers and their ancestors. Humility is what saves a man from falling victim to pride. There

is a bedu proverb which says: 'A proud man's fate is perdition.'
The non-nomads have another proverb which they cite if they
see a proud man: 'The only thing that gets big is a manure heap.'
That's the one quality that the bedu regard as essential: humility.
But also good manners. If a person passes another and greets him,
the other should return the greeting humbly; he should also guide
him on his way. So humility is probably the only value of all
those my father taught me of use to people nowadays.

In the far distant past, the people of Syria, Iraq and Egypt—
even the people of the cities—were all bedu. Then they possessed
the qualities I have mentioned. But with the passing of time and
as people began to mix, so these qualities were lost. Not all of
them, of course. Loyalty was and still is an Arab virtue. There's
no doubt about that. I don't think the Arabs will ever lose this
entirely.

When I travel to Dukhan, I see many changes on the way.
First, the bedu tent has been replaced by houses of brick and
cement. Then, the road I used to travel on in the past was unsur-
faced: it was just a camel track. Now it is asphalted. In the past
it took us three days to get to Dukhan. Now it takes one hour. In
the past when I got there, I would find only dates and a little
buttermilk. Now, I find meat, fruit, everything. Then, there were
no oil installations; I would see only bedu tents. Now, when I go,
I see lights everywhere, and towns like Umm Bub, Jehila etc.
Perhaps I wouldn't even be able to find the place where I used to
graze my sheep now! (*with a slight laugh*).

In the past, you would find only one or two houses or tents
together. Now all the bedu have gone to live together in the same
areas. They've been provided with plenty of water and electricity
and such things. And, in contrast to the way they were before—
because of the bounty that was bestowed on them—they have
become more comradely to each other. In place of the recrimina-
tions that used to occur in the past, they now have a more friendly
relationship with each other. They will say: 'Peace be unto you'
and 'Please come in. I've got so and so visiting me. Come and
visit me.' So it has become and we praise Allah for it.

Another change in manners and morals. In the past, if a bedu saw anyone, he would say: 'Where have you just come from?' Now it has become ill-mannered to ask such a question.

Bedu are now paid salaries by the State. Or they work, in the gas company, the cement company etc. I was employed as a driver for three years. Then I got a truck and went back to live with the bedu; I lived like that for a long time. In the *badia*—the desert—there were no springs of water. There would be one well with a bucket that was generally a long way off. I transported water in my truck, also sheep and wool, from one place to another. I bought the goods I needed in Doha. When broadcasting started, I began to present radio programmes and became an employee. I have been broadcasting since the year it started, which was 1969.

The programme I present is called 'Bedu Corner'. It tells listeners about the bedu way of life in the past: the people, the stories, daily life, the poetry. I have recorded many programmes on bedu subjects. There was one called 'Bedu justice'. And 'Bedu medicine', and 'From the bedu heritage' and 'Bedu stories'. Also 'A letter from the bedu', 'Bedu life'. The programme is very popular, and not just in Qatar but in Saudi Arabia, Kuwait, the Emirates—the young people are still interested in poetry.

Apart from my work for the Ministry, I have another job in the Nabati Poetry Club. This is also part of the Ministry of Information. Its purpose is to introduce plays to the bedu; we also record poems by Qatari poets and edit books of their work. I have a commercial business and I have a shop—I deal in spare parts for cars.

I have travelled abroad: to America, to London and France. What I like about the people there is the fact that they tell the truth. But what I don't like is the way thieves are allowed to operate, to rob visitors to the country. Why don't the Governments eliminate them? Why don't Governments seize the thieves and exact reparation? Another thing I don't like is the way a girl goes out when she reaches sixteen or seventeen and enjoys complete freedom. Why don't they keep her under control? Isn't she her father's daughter? Why should she go out? I don't like the way wives are free after marriage. Husbands don't care about their wives or their children in these countries. Everyone is free to do as they like. Another thing: the young men and even adult men spoil their appearance. They have long hair. They wear patched clothes. I don't know why.

Then there is envy. I've noticed some of them envying us. Some envy anyone they see wearing decent clothes or who has money. Why should they? It is the Lord of the worlds who decides. I've seen a lot of them who envy the Arabs for what Allah in his bounty has given them: oil, clothes etc.

The people of the Arabian Peninsula all cover up their women. When a woman shows her face it is a kind of shame; she feels shy about showing her face. Of course, according to Islam, to expose her face is not nakedness. No. In God's eyes, an exposed face is not naked. But we've adopted this habit from our grand⁄fathers and great⁄grandfathers; it's a tradition. For this reason, her mother, father and brother put pressure on her. It is pressure in matters of honour, not in material things. She can choose her husband. She can come and go, but she must be covered up. There's no difference in this respect between the bedu and the settled peoples. My wife still wears the *batula*. I'd slit her throat if she took it off. That thing on her face is a protective covering. Nobody lets his wife go out without it. My daughter, possibly. It makes sense in my daughter's case. She's been to school and studied. Also, now I've seen more myself, and understand more, for example that an exposed face is not naked, I might allow my wife to go out without the *batula*, personally, but her brother and father would not like it. We are undergoing a change in life⁄style and traditions because a girl goes to school nowadays. She has colleagues at school who do not wear what their mothers wore. There is still some pressure on her, but it is getting less. I think that in a few years the *batula* will disappear completely. It was our ancestors who started the habit of covering the face. Why? So that when a girl grows up and is ready for marriage, she might be thought to be beautiful. Cousins might kill each other in order to marry her. If she were known to be ugly this might prevent her from getting married. That's why the veil was introduced. No other reason.

If our oil ran out, my children could return to the old bedu way of life. Because I will leave them camels, sheep and horses. They can ride horses and camels. They eat dates—they still have dates —and milk. I've brought them up this way. Not only me. There are a great number of bedu who settled in the towns who have also taught their sons these things. Maybe they won't be able to find meat. In that case they can drink milk. If they can't find vegetables, fruit or anything, they can eat dates and milk and live like their ancestors. I am sure they will lead comfortable lives.

The Student Teacher

Ali is a bedu in the pure romantic tradition: immensely warm and generous, proud, independent, scornful of cant—a real dare-devil. He is also grossly unpunctual, frequently failing to turn up at all, and quite appallingly prejudiced against outsiders in general and Iranians, Palestinians and Egyptians in particular. However, he is always ready to love his friends, even if they are Iranian, Palestinian or Egyptian and this, in some measure, excuses his prejudice.

His face, in repose, is as fierce as that of a character in an Eisenstein film: the features are strongly marked, the moustache abundant, the eye whites very white, the eyes acutely observant, suspicious. In fact, although it is not immediately evident, he does squint and this greatly reduces the sinister quality of his gaze which sometimes appears to be directed towards the end of his own nose. A very individual person by any standards, Ali is particularly interesting because he grew up in a traditional bedu background and, at the same time, has been formally educated, not just in secondary school and at the training college—he has also met many foreigners and travelled outside Qatar. He is training to be a teacher because there are too many non-Qataris teaching Qatari pupils, he says. Beyond the usual bedu pursuits of hunting and fishing, his main hobby is acting: he spends most of his time in the evenings at the theatre. During the week he lives in a hostel in Doha, at week-ends he goes north to where his parents and young wife live.

The road to the north, like the roads very young children draw, is one long straight line. It is January and the desert looks alive and cheerful; there are pools of water everywhere and a new growth of grass, as sparse and silky as a young man's beard. The sun dodges between the clouds which appear for only a few weeks in the year, and great arcs of light swing across the shaded desert. There are a couple of agricultural schemes, but otherwise no trees on this road. The conversation somehow turns to Adolf Hitler who, everyone agrees, didn't have much to recommend him. 'Yes, but . . .' says Ali, 'wasn't he brave?' Suddenly, at a particular point along the road, where the desert looks no different to the untutored eye from the desert over the past thirty kilometres, Ali begins to beam happily. This is, as he puts it, his country.

Soon our destination appears on the horizon: *medinat al shamal* or the town of the north, a Government-built 'new town' where the bedu have settled. Ali's cousins, aunts, uncles etc. are thick on the ground. When not at home they tie their outer gate with a white cloth. The local sights are pointed out. 'The owner of that house' Ali waves his hand at it, 'is being treated in the London Clinic.'

The first port of call is Ali's wife. Her mother is sick so her father will not allow her to leave home. The situation is obviously rankling to Ali, but he takes a cheerful view. 'Once we have a few babies crying their heads off they'll be quite happy to let us go.' His wife is a slim-waisted girl with long black hair parted in the middle, a direct gaze and a laconic air. Ali teaches her to read and write, doesn't he? Yes. She observes him affectionately, ironically. Everybody adjourns to Ali's bedroom; tea and a plateful of biscuits are brought in. Ali opens the wardrobe and points to a rifle. 'There is a rifle in every room of the house. For hunting, you know. Or maybe thieves might climb over the wall,' he says hopefully. The family party sit around on the floor, friendly but watchful. Ali's aunt recalls meeting a European woman ten years ago when they were still living in mudbrick houses. This woman was very sorry to see them live such miserable lives. The old bedu woman laughs.

It is dusk now and the men in the village have begun to gather at the outside *majlis* of the local educational headman, a relative of Ali's. He is a rather handsome, serious man in his thirties with a short black beard and dark eyes who manages to remain dignified while being clambered over by a small dark daughter in a scarlet dress. Ali pours the coffee, since he is younger than his relative. About half of those who crowd into the small room seem to be poets. One young man pulls a typewritten sheet out of his pocket and offers it shyly. Then everyone moves on to Ali's house where his parents have prepared a feast for a friend who had just come back from hospital in Europe.

All the men crowd into one small room of the low concrete villa. They sit on the floor round two large mats. Then two enormous steaming platters are brought in from the kitchen; there is one lamb on each laid out on rice prepared with special spices and dried lemons. Before tucking in with their right hands, the men pull the mat over their knees in case the rice should spill. Father and son serve; they will eat later with the family. The lamb is delicious but very hot and, on this occasion, not too easily detachable from the bone. You pull and pull at different places, but to no avail. Everyone is, of course, watching out of the corner of their eye—although they politely pretend they are not—and soon titbits begin to rain down on the portion of rice in front of you. By now the whole company is smiling, like indulgent starling mothers feeding a rather dumb chick.

The meal is over quite quickly. Everyone washes their hands carefully and wanders off; it is not polite to hang around after eating as we do in the West. The remains of the two sheep are carried off to the next room where husband and wife heap tin plates with meat and rice and carry them off to all the houses in the neighbourhood. These are presents for the families of the men who have not been invited to the feast. Only when a dozen or so plates have been sent out do the family eventually sit down to eat.

When we were children, we bedu knew nothing of Doha. If one of us bought a new *thaub* everyone in the village would go to his house to see it. We played, went to school and slept in the same clothes.

The habits and traditions of the bedu are better than those in urban areas. The bedu is unspoiled. Unlike city people, who have mixed with others and travelled abroad, he is not affected by external influences. He is braver and more gallant than townsmen. He is generous. Yet, townsmen consider the bedu hot-tempered and uncivilised.

Frankly, when I'm with my family, I say I'm a bedu but when I'm in Doha I say I'm a townsman. I live like a townsman. It is true that the bedu are good hearted, gallant and generous, but they have their defects. For a start, they don't allow you to go out with your own wife. Secondly, they expect people to be generous even when they are poor and have nothing to give to guests. The bedu don't allow any individual to reject a tradition or to attempt to change it. When I go home I have to wear my *thaub*. I have to get up at dawn to pray. I can't shave my moustache. They want everyone to live just as they do. Here in Doha I can do what I want. Some bedu reject education. There are families even now who will only allow their children to learn the Koran.

But some bedu traditions are still strong in me. Once I went to the airport. I found a man lying on the grass. I took him home with me, fed him and offered him a bed although I didn't know him. I also obey my family. I don't like to do anything to upset them. If anyone killed a member of my family, I would have to kill him. It's true—I carry a weapon in my car.

A bedu's wife does nothing but cooking, washing, etc. My father treats my mother as if she were a machine. But I am different. I am a liberal bedu. Though my wife is not educated, I don't ask her to wash my clothes. My clothes are washed at the laundry. She doesn't cook for me since I live for most of the week in a students' hostel in Doha. I go to the north on Wednesday after-noon and come back on Friday evening. My mother does all the cooking. If I lived in the same house as my parents, I couldn't treat my wife as I would want to. I would treat her like my father treats my mother, only less strictly. I will teach her how to read and write—I do that now.

As a matter of fact, we—the bedu of the north—are not popular here in Doha. Townspeople consider us as backward and heart-less. They think that a bedu would give up a friend for any quite trivial reason. This is not true. But still, by God, I have had to put up with a good many nasty remarks in Bahrain and even here. Once, in Bahrain, someone said to me that if I went into a shop I should speak in classical Arabic. Can you believe it?

There's a big difference between the traditions of the bedu and the traditions of the town. I was once invited to the house of a town family. The host brought the incense and as I was a guest he should have given it to me first. Instead, he handed it to some-one else who held the incense pot underneath his clothes. This is shameful. I protested vigorously; I did not hide my feelings. Then we went inside to eat. While I was eating, the person beside me held a bone and crunched it. To a bedu, only dogs crunch bones. When we eat, we say to the host: 'May God enrich you.' That fellow, when he had finished eating, said nothing. When a bedu is invited to a banquet held in honour of a guest, he should invite that guest and fix a date for the next banquet. But townsmen go home without inviting the guest to dinner, lunch or even coffee. When I argue with them about such traditions they claim that I am ignorant.

When I first came to Doha from the north many of my friends were there too. In school you find that the front benches in any class are occupied by the northerners, the central benches by the pupils from Doha, and the Palestinians and other non-Qataris sit at the back. Sometimes the teacher even told us northerners that we smelt.

Even the way we salute each other is different. A bedu greets his friend by placing his nose against his friend's. I always do this. Someone of my father's age, I kiss on the nose, forehead or head. I kiss my mother's hand or head. I shake my sisters by the hand. Townspeople kiss their sisters on the cheek.

Bedu in the north get up at 4 a.m. to say their prayers. If you don't get up your family wakes you forcibly. After that the bedu go to work, either as coastguards or as shepherds or as government employees. He returns at noon to have lunch and then he sleeps. In the afternoon he either sits in his *majlis* or looks after his falcon. He sits chatting for hours on end about sheep or any other subject. After evening prayers he goes home and has dinner with his wife. After dinner he chats again and then finally says his night prayers and goes to bed. Usually people talk about traditions or falcons or something. Some bedu are given jobs by the government, but they don't have to go to work. Their names are registered on the payroll and at the end of each month they receive their salary. They are appointed as foremen, coast-guards, watchmen or drivers. My father is a mechanic and driver because he used to work at Shell. He likes to go to work.

But many bedu don't have to rely on their salaries. Some rent out houses in Doha which they own. Others loan cars to the government. My father receives a salary of 1,500 *riyals* a month from the government. I live on a scholarship from the government and have an extra allowance from my family. My scholarship is 1,150 *riyals* a month. I work at the radio station on a committee that checks on the texts of plays for serials. For that I am paid 1,353 *riyals*. My father has houses, shops, taxis, cars and land. The taxi licence is sold at 120,000 *riyals*. At the student hostel, accommodation, food and laundry are all free.

As a child, I remember, I used to get up early. In the morning I went to school and in the afternoon I trapped birds or went fishing. We played many games which are unknown to towns-people. Al Saagair is a game in which one person plays a criminal and has to be caught by the others, but by his head. We also used to ride on palm branches as if they were horses and play at having battles. We made catapults of rubber and wood. We got the rubber from old tyres. We played hopscotch. We collected seashells and we played football. We made traps for birds with animals' intestines or animals' horn. We fished in forbidden ways. We used poison although we were not supposed to. We used to go in groups, men, women, boys and girls, to spear the fish in the shallow waters. The ends of these spears were as thin as needles. We also caught fish by using palm leaves and branches to form a sort of dam during high tide. When the tide began to ebb, the fish could not penetrate the barrier.

Our provisions came from Doha. We bought sugar, rice, tea, petroleum in drums. In 1959 and 1960 there were cars. I remember they were orange.

The house we lived in was made of stone and mud. The roof had wooden logs covered with animal wool, to protect us from the rain and the heat. Sometimes the roof was covered with straw or with bamboo. The rooms had one small window. It was barred with two sticks in the shape of an X to prevent cats and dogs from entering the room. But scorpions and snakes could not be kept out and they were very dangerous. We had a small cupboard called the *Rawshena* where such things as brass jugs and incense pots were kept. Clothes were hung on wooden pegs or nails. From within the room was coated with a thin layer of gypsum which was white. This kind of house was well suited to the climate. If you live in a room made of brick, it's hot in the summer and cold in the winter, while rooms of mud and stone are cool in summer and warm in winter. We kept a drum in a corner to wash. The WC we called *al Adab* and that was outside. The floor was covered with a rectangular reed mat. They were bought at al Ihsa or Bahrain. We had a carpet made of plain or coloured wool. There was, of course, a storage place for the rifles. It was either in the *majlis* or else in a corner of the room; the rifles were hung next to each other. Each house had a shed for sheep and a stable for the donkey. We travelled by donkey to the farming areas. The best farm was the one with the highest palm trees and that was ours.

At home I can say that my life now is exactly the same as when I was a child. It is true that we have a modern house but I live just as my parents have always lived.

I love my parents equally, but sometimes if my father beat me I preferred my mother because she would always protect me when he tried to hit me. Not that he did very often. Also I love my father because I feel he is the protector of the family. As for my parents, sometimes they were happy together and sometimes they would quarrel. For a day or two they wouldn't talk to each other but then they made it up. They knew neither could do without the other. The difficulties of life made both of them exaggerate problems.

My father used to beat me if I quarrelled with anyone or if I went out without permission or stayed away for five or six hours. He didn't like me to go out with the older boys. Some used to steal pigeons or fish from the fisheries. We all used to steal from the fishermen and we were beaten for that, also for hitting younger brothers or sisters, or taking a rifle out. I was beaten most often for not going to the Koranic teacher. I used to smoke secretly. I remember the first cigarette I smoked was 'Navy Cut'.

When I was a boy I loved the sweets that came from Bahrain —they were famous throughout the Gulf. I also liked a sweet made of flour baked with cardamom and saffron and a cake called *al ogeili* which we baked at home with flour, saffron, eggs and milk. It was baked on charcoal, but only at feast time. I also liked porridge with sugar, and macaroni.

Our mother sang songs and lullabies. They varied from tribe to tribe. She told us about the man of the sea to frighten us, for we believed that there was a ghost living in the sea. She also asked us riddles. I remember one was: 'They are unwrapped at night and you do not find them in the morning.' She meant the stars. She told us also of a green tomb with a golden lock and an iron key. This was a watermelon; the iron key was the knife.

I remember that mothers often told fables about wicked step-mothers to keep their children attached to them. One was about Serour who was killed by his step-mother and served up for dinner to his father's guest. The boy's own mother had died and his father had married a wicked woman. She was very gluttonous. When the father killed a lamb she roasted it and ate it herself. To conceal her shame, she served up the boy for dinner instead of the animal. The man, of course, looked for his son. He went every-where shouting 'Serour!' From her grave his dead mother called out, 'Serour was killed by his step-mother. His legs and bones are under the stable.'

I began to go to school in the north, but after the fourth grade I had to go to school in Doha. I stayed there until the end of my first year in the secondary school and then went to live with an aunt in Bahrain. After secondary school I worked in the Ministry of Health for just over a year. My cousin was a director there and he found me the job. But I went back to Bahrain because I was in love with a young girl there.

I met the second girl I loved at a wedding party. She was my cousin. I used to go to the area where she lived to meet her. She always used to ask when we were going to get married. If we had the slightest tiff she would tell me that I didn't love her. So one day I went to a nearby village, bought three needles, found some soot, mixed it with a herb and tattooed her name on my skin. The next time she said I didn't love her, I told her I could prove that I did—and I showed her the tattoo.

It was love at first sight. This, of course, was after the memory of my first love had died. I always wanted to marry a beautiful and educated girl. But my family refused to allow me to marry her. This was because she had been brought up by her divorced mother. Some bedu believe that if a woman alone brings up her daughter, the girl is not respectable. Frankly I was not convinced and still am not. I think a woman can bring up a girl to be well- bred and honourable. There are many tough, fierce men whose daughters wouldn't hesitate to do anything behind their backs. I am educated and so I think for myself. But I gave in, partly because the girl got married herself. So what could I do? I married my other cousin. At that time she loved me, but I did not love her. I knew she loved me because my sisters told me. I thought if I married her I would be freeing her from her father who's a difficult man. Now I respect and love her.

I want to go out with my wife but I can't. It's true that some people do so when they travel abroad. Here in Qatar someone is needed who will break the ice. But who will have the courage to do so? If you go out with your wife, people talk. Or they might whistle. If anyone did this to me, I would . . .' *(threat too terrible to be uttered. Author.)*

Education changed me a lot. Also I became friendly with foreigners, started going to football matches, to drive cars, to move around and travel abroad, so that gradually the influence of tradition became weaker. But I have not changed in all ways. I treat my guests in the same way as before. I go hunting.

I had no particular desire to go to the College of Education, but once I did I was keen to get good marks. I didn't want to study abroad, because I get homesick. I like to read, but I hate the very word 'examination'. Napoleon used to say he was ready to fight ten battles but not to take one examination. That goes for me too.

When I went to school, my mother used to say to me: 'May the

Almighty let me live until I see you become a clerk.' That was her ambition. Good heavens! in their eyes a clerk held a really unbelievably high position. Later I discovered that there are doctors, engineers, army commanders, ministers. My family wanted me to be educated to become a clerk. But I now know that I have been educated to learn about my country's problems and to find solutions for them. I am educated so that I will know how to deal with other people and how to lead a worthwhile life. I am more liberal now. In the past, I stayed with my family all the time. I met guests twenty-four hours a day. Now I live in a hostel and spend only two days a week in the north. I joined the theatre and spend most of my evenings there. But I want the theatre to improve people's way of life rather than to change it. I think we should be trying to maintain our good traditions while also trying to make people think and to raise their standards generally. In the theatre we reveal the Qatari's problems and either we suggest solutions ourselves or else we leave it to the audience to do so. We put on plays which show the Qataris are no angels.

I want everyone in this country to perform their duties faithfully and to improve themselves, and not to take on three jobs and do nothing. Such people are useless to their country. I want this country to become cleaner. You saw our houses, you saw the wood and the goats in the back yard and all that rubbish. Although the government has built modern houses so that people can live in a civilised fashion, some of them stick to their old ways. You saw the disorder. What I want is for everyone to think more about hygiene. I'd like them to be more educated and to learn to speak more foreign languages.

The Educational Headman of the North

The things I'll never forget are the days of spring when there was greenery and plenty of food and young lambs. Greenery is dear to the soul, there is no doubt about that. But we loved spring all the more because when it came there was more grazing for the animals, more prosperity.

I remember, too, how we used to turn back for home at the end of the diving season. We would go diving for two months; I went, too, although I was only a child. One day my father would say: 'Come. In two hours, time or tomorrow we are going home to the desert to see your mother and the other children.' These were the happiest occasions in my life, because I couldn't bear these two months. I couldn't bear them when I was only nine or ten years old. These are things I shall never forget.

We would come back and find my mother. She would be standing waiting for us on the sea-shore, ready to receive us. I would want to go and see my home and everything around it. After that I would run to see my friends who hadn't gone diving and we would play games together. But there were no celebrations when the boats came in; there were few celebrations in Qatar then. On Eid days my father would perform a folk dance with swords called the *'Artha* and also teach me it.

I was born and grew up in a place in the north called Al-Chumail, one of many small villages there were by the sea because, as you know, people in those days lived mainly by pearling. In the winter they looked after sheep and other animals in the desert.

My origin is bedouin. My grandfather was a bedu. I consider myself a mixture; I am half bedu. But I have lived a bedu life and I am proud of my origin. Bedu values make you proud of being a bedouin. First of all, the bedu has a pure origin. The bedu are not camel-drivers as we imagine. You will find all the Qatari tribes—al-Thani, Kuwara, al-Kubaisi, al-Muhannadi—all of them are of bedu origin; that is to say, that they come from the Arabian Peninsula. The qualities of the bedu are truthfulness, faithfulness, willingness to help others, gallantry, nobility. All these virtues we derive also from our religion, but we were bedu before Islam.

The bedu have one custom in particular which is different from those of non-nomads. They put aside a certain sum of money to be used in case anybody is killed by another man—by mistake, that is to say. If this happens, the bedu put together this money and pay it to the person who needs it, as blood money, in the name of the tribe or the group to atone for the dead.

We bedu have a direct relationship with our surroundings, a direct economic relationship. Especially in desert places like Qatar, rain would come only very occasionally. Some years there would be no rain. Other years it would come and bring greenery and happiness. Even nowadays I can tell if it's going to rain or not. I know which kind of clouds and which winds bring rain, and which don't.

After I left secondary school, I took a diploma from the Institute of Management in Doha and went on to work as a secretary in the Department of Religious Affairs. Then the Ministry of Education began to look for an educational officer for the northern area. Now the people in the Ministry were all Arabs, but they were foreigners from outside Qatar—and you know the problems with these people here in the north, you have to go to them and persuade them. When the Ministry found that I came from the region myself, they thought that if they sent me I might be able to make the changes they wanted to see. And, praise be to God, I have fulfilled their faith in me. I changed everything in the north. The transformation you see here all happened after I took over. I was able to achieve what I did only because I was patient with the people and persuaded them gradually. And because I was one of them myself.

I started ten years ago, but I have not spent ten full years in the Medinat Al Shamal. I spent five years struggling, before I was able to move up here with my family. During the first five years when I took over the north I lived alone because the place was only half-built, there were no comforts. I lived with a paraffin lamp and used a primus stove to cook my meals.

Our aim was to persuade the bedu who lived in dozens of very small villages to settle together in one place, Medinat Al Shamal. Unless we could do this there was no way of providing them with modern facilities, with water and electricity, healthy dwellings, hospitals and schools, especially secondary schools. Now we have achieved what we set out to do. But we had to overcome many difficulties at the start.

First of all, I had to face the problem that people were proud of their village. They were attached to it. They would say: 'This is my village and my father's village and my grandfather's village, how can I leave it?' So I tried explaining to them that the State was trying to help them by educating their sons and improving their living conditions. Then I collected the people together and brought them all to the Emir's office; the Emir, God preserve him, said much the same as I had been saying and also promised that they would be well cared for. Eventually they agreed and moved together into the town, but it was an exhausting business.

Now they are happy here. The State kept its promises and provided everything they needed: it gave them jobs, it installed the services. But people still feel drawn to their villages; they haven't really settled down yet in the town. They don't feel that this is where they come from and they don't feel any strong attachment to it. I'm still persuading them, but they're a little reserved on the subject. During this fifteen-day holiday period we're in now, they have all gone back to their original villages. Everyone puts up a tent and stays in it. Besides, every Thursday and Friday, they leave the town and go back to where they came from. At the weekend they just stay in their old houses. But in longer periods, such as at the moment, they go to some green area and set up their tents there, but modern tents not the old hair ones. The adults still prefer to go back but, as far as I can see, life here has become natural for the children.

The former bedu get bored with life here; the Government housing is good but it gives them the feeling of living in a camp. They sometimes get fed up here and they enjoy going back to the old way of life in the desert, of being close to nature. Here there are no facilities for entertainment and not much comfort. You're shut up in your house. So they feel they want to get out and enjoy the greenery at least.

Now that we've succeeded in bringing the people together here,

I am responsible for their education. My office is the connecting link between the Ministry and the local people. My daily work consists of signing official papers, inspecting the teachers, and educational administration generally.

I believe that education has become as necessary to everybody as water and air. Because it's through education that society changes. I want change, I believe in change and I work for it. I believe, for instance, that Qatari mothers should not be illiterate but educated: that Qataris should be fully and not just half-educated. I believe that we must have Qatari doctors and engineers and that all this will come about and, in turn, further transform our society. I believe in an educated society that retains its customs, religion and traditions.

Where education is concerned, we face some resistance, even now. But I try to make them think about it. About the doctor in the hospital, for instance, I say: he was once a child who knew nothing, but then he was educated and now he can cure sick people. But most of the opposition is to girls' education; we find that there's no real objection to the boys being educated. Someone might say: if I allow my daughter to be educated and she learns how to write, she might write love-letters to somebody without my being able to understand what she's writing. That would be some father's opinion, if he was illiterate. I tell them that if the daughter is not educated and the son is, then the time will come when the daughters won't be able to find husbands. At least this is what I used to tell them. Most of them were persuaded and are now sending their daughters. We've got over the biggest hurdles; now only the lesser problems remain. They tend to marry off their daughters at the preparatory school stage, for instance, when they are only fourteen or fifteen, to half-educated men. But this is a problem which we shall get over in time.

In general, women in Doha have more freedom than women in the north. In Doha a modern woman, especially if she is educated herself and married to an educated man, enjoys her liberty; she goes out with her husband. But tribal women, especially in the north, are more restricted. They had more

The bedu student teacher

Gulf hunting falcon

Qatari girl in
national costume

freedom in their villages, before they moved into the town. What was the village? Some villages had just ten houses and all the people living there were related to each other. They were as one family although each household was independent. The woman could be free with her relations.

I myself think there is no need to be excessively strict. Besides, even if I were strict, if I trusted my wife I shouldn't care if one or two people saw her and looked at her. The rest of the tribe, the younger bedu, have begun to break the chains. They all take their wives with them to market and they shop together. But they are still afraid that the older members of the family, her mother or her father, might protest. As far as my own daughter is concerned, I must remove the shackles that bind her. I must allow her to face the world, to face society, to work in a working environment, but at the same time to retain her customs and traditions. Every woman must be allowed to develop her character and personality, then many problems will disappear. Character and knowledge—these are what matter, nothing else.

As the old problems recede, new ones arise. I can see that it's necessary to get this region moving economically, so that people don't depend just on Government employment. Prices are rising and people need more money. We must set up factories in the north. We would like to see some of the factories up here rather than at Umm Said or Dukhan. There is already a small port here; we could expand and develop it. This would prevent Medinat Al Shamal from stagnating, and allow it to increase and grow.

People here depend entirely on the Government for their employment. Everybody living here works as an employee of Government services and agencies. Most of them earn salaries of around one thousand five hundred *riyals* a month. One person might work in two jobs; they work in the morning and in the afternoon and they earn two salaries. The Government allows this sometimes if people need extra income. They can also earn more money by hiring out their car, if they have one, to the Government. The Ministry of Education, for instance, hires around twenty-five cars here on a monthly basis and pays one hundred and twenty *riyals* a day for each one. All the cars here are on a list and everybody has a turn at renting to the Government for one month every two years. This is another form of Government assistance.

By God, here in the north, the people spend all their income. It melts away. They have more money to spend than they need to live on, but if they want to buy a car or a television in instalments, their savings soon disappear.

If they are sick, they travel abroad at the State's expense. Here in the north people don't travel just for pleasure. But many, old and young, have been abroad for treatment and they talk about what they have seen. The old say they saw strange things. They are particularly surprised to see the women uncovered, or nearly naked; by the dancing halls; and the way that alcohol is just drunk in the street. Of course, these are extraordinary things to them. The young like what they see and think of transforming their own society to bring it in line with European societies. But neither young nor old spend long enough abroad to be really deeply affected.

My hope for the future is for this town to expand and for factories to be set up here. I must convince people of the impor-tance of the north, and we must all work to remove the differences between the people of the north and Doha. *Insh'allah*, there will soon be a second town up here. We could also develop agri-culture. I like agriculture. This is the most fertile part of the country and there are many farms up here, but the people need to be stimulated and given assistance.

If the factories are brought in, the people here will work in them. They won't refuse; they are not bedu to that extent. All the people here, all the Government employees, are prepared to work. We've got technical people, we've got electricians, we've got pipe fitters, we've got everything. Our town is no different from Doha as far as work or jobs are concerned. It differs from Doha only in its customs.

I'd like to see the Government build a village based on the old bedu way of life. They could build this village the way they built the museum in Doha. Tourists could visit it. In America they did that once: they built a whole town as it used to be in former times. Here in the north they could build a large village of, say, forty or fifty houses. They could also develop beaches, because the beaches around here are the finest in the country. This is the best area for tourism, if only they were to care about tourism. Apart from Doha, where can a tourist now go? We must make centres for them. The north is rich in beaches.

The Falconer

You generally become interested in falcons if you grow up with them. If, as a child, you have lived amongst people who have owned birds and hunted with them, you will develop a great love for them and want to protect them and carry them around on your own wrist. I began to be familiar with falcons when I was six or seven. We often went out to the desert to hunt.

Hunting falcons is not easy. They migrate to this country from mountainous areas such as Iran and land on the shore. But to catch them you have to trick them, for falcons are more prudent than men. Above all you have to be careful not to make a noise or to call out; they are afraid of the human voice.

In the end we trap the falcons because we are cleverer than they are. Once the bird is in our hands we immediately sew its eyelids together with fine thread, though this is later removed. Then we cover the head completely with a small hand-made helmet or hood from which only the bird's beak protrudes. We give the bird a name and for the first night or two a falcon trainer has to stay up with his new catch gently echoing this name. This goes on for several days until the bird becomes attached to the man. During the first four or five days the falcon will try to bite the string tied to its leg, then it will become tame. But we don't allow it to fly freely at this stage: we keep a string tied to its leg. Our aim is to train the falcon to find food for itself: we do this by keeping the bird hungry and calling it by name to discover the raw pigeon we have prepared for it. We untie the string on the leg only when the bird is ready to hunt.

The best quality falcons are called the *shahin* or the *al hur*; they are quite different. The first is renowned for its speed and can track down its prey in any circumstances. The *hur* is rare, it is bigger and better-looking with a broad chest and strong legs. There are also big differences from one bird to another. Some are young, some old. A falconer can always recognise the best, but he must see them in action because some falcons only come into their own on the hunt.

The longer the bird is together with the falconer, the longer it hunts with him, the more familiar it feels with him. Slowly, the bird comes to understand that the falconer is his colleague and that they must co-operate when they hunt. It gets used to sitting together with humans who look on the bird as a companion rather than as an oddity or a savage creature. As it grows tamer, it loses its fear of men and dogs. This point about dogs is important. The falcon and the dog are given food together and they come to look on each other as mates: the bird knows that the dog is helping it. Neither is afraid of or aggressive towards the other.

There are some birds that scratch and bite, but this is only because they don't receive enough attention. Whatever you do to try and teach such a bird, it will not learn. That is why it is so important to carry it around on your hand all the time. Unless you do, it will become unmanageable, squawking, beating its wings, scratching. You must take it with you everywhere, even when you go to drink tea with your friends. If, for instance, you bring food to an untrained bird, it will try to wrench the meat from your hand, and eat off the ground.

Being a falconer is a full-time job while you are doing it. Each bird has to be carried for three months of the year. During these three months, if the bird means something to you, it should never be separated from you. You should feed it with your own hands and so it will come to love you. If you are driving a car the bird must be put on the seat beside you. If a falconer has two or more birds, the training becomes very difficult, since he has to put one down before he can carry the other and so on.

After the three-month hunting period is over, the falcon is shut up with others in a darkened room where it is fed regularly. But no one looks after it or speaks to it or holds it on the wrist any more. It is locked up for around six months and only allowed out again two months before the next hunting season. In that time, it forgets everything, all it has previously learned, even its name. So it has to be retrained from scratch.

This bird which I have named Marzouk is a *saker*. In the summer it cannot even find a piece of bread, because birds do not like hot weather. That's why we lock it up. Each year it grows new feathers and it is by looking at these that we are able to tell its age.

This kind of rapacious falcon comes to us from Iran and Russia —from cold regions. They come to us because it is warmer here than there, but when the really hot season starts they leave. So we have to imprison them. They should also be kept as cool and quiet as possible.

One falconer can teach up to five birds at a time. During the hunting season they may bring me a bird, I train it, send it out to hunt and then train another. The trained bird is given to another falconer who hunts with it.

When we are hunting the bustard, we have to take several falcons with us, say four or five. If one flies off to look for bustard, and doesn't find anything, it may get lost and so a falconer who leaves the camp with four to five birds may return with only one.

When our bird attacks the bustard, it carries it off instead of returning with it, so we carry drums with us. We guess where it might have landed, drive there and wait. We also carry with us bustard wings as a bait and we wave them meanwhile, calling the bird's name. If the bird is near and unable to catch a bustard it comes back. If it has caught its prey, it will spend the night outside after eating and we have to start calling it again in the early morning.

Falcons do not recognize bustards by themselves, as a matter of fact. So we have to make use of the bustards' wings to teach them. The bird is kept hungry for two days. On the evening of the second day a piece of meat is placed between these wings. It is called by name: 'Marzouk, Marzouk . . .' When it hears this and sees the wings it lands and finds the meat. This is how it comes to realise that it will find food in these wings when it is hungry.

It is true that some breeds of falcons are better than others. But finding a good bird is also a matter of luck. Some lower quality birds which may have proved difficult to catch and difficult to train may turn out to be very good. Part of the reason is that a bird doesn't hunt for its master. It is kept hungry and when it hunts it does so for itself.

Falcons can cost a lot of money, say 30 to 135 thousand *riyals*. This is why if it goes off after a bustard, fails to catch one and then gets lost, we are very unhappy.

When a bird has been with us for one or two or three years it becomes very dear to us, and we will take great care of it even if it is not very expensive. Marzouk, for example, is not expensive. He is worth only 6000 *riyals*. He is not a very high quality bird and still untrained. So far it has not yet attacked a bustard—its price will increase when it does. Marzouk is a male bird, but there's no real difference between the sexes. Some say that the females chatter a lot, but I don't believe it. Anyway, *shahins* are all silent. They are very impressive the way they swoop, quite unlike other birds.

Hunting here has changed a lot. In the past there was plenty of game in Qatar because there were fewer people and cars, less noise and not so many hunters. Now, the hunting season is over in about fifteen days. We heard once that there was plenty of game in Saudi Arabia. So all of us went there but we found nothing because so many Saudis were also hunting. We also travelled to Iraq where you can find plenty of game and bustards. This year we went there in the early winter when no one else was around. We hunted a lot, a record amount. One month later we went back there again but there were so many other hunters that we found very little. The first outing lasted for 45 days and we caught 1,187 bustards. The next time we caught many less. The number of game birds has just declined from one year to the next. In the past there were plenty. Now there are virtually none and there will be less and less.

I wish I could get out of this hunting business. It's an awful job. First, it goes on in the cool season, when temperatures in the desert are often below zero. Second, it's so dangerous. You could easily lose your life. And these birds tear at your hands with their beak and claws until they bleed—my hand is covered with wounds. It's all very difficult, especially when it's cold too.

Of course, it's satisfying when your falcon catches a bustard or when you shoot a gazelle or deer. But you may also have to face lions, tigers and wolves. There are plenty of these in Iraq. Every day we meet two or three.

I wish that hunting would come to an end so that I could lead a peaceful life. Sometimes the drivers are so busy scanning the sky that they overturn the car. That happens often. Or else the car may break down. Until they rescue me, sometimes only several days later, I have to do without food and water and am exposed to the greatest dangers. I do hunt goats and roast their meat, but we run out of tea and coffee and water and it's not comforting to think that nobody knows a thing about us, especially when the car is damaged.

When you're hunting, you have to get up at 3.00 a.m. You drink your coffee, then take your car to the petrol and water tankers and check what you need. You also have to take a stock of food, usually biscuits or dry food. You say the dawn prayers and set off. If you've gone south the day before, then you go east today. You have to drive off before sunrise or else the bustard will see you and since they're feeling energetic at that time they will fly off.

When you've spotted your bustard, you remove the falcon's hood and send the bird in the direction of its prey. When it catches a bustard, you cut off the head and give it to the bird, some of it but not too much. If God is helping the hunt the falcon may find as many as fifteen bustards.

A falconer will fly only one bird at a time and will carry a gun. At 10.30 we usually stop for coffee and sleep for a while: we don't like to exhaust the bird during the hot part of the day.

You might come back to camp at any time: six, seven or eight o'clock in the evening.

In the morning the falconer chooses a different direction. He must take good care to mark the road and the trees so as to find his way back in the dark. He has to assess the amount of game in the area and keep the others informed.

He may easily drive into a soft muddy place as I did this year. There were three of us. We got our clothes all muddy while we were trying to extract the car, and it was freezing cold. It was four days before we were rescued.

Still, this bird is part of my life and I devote all my time to it. At certain times I do nothing else but look after it. It becomes like a child. If I am thirsty while I'm carrying it, I would rather wait for a colleague to turn up and give me a glass of water than abandon it. If it goes sick or catches cold or is hurt, I am sad for it and nurse it. I take it to the vet if there is one nearby. Falconers develop a special sympathy for their bird, as much sympathy as they feel towards their own children. You find you're always asking whether the bird has had its meal or if anything is wrong with it.

As I said at the beginning, most falconers' interest in the bird dates back to their childhood. But falconry takes place for only three months of the year. So for the rest of the year, a falconer has to have another job. I, for example, work as an employee in the electricity department. Four months before the hunting season, I am called from my work and my only job then is to take care of the bird. The sheikh for whom I work pays me a salary and takes care of me and the bird. He provides us both with food. I go back to my job when the season ends and then back again to the sheikh whenever I am needed, because I am a well-known falconer.

3. OLD MEN REMEMBER

The Poet at Al Khor

Al Khor is a large old fishing village set on a bare incline above a
turquoise bay. It is spring; the sun, standing high in the sky, is kinder than
usual to the modest strands of colour—silver, beige, buff and charcoal—that
criss-cross the Qatari flat land. For a few short weeks, the desert appears to
have been spread over with a soft Scottish tweed. A line of fragile young
trees, doubly protected by wooden fences and barbed wire, appears at the
outskirts of the village. And above the mainly new, straggling concrete
houses loom a cluster of minarets, not slender and soaring like English church
steeples but low, homely and rounded, for Islam is preeminently a practical
religion.

The poet lives behind a high, white wall, punctuated by a wooden door.
The courtyard behind is spotlessly clean and presided over by two patriarchal
goats and a jubjub tree. In the centre stands a low, whitewashed, one-roomed
building where the poet lives by himself. In a country where no-one seems
to be alone, ever, this solitude seems somehow remarkable. The room itself
has long, narrow windows built into the thick walls which allow any passing
breeze as well as the sounds of Al Khor—birdsong, goat bleat, child cry,
motor engine—to enter. There are cushions round the walls, low tables and
large cardboard boxes used to store things in, marked Sony and Kodak.
Like many a bachelor quarter, the room looks dusty and disorganised. But
the cups into which the Arabic coffee is poured are taken straight from a
covered tin bowl filled with clean water.

The poet is old. He has a sharp, thin nose, black hair streaked with grey,
and watchful brown eyes strangely flecked, like a bird's wing, with specks
of blue and grey. He apparently believes that all foreigners are Jugoslavs.
Beyond this slight eccentricity, his mind is clear and his memory unimpaired.
In the old days he worked at sea. 'Life at sea was really terrible,' he says, 'and
we longed to quit it.' Later he worked as a guard with Sheikh Hamad,
the father of Sheikh Khalifa, who helped the needy or if there was a death
in the family or if anyone got married. 'I used to eat and drink with him.
He was not haughty.'

An individualist in an intensely social society, the old poet keeps the
village at arm's length. No, he does not commemorate people who die there
with a poem. Why should he? They are not his family. When guests leave,
he carefully locks the wooden door behind them.

When oil was discovered, I was working as a watchman with the first oil company. Then the Second World War broke out and the well was closed. We had no work for eleven years.

We were told that oil was black gold when we asked what it was. We had no inkling of how it would change our lives. In the past the kind of oil we knew was different. We used to catch a big fish, take out its liver and from this we extracted oil to paint out ships. We did not know that the oil of which they spoke would bring us an income of even four *annas*. At that time we were all working as watchmen for threequarters of a *riyal* per day. When the pipelines were extended and big ships came to take the oil away—only then did we feel that our lives would change.

I was born here at Al Khor. The village then had about five hundred houses, made of mud and stone, not of brick like now. The roofs were low and covered with palm leaves. We wore a white gown only when we visited the town. In the houses we kept sheep, cows and—God bless you—donkeys. The donkeys used to carry stones and also water from the wells. They left at noon and came back at sunset. The water was carried in goat skins.

When a Qatari was born he was rubbed with a kilo of salt; this was to strengthen his skin. After seven days the salt was washed off. From then on the baby was only washed when it dirtied itself.

The bedu in Saudi Arabia did not have a bath for six months at a time. In Qatar, too, in the old days, the boys never washed during the five or six winter months. The Lebanese used to bathe of course, and so did the Egyptians, even at that time, but we never did, not even in the sea. We only went into the shallow water to collect our fishing nets.

When we got up in the morning we used to wash just our eyes with water, for children do not pray. Then we were given the bread which remained from supper, together with some milk and ginger. We breakfasted at dawn. Those who studied went to school. One teacher taught about fifty boys and girls the Koran and the Arabic alphabet. We had to pay four or five rupees every four or five months. In the summer we sat outside by the wall. Each of us brought along something to sit on—either a piece of mat or a sack. The teacher used to place the Koran on a chair to keep it undefiled. I learnt the Koran by heart as my mother had done before me, with the same teacher. Sometimes the teacher beat us with a fish tail—the tail of a heavy fish that hides in the sand at the bottom of the sea and tries to crush men by lying on top of them.

Islam taught me to pray, to pay the *zakat*, to be helpful to strangers and generous. The Koran had a very great influence on me. Is someone who can drive a car the same as someone who cannot? Is someone whose eyes are open like a blind man? The Koran is a great guide; it taught me how to avoid sin.

My father, God grant him mercy, was a poet and an eloquent man. He loved to mix with people. At that time the Qataris were good-hearted and had little to occupy them, no buses, no cars, no contracts. When they came back from the sea, they visited each other's houses in turn and drank coffee. They talked about falconing, about diving, about courageous warriors, about camels, about the desert and the sea.

I sat with them from the age of seven. When we had finished our lessons we joined the adults in the *majlis*. This had an important effect on me because learning at a young age is like carving a stone; when one is old, to learn is like trying to sculpture the sea. The prominent poets taught the others to write descriptive poetry on falconing, bravery, etc. When my father's scribe died I started to write down his poems for him. I also wrote his messages to the rulers.

In those days boys used to have an attachment to some animal —a gazelle, a camel or a dog. I had a gazelle and my first poem was to a gazelle.

My mother was the one who told us stories. She would speak of lions and wolves that devour little boys who go out alone in the desert. This was intended to prevent us from straying away from the tent area when we went out into the desert. There were other fabulous tales like the one about the orphan girls who had a camel which brought them food.

When a mother wanted to make her children sleep quietly, she would tell them that if they were good, the following morning a gazelle would come and she would milk it to make tea for them. We used to see gazelles in our dreams.

I have written poetry on a great many subjects. Some are for the Ruler: rulers are like swords—their subjects should furbish them with their praise. Some are for my friends, some are about love, some about religion. I compose popular songs. In the past I wrote sea shanties for people to sing while they worked. I wrote songs which people sang when they went out into the desert. These might be addressed to camels, or to water, to a camel while it was drawing water or while grazing. I write poetry for cere-monial occasions and also at other times. But poetry is like the sea: the tide ebbs and flows.

The young men of today know and sing my poetry, even on television. Sometimes singers come to me and ask me to write them a poem on a particular subject. They then compose the music themselves, present it to the Ministry of Information which approves it and pays the singer, the composer and the poet.

But there were more poets in the old days. Each village had three or four. There was at least one poet in each tribe. In those times poetry was used to satirise people and indeed it had more effect than a spear. In the past poetry was used as a weapon, especially when there were rivalries between tribes. Nowadays poetry is only sung on musical occasions. So now we write lyrics to suit such occasions. Poets are like tailors: they fashion their poetry to fit their subject.

We were different in our generation from the young people of today. In the past there were only three watches in this country; the teacher owned one of them. Maybe only six people had shoes. We wore three pieces of cloth, one of them round our waist, and one draped over each shoulder. These *thaubs* we wear now are not ours, they are Egyptian.

But how can people here ever go back to the way they used to live now that they have learnt in Egypt, in London, in America, in Austria? Some things in the present are good, God bless you. People are more comfortable, but their minds are not.

When I was young, if anyone had saved ten rupees he felt as wealthy as Croesus. He went out, bought himself rice, dates and coffee and cut some wood in the desert. He'd get water from the well and he drank without purifying it. He ate the fruit from the trees and was happy. He asked no questions, nor looked for answers.

Now one hundred rupees are worth no more than one *riyal*. This *thaub* I am wearing cost me fifty *riyals*, but in the past it would have cost just one *riyal*. You could buy two women's dresses for a *riyal*. A man could marry his wife and pay no more than forty *riyals* in all. I swear by God, only forty *riyals*. People used to help you. A friend or a brother would give you a goat; someone else would offer a lamb. Then you would prepare the grain and marry your cousin. Nowadays it costs fifty thousand *riyals* to get married; but not in our day.

It is not good to have two wives; it is good for neither the heart nor the mind. The heart loves one person only, not two. If you aim a rifle, does it strike twice? No. It hits only what you aimed at. In the Koran it is written: 'God did not create two hearts in a man.' If you love one person, you should carry on loving that person to the end of your life. When my wife died I did not re-marry. I am old now.

I have one married daughter who lives in Doha. I have a pension from the State. I have been abroad, once to Kuwait and twice to Shiraz. I visit Doha maybe once a year. But usually I go nowhere. I spend all day at home. Just before sunset I visit my neighbours or they visit me. I watch television. Television shows us all the places we have never visited: Egypt, America. I bought this television four years ago. I also have a radio and a tape recorder.

If I were young again I would do what all young men do—I would get married. But let me tell you, if a horse doesn't find a mare he would not go with a she-camel. Nowadays our type of woman no longer exists.

Said, From Poor Diver to Prosperous Old Age

Despite his regrettably exploitative attitude towards women (openly admitted), Said is in many ways a grand old man and the best driver in Doha (author's prejudice openly admitted). The features are well-cut and quick to crease with a charming open smile, the small form—he is slim and no more than five foot three inches tall—energetic and very upright in spite of his sixty-five years. He wears beautifully laundered white *thaubs* and drives a green Chevrolet which he owns himself; he is always punctual. He seems to know everybody in Doha, if not in the whole of Qatar and, like the old bedu that he is, never gets bored waiting, for he can talk ceaselessly for hours on end. It comes as a surprise at first when he marches into every office, from the highest to the lowest, with you to shake hands with the occupant. But then he disappears as discreetly as Jeeves. Unlike Jeeves, however, Said is never deferential; he is an equal.

I was born and brought up on the northern coast of Qatar. My father died when I was eight or nine years old. My three brothers and I worked. I also have three sisters. We had difficult times at first. We cut the long grass and we sold it. In the summer we went to sea.

We didn't have much food to eat, but we were healthy. We were blessed by God. God says he protects the weak. We didn't suffer from any diseases. If we didn't feel well we drank herbs as laxatives which helped to clear the system. Or we used fire to cauterise. After taking the herbs we felt better.

These days were hard. We went to sea first as *tabbabas*. The *tabbab* was the one who served older divers. We worked for no wages, just for our keep. This went on until we grew up and worked in different fields. We also bought and sold camels until we grew up. I worked mainly as an entertainer, a *nahham*, on the pearl boats until the companies were set up. Then I started working for a company as an electrician. I knew nothing about electricity but the company trained me. I worked for two or three years as an electrician. Then I took up driving which took me a month to learn. I became a lorry driver. There were very few drivers in those days.

I remember my father, though I was small when he died. My mother was happy with him. In those days there were no doctors to treat people. My father fell ill. When he went to sea, his stomach swelled with the high tide. When he stayed away from the sea, the swelling disappeared. He stayed with us for a month. We took him to a doctor in Bahrain. But there was nothing the doctor could do. He died there. We brought him back and buried him in Qatar.

My mother treated us well. But life was hard because we were very poor. Life was difficult even for the sheikhs. When we were at sea our mother and sisters lived on what we gave them. The *tabbabas* were given tiny pearls as a bonus, which we sold for up to ten rupees. Also, after the *tawash* had bought pearls, he would usually give us a small present for serving meals and coffee.

In the past we lived in tents. The women made a living by weaving. My mother and sisters made carpets and sometimes did some knitting for a fee. In those days everything was cheap. One could live from winter to summer for about one hundred *riyals*. This was before the war. Soon after the war there were plenty of cars. But before that they used camels and donkeys.

The camel eats and drinks a lot. When we took the camel to pasture, we let it graze while we gathered twigs, lit a fire and cooked our meal. Food and water will keep a camel going all day long. If it had nothing to eat during the day we would feed it at night. We gave it water from the wells we found on the way; we also filled our leather bottles with water. It's not true that the camel is indifferent to man. The camel shows interest in man. But when it is in rut no one can approach a camel, especially a male camel, unless the camel knows him. If a temperamental camel doesn't do what it's told, the man beats it with a stick until it obeys him. The camel responds to the way people treat it. The male camel can be difficult to handle; the female is friendlier and easier to handle. The camel has no time for nonsense, it is not friendly—like the dog. The dog is a poor thing. Once we had a camel; when we rode on it, it would only stop when we pulled the bridle. It was gentle and good. If we wanted it to sit down or to change direction we poked it on the neck and it did whatever we wanted it to do. But when it was in rut it wasn't easy to handle. Sometimes camels have fits of madness and people avoid them when they see them in that state. The females are in season for only a few days in the year—and not every year at that!

In the past we had different names for summer and winter. We had two seasons: *Qaid* (summer) and *Shita* (winter). Each of these seasons lasted six months. We didn't celebrate the coming of each season. We celebrated the Eid and the coming of Ramadan. We also celebrated the coming of the *Wasmi* rain. We praised God for the rain. In those days we had no air conditioning and in the summer it was very hot. We stayed in the country. We didn't go to town.

The men and the women lived together in the same tent. We divided the tent with a partition. But the women stayed together and so did the men, the men slept separately. But man and wife slept together in a separate place which was also used for guests. Once a woman had reached the age of puberty she wore a veil and a face mask. Women wore those things to protect their bodies. The veil brightens a woman's face. When she gets married and removes her veil, her face appears as bright as a light. Those bedouin who could afford it had more than one wife, up to four. Not more. But if the man divorced one then he could marry another one.

I have been married three times, but with only one wife at a time. I divorced one and married another. Once I'd had enough with one, I divorced her and got myself a new wife. I have no patience. The women would have been at each other's throats. I have no mother. She died soon after my father. If my mother were alive I could have had two or three wives. My mother would have controlled them and would have seen that they were all treated equally. My sisters took care of the house after my mother died, but they wouldn't have been able to control the wives; in any case they would have married. Mothers and grandmothers usually controlled the wives and treated them fairly.

The advantages of having more than one wife is that you can

have more children. Also when the turn of one of the wives comes, she would prepare herself in a way that would please the husband. And the husband would have a jolly good time! On that night the husband sees her like a bride. Each woman tries to win the attention of the husband. The women don't like this system. When a wife finds out that the husband is engaged to another woman, she becomes depressed and sick. The woman feels that the husband will favour his new wife and she will be regarded as the old wife.

I divorced my first wife because I saw a good and pretty woman and wanted to marry her. My wife was getting on in age. Whom would you prefer, a woman with two or three children, or a girl? Obviously, you'd prefer a girl. If I were not concerned about my children I would have taken two wives. For if I get more children I might not be able to support them. My first wife did nothing wrong. Nor did my second wife. I divorced the second for the same reason I had divorced my first wife. My present wife is about thirty years old. When I married her she was about sixteen. I'm about sixty-five now.

Times have changed. We are happier now. There was no peace at sea; the work was depressing and dirty. We drank water while our sweat was dripping into it. The food wasn't clean. The clothes we wore were also dirty from sweat. In the past we couldn't afford more than two or three *thaubs* a year. If you could buy two or three dresses you were regarded as a sheikh. Now the wardrobe is full of clothes. Now we have thirty or forty *thaubs* in the wardrobe. We must wear nice and clean clothes to compensate for what we missed in the past. We had hard times in the past, but now, praise be to God, we have everything in plenty. In the old days when one wore a clean dress people would say: 'This man's used soap to wash his dress. Where did he get the soap from?' I must always be clean, because a person who is dirty is avoided by people.

Life began to improve because I had a steady income. When I first started working for the company my salary was 75 *riyals* a month which was a lot in those days. Before working for the company it would have taken me several months to earn that much. I also did overtime. Since then things have improved. After two years my salary increased to 200 *riyals* until it reached 500. I was given an increase every two years. I worked for the company for twenty-one years. I couldn't save while I was working because I had to support my sisters. But when I left the company they gave me 65,000 *riyals* and a house. With that money I bought a house and land. I sold that house and made a profit. The house cost 18,000 *riyals* and I sold it for 22,000. The land cost me 8,000 and I sold it for 15,000. Since this venture things improved and now I own houses and live on the income from my property. I don't have to work now, I have everything in plenty, praise be to God. I have three cars.

I married when I was working for the company. I divorced and re-married while I was still working for the company. Marriage and divorce cost a lot of money. When you divorce you must give the wife about 1,000 *riyals*. You have a lot of expenses when you get married, such as a new kitchen, jewellery, dowry and so on. I paid 8,000 *riyals* as a dowry for my present wife. For the second one I paid 400, for the first one I paid 80 and jewellery worth about 100 *riyals*. The present wife cost me a lot. She's a relative of mine. I have four children from the previous wives and eight from the present wife, the ninth is on the way. My eldest son is still at secondary school. I have four boys and four girls from my present wife.

My eldest son can do whatever he likes. I want him to support himself. My other sons are still at primary school. They will choose their own future. I never went to school. So I didn't know what was good for me. In the case of my sons they will know better because of their education. I wish I could be young again and had the same opportunity as my sons. I would study to become a doctor or a director, the number one boss, second only to a minister.

The Merchant in the Market

In the old days this town, Doha, was just a village. At the time I was born it numbered no more than 8,000 souls. The ruler at that time was Abdullah bin Jassim al Thani, God have mercy on him and accommodate him in Paradise—he was the father of Sheikh Hammad, the father of the present Ruler. There was no work in Doha except pearling. At the end of the season the boats were pulled out of the sea and painted; they would be kept ashore until the next season. During the remaining six months of the year the only work for Arabs was buying pearls, because they considered any other form of trade to be shameful.

In the winter, people would do various jobs: some of them would catch fish, others would go out into the desert. In the desert they would own she camels, sheep and goats, and birds for hunting, and dogs for tracking down hares. They would enjoy themselves in the desert and visit the town occasionally to buy the necessities of life, such as rice and dates and coffee and such things. In the spring the bedu brought wood from the desert, which was an important fuel at that time, used for cooking mainly. They also brought clarified butter, and a stiff kind of yoghurt. They brought truffles; in the old days we had many more truffles than now. Truffles grow in the ground like potatoes, only they are better. In fact they are delicious and very expensive to buy. You can only find them at particular times of the year: they grow if it rains in the autumn. If the rains come late there will be no truffles. It's no use if it rains heavily later, the ground must be wet at the time when Scorpio is in the sky. People in the desert lived quite comfortably in the spring. They killed the male goats, but they kept the female ones for breeding. They were in very good health, because they only ate natural products, such as yoghurt, dates and rice, and the meat of these small goats and sheep. They would stay in the desert until the end of spring, pack up their tents, take leave of their camels and sheep and goats, entrusting them to the herdsmen. These divers would then go back to their main work of pearling. People in those days were happy, even if their income was small.

We had nothing really until God opened the door of prosperity and the oil companies came. Then people started to work in the companies. They would start off as labourers, then learn a bit, and progress to driver, then learn a bit more and become a mechanic, then learn English, so they would become clerks, and so gradually our standard of living began to rise, until we reached our present level. Now, praise be to God, our Ruler has made everything easy. We now have embassies in every country, and these embassies are there above all to look after sick people. In my opinion, we were living in darkness in the past, and our condition has changed from darkness to light.

When I was young, I always wanted to go into the town—in their youth people always liked to be in the town. I had a boss called Mr Steve and I asked him to try me out as a driver and I said 'If I succeed, I succeed. And if I fail, I fail'. He grew very fond of me and didn't want me to stop working for him. But he gave me a test: I had never driven a large vehicle before, only a car. So I got into the car, and they put barrels, which they brought from Doha, on the ground and two candidates passed. When my turn came, I took a strong grip of myself—and still today I don't let work get on top of me—if I succeed, I succeed, if not. . . . Anyway I got into the car and drove around in between the barrels and was told 'You've passed'. So then I went to my employer and asked to be released, but he refused. I said 'You shouldn't deprive people of opportunities that are offered them. I know you're fond of me and I respect your problems, but at the same time you must realise that my circumstances are pressing. I have a family and if I become a driver I shall earn three more *riyals*.' So he gave me permission to leave and I worked as a driver.

I worked as a driver until the Second World War. The company's oil operations in Qatar were closed down, so I went and worked in Saudi Arabia with the oil company there. I worked so as to have access to lorries; I was then able to buy and sell dates, flour, tobacco, in different areas, because my salary was much too small. In the end I left Saudi Arabia and returned here for this reason. I began to trade with Muscat, Suhr and Dubai. I opened a shop in the Souk Khaled; I bought it for only 2,200 *riyals*. Gradually business improved. Dealings with people then were straightforward and honest, there was no double dealing or trickery.

When the business was starting, I had 35,000 *riyals* which, in those days, was a large amount. For that sum I bought a lot of canned meat and beef sausages and stored them in the building of Sheikh Fahad Bin Ali. There was no air conditioner and it was hot—you know what Doha's like in the summer. To tell you the truth, I had borrowed a sum of money from a trader in Bahrain who ran a similar business there, so I went to Bahrain to see him and said 'Oh brother, I have some money which belongs to you and you've been carrying goods for me to Saudi Arabia, so I'll sell the canned meat I have to you three *riyals* cheaper than you sell it to Saudi Arabia'. And I decided if he wanted it, I would have it transported from Doha to pay off the debt which I owed. Anyway, he didn't accept my proposal. So I said to myself, I think I'll leave this kind of business. God got me out of this pickle without any loss. And I gave up selling canned goods because there were too many competitors and the town was small. I thought to myself, I shall now work properly: I shall work as an agent. Anyway I discovered it was very difficult to become a successful agent unless you could grease the palm of the inter-mediaries. For example, an intermediary would say 'I'll bring you an order for thirty cartons; I'll take twenty and leave ten, of these ten half of the price will go to me and half to you'. That's not the proper way to do things. Look at this clean *thaub*, I wouldn't want to dirty it. As God made me rich, I must preserve my integrity. So I am forced to switch from one business to another, in search of an honest loaf of bread.

I was hardworking and, praise be to God, I succeeded in my work. And now, praise be to God, I have some building com-panies. Where did they come from? All of them came from God.

And I have shares. All of this I acquired through trading. I am one of the founders of the cement company, the flour mill, and the fish company, but I have never had anything to do with banking. I keep away from things which are dubious. I avoid taking interest on money: all that I have earned comes from commercial enterprises. I have nearly seven million *riyals* in one bank, but I don't take even seven *dirhams* interest on it. Although I keep money in the bank, often if I have five to six thousand *riyals*, or one million, I buy a piece of land with it. We have a lot of land that we've bought; at present we just buy land, we don't sell it, because land will always have a value. I used to be concerned solely with trade, but then I followed this new path and, praise be to God, have derived a lot of benefit from it.

I have shops, not just one shop, and I have a money-changing business. There's plenty of prosperity, and we know that God will go on increasing our wealth, and never decrease it—as long as we continue to pay our *zakat* and perform all the duties that God asks. We travel a lot and spend a bit of money here and there, but, praise be to God, at the end of the year we find we have made more profit. If there is ten *riyals* more profit from one year to the next, we say '*alhamdulillah*'.

PART TWO

The New World

THE TECHNOCRATS

Mohammed—Like Any Western Technocrat, Almost . . .

A young woman nuclear physicist goes off to a foreign country to complete her Ph.D leaving her husband, with his consent and encouragement, to look after four small children, two of them twin girls of eight months— the circumstances would be impressively enterprising and unconventional in Western Europe or the USA, let alone small, traditional Qatar. Yet it is hardly the talk of the town in Doha, neither a showpiece nor a scandal. People who know Latifa merely say that she is 'quite a girl' and leave it at that. Photographs show a lively, attractive woman in her early thirties with a dark bobbed hair-do.

While she is away studying, there are two Indian nannies and a cook to look after things at home. The Government pays for her studies and for some travel. Any additional travel plus the very expensive weekly twenty-minute telephone calls to the children from Cairo are amply covered by a very substantial family income. For her husband, Mohammed, is director of a Government department and also owns property. Latifa chose to do her doctorate at Cairo rather than at one of the top British universities which also accepted her because the residency requirements in Cairo are no more than three months in a year. For the moment she has gone for six weeks and will be away for a further six. After a month or so in Qatar, she will move— babies, nannies and all—to a rented house in Surrey, for Cairo lacks certain vital equipment and she has further research to do in England. In the meantime, the question: 'When is mummy coming back?' is easily fielded by her husband with the answer: 'Next week'. Small children, fortunately, have a notoriously defective sense of time.

Like its occupants, the family villa has a firm sense of its own identity. Unlike Western-style rooms in some Qatari houses, the sitting-room is neither barn-like nor stiffly regimented; it is a pleasant size, with a few low, comfortable modern chairs, casually placed. There are fresh roses on small tables and a notable lack of knick-knacks. The one characteristically conventional Qatari note is struck by the bookshelves: the *Encyclopaedia Britannica*, some beautifully bound Government publications and a copy of General de Gaulle's speeches. The latter attests however only to the recent cultural assiduity of French Embassies in the Gulf. The books that are actually read are all upstairs where the family lives, amidst babies, toys and television.

Foreign guests are received in the sitting-room and Qataris in the Arab *majlis* on the opposite side of the hall. 'We feel more comfortable here in the *majlis*,' says Mohammed. The *majlis* is a fairly large room, capable of seating twenty-five people comfortably. It is, of course, unfurnished except for the usual large, expensive modern Iranian carpet and the habitual white-covered cushions with blue patterns round the walls. But the old rifles, collected by Mohammed and hanging on the wall, are an unusual feature. There are more Arab antiques in the hall: a fine old Kuwait chest and a number of old brass coffee pots. Also rare is the profusion of lovingly tended plants. Even the most prosperous Qatari households tend to favour plastic plants.

Mohammed is in his mid-thirties and is director of the Electricity Department. At first sight he seems very Western, the model of a modern university-educated technocrat. He wears British suits, has a short hair-cut and speaks idiomatic English. His manner is informal and relaxed. He has a ready sense of humour and a general aura of efficiency. And, like the best of modern technocrats, he allows himself the minor vanity of making his literary knowledge known. Yet under this easy-going exterior there lurks a very sharp mind which is more Arab than Western in its working, never moving on one level only, never accepting anything at its face value. As mobile as quicksilver, it explores every motive, assesses every possibility, dissects every phrase, interprets every gesture. In Arabia nothing makes an outsider feel more alien than to have their most straightforward remarks or reactions subjected to such a continuous silent critical scrutiny.

In other respects, however, Mohammed is the robust, direct character he appears to be. In this small community he is one of those who are most

readily outspoken, undeterred by the familiar fear of the what-will-the-
neighbours-say syndrome. This is partly because the natural inclination of his
temperament when in difficulties is to have things out, to force the issue—
if need be. But his independence is also explained by a factor new to the
Middle East: this is the sense of security felt by people like himself because
they know that their qualifications will now ensure them a livelihood almost
anywhere in the world.

My father was never involved in pearling or anything like that.
He was a mechanic. This is why I have an engineering degree.
In fact, I am better known as Mohammed Mechanic than as
Al Ali; Al Ali is a family name which is forgotten because of the
trade name. The same thing happened, as you know, in Europe
during the Industrial Revolution—people assumed names
connected with their profession, such as Smith, for instance. The
same thing happened here. We still have names like Carpenter
and Goldsmith. But there is usually an Arabic word for most of
them, except for mechanic. This explains why I am best known
as Mohammed Mechanic.

Anyway, my father was an auto mechanic. He learned his
trade in Bahrain and he learned it the hard way. He had to work
for almost nothing—just for food, and I think he was given a
new set of clothes once a year. He had to learn without being able
to read catalogues, instruction booklets or maintenance manuals,
since he was not able to read at all. But he learned well and
became quite famous—or, at least, well known. You might even
say he was famous actually, because he was the only mechanic
here at the time! Yousef Mechanic, they called him. From Bahrain
he came back to Doha and joined the Qatar Petroleum Company.

Later he had his own garage. It was the biggest and also the
first fully-equipped garage in Doha. That was in 1954, or maybe
in 1955. There were already quite a few cars by then because oil
had been discovered and people, especially the sheikhs, were
buying cars for hunting. These cars had not been built to suit the
country so we had to modify them, rebuild the suspension and
make the clearance higher, for instance. So I grew up learning
from my father at that garage. I used my hands a lot. This may

be why I am more practical than theoretical. In the end I had learned how to do everything and could fend for myself: I must have been around eleven or twelve years old at the time.

Then, when I was fourteen, my father used to leave the whole garage for me to run while he went off on hunting trips with the sheikhs for two or three months at a time. It was a rough job, believe me. Here you had a fourteen-year-old boy controlling a large garage and all the people who worked in it. The workers were real toughs: most of them were Iranians, Pakistanis, Indians. Their hobby after working hours, you know, was weight-lifting! Sometimes I was a bit frightened, but it usually worked out all right until my father came back.

I think sheikhs at that time were a class apart, but they had only become so after the discovery of oil. Before oil, the only person who was called Sheikh was the Ruler, the governor, the head of the whole community; his main role was to levy taxes to cover official expenses. But his relatives only became a separate class after the oil; from having been quite poor they became very rich. I know some sheikhs who used to be truck drivers, tyre repairers —anything. Suddenly, they acquired a lot of money, at least relative to the standard of living at the time and, of course, that changed their character and outlook. But this situation was transformed again as other people began to become rich too. Now sheikhs and non-sheikhs are on the same financial level—in fact, the sheikhs are often poorer than many, probably than the majority, of the big families here. I never regarded myself as any different from the sheikhs, neither better nor worse. The balance of power in society in earlier days was totally different: the sheikhs needed people to fight for them and to support them. In fact, nobody paid attention to anyone but the Ruler, the Sheikh, and his son who would help his father by acting as adviser or minister. His immediate family, brothers, brothers-in-law, formed a kind of *élite* and had some political influence; the rest didn't. Then, after oil, the others were influential for some time, but this influence has gradually declined. I, personally, take notice only of the higher authorities—the rulers, that is.

This country used to have a very simple social structure. But nowadays you hardly ever meet your friends except at Eid. You are busy most of the day and at night you now have all these parties, unfortunately usually business parties. In the old days social habits were different. Then you used to go and meet so-and-so because you liked to chat to him on any subject, unrelated to work or business; because he liked your personality and not your pocket book or your position. Now our society is acquiring some of the same characteristics as European society: the pace of life is very fast, people are running after money, money, money—this is all they think about. I guess this is inevitable and one of the by-products of affluence.

It is true that our country is still a young country. And it's worth remembering that someone of my age would not hold the post that I am now holding in many other countries. Most of the active working population here is young. But for the time being, as we still don't have an intellectual *élite*, what older people say is what gets done. The younger generation still have no real influence.

Definitely, there is a generation gap. I'm no sociologist nor a psychiatrist and what I say now could be totally inaccurate. I think teenagers now are exposed to a lot of television films and movies: they see detectives, Kojak and Kung Fu. You wouldn't believe the effect of that Kung Fu series, about this Chinese man who goes around as a pacifist but can handle a lot of people if peaceful ways don't work. People are imitating him, admiring the way he behaves. Children are copying his poses. A teenager sees life as a means of imitating the films he sees. But he hasn't seen life outside the television screen, so he doesn't have a yard-stick to measure it against real life. There is also the effect of affluence. There is no poverty here. People work hard but not that hard. Today the money comes a lot easier so the teenager gets a car when he is very young, he has lots of facilities at home, his own TV, his own stereo, tape recorders, cassettes. You can buy them as easily as a box of biscuits. He and his friends live in a world of their own. They all have the same mentality, they've read the same magazines, about so-and-so who has won the Monte Carlo rally, about the stars and what have you, they've seen the same movie last night—this is the shell they hide in.

They no longer go out with their fathers to meet his friends, so they don't integrate and learn from the older people. They are anti; they say, 'Why should I go with my father and sit in the *majlis*—they only talk about land and shares'. The younger people are more interested in the movie they saw last night, but if they talk about these things in front of their elders, they will be laughed at. And if they go and listen to the old people talking about falconeering, or about one of our old stories, or about land prices—it is really boring.

I think eventually that gap will bridge itself. If I sit down tomorrow with my son, we will have a little bit more in common than my father had with me. My son will be six in April. I take him with me in the evening; he loves to come. At that age they do. I am encouraging him to acquire a hobby. Fortunately he is interested in radio control and I am too. When we were in Japan he wanted me to buy a very big model of a complete radio-controlled helicopter. But I thought it was really too dangerous for him. Instead I bought him a model aircraft and a small beach buggy with petrol engines. I have a Range Rover, which he calls his own car. The Mercedes is my car. I want to make him my friend as well as my son, you know. I think that's a good relationship to have. I think this is in line with our traditions. Here, from the age of six or seven, a boy is told, 'Don't behave like this or that, now you're a man, you're no longer a kid'. The sense of manhood is from there on applied to him. Of course, this is idealistic, it fails in many cases. A lot of sensible older people don't treat their children as ignorant, saying 'Oh, shut up, don't be silly'. They argue with them from their own different point of view. That's good I think. Treating them as ignorant only discourages them from communication even with their own people, later on, when they may be afraid of saying something bad or something which is not sensible.

As for my daughter, she is in my wife's care. As a father I give her as much attention as my son, but as she is a girl I prefer her to get closer to her mother than to me as a father. Maybe I'm being influenced by tradition here. There is the belief in this country that the girl loves her father and her father loves her, and the boy the mother. But I think that, as a girl, she should learn from her mother.

I think that the problem of spoiling children is not a matter of whether the parents are educated or not. I think it happens in both kinds of families. A kid will get spoiled—and this is the case with most Qataris—if the father can afford to buy anything it wants. In some more developed Gulf countries it's really a problem. Once a father realises that his son is eligible to drive he will buy him a car. It is no longer a Datsun, Toyota or Mini Minor, it's the big ones now.

As for our generation, we are the sons of the fathers who had to work hard, and we just made it, to complete our education. So we know the problems of the old way of living, and the difficulties of obtaining even the necessities of life. So we appreciate our present comfort even more. The younger generation came at the beginning of affluence. They have no idea of the difficulties of the past, they cannot imagine the hardships of pearl diving, for instance; in fact, pearl diving might seem to them something poetic to write stories about. They are very romantic about the past because they have no connection with it.

My father is dead. My mother is still alive and living next door to myself and my brother. I am actually one of six children: we are three brothers and three sisters and I am the eldest. And now, by virtue of being the eldest, I have run the affairs of the family since my father's death. You see, according to Islamic law, when the father dies the legacy is divided according to certain rules. But when the brothers and the sisters and the mother are as one family —if they are a *real* family—they usually don't like to split up the inheritance, so they keep things as they are. When my father died we had a house and a couple of cars. We sold the house and with the money we bought land near to where we live and have now built a three-storey building. Also we built another two houses adjacent to my house; we've rented one to an embassy and my mother moved into the smaller one. The rent from all this property goes to the family and I manage it. I also buy and sell property. My loan from the bank for building carries interest of, I think, around 4 per cent. Normally, round here, we recover the cost of building within ten years, but I think I shall do it sooner, say in six years. After that everything is pure profit.

I have a brother who is studying in Cairo who also has to be helped with money. My sisters don't get the same share of the inheritance as we brothers do legally, they get half as much. Sons get twice as much as daughters do: I'm not defending the Islamic law or anything, but I think there is a lot of merit in it—well, at least a case for it, because usually in our society a woman is a dependent. So nobody would abandon a woman whether she has money or whether she deserves it or whether she doesn't. Whether I have money from my father or whether I don't, my sisters are my responsibility, whether I like it or whether I don't. This is a *social* obligation; it's not a law or anything. I just wouldn't dare, I just can't imagine myself telling my sister you just manage by yourself, even if I had no money at all. But the son usually has dependents and the law supports him.

I have a teenage sister aged fourteen. She is different. She has a mind of her own. I don't know what she wants to do, but she likes painting and she won the silver medal in a Unesco competition. If she were to ask me I would encourage her to go to an art school. I wouldn't mind sending her to Cairo if she wanted to go.

I myself went to a proper primary school, as well as the Koranic school. We used to be paid, actually, to go to the Government school, I remember. They used to give us a midday meal, summer and winter clothing and a monthly salary. At the beginning the sheikhs' sons didn't come to the Government schools; sometimes they had private tutors. But then later they did. Sheikh Abdul Aziz, the Emir's son, just went to an ordinary school.

After school hours and during the summer vacation I carried

on working in the garage. In the late fifties I began to work for myself and my father encouraged me. I was then sixteen. I bought a truck with what I had earned from assembling Vespa motor cycles, new ones, for a merchant who got them partially dis, mantled. The Government at that time used to hire vehicles by the month, mainly to carry labourers to and from work. It was an easy job and the pay was good; also I had my father's garage service to back me up in case of problems.

Then in 1960 I decided to try some commercial business. I went to Bahrain to bring back a lot of second-hand tyre rings. The USA at that time used to make the rings 15 inches in diameter, then for some reason they went down to 14 inches to fit smaller tyres. Now these tyres were not suitable for hunting trips so when people bought new cars, they would take off the 14-inch tyres and fit the 15-inch. We used to buy old second-hand or scrapped cars and polish and paint the tyre rings and sell them —at a very high price. I remember the net profit was about 500 per cent!

After that we had a club. We intended to have a social club but different from the other clubs at that time, because they were sports clubs and I don't think they had the right atmosphere for young people. You see, there were very old and young people mixed and they didn't fit—the old who were not educated and the young who were. So we started a social club for people who all had to have been at primary or secondary school. We produced satirical plays criticising things around here.

At that time we could see how people's character was beginning to change under the impact of the oil money. I remember that we once produced a play on this theme. The main character was someone who was important within the community because he was a good man, because he was kind and generous. He was like a father to everyone: they used to come to his house which was like a club in the area. That was the setting before oil began to make people rich. There was a Palestinian in the club who was fairer in complexion than most of us, so we called him Mr Jones; he symbolised the oil companies and the colonial powers. In the play he acted as an Englishman. I remember that we found him a hat to wear and a stick, or it might have been an umbrella— we were not sure which one was right. Certainly, he had a brief, case. I remember that very clearly! He was tall and thin and fitted our image of an Englishman perfectly. Anyway, what happened was that the good man became rich and no longer cared a damn about anybody else. He used to kick them out when they came to see him because they were poor and he was rich. In the past the only difference between them had been that he had had a better character than they had. I acted the rôle of the Qatari who turned nasty.

We had a funny play too, about illiteracy classes for old women. We hoped that people would talk about it at home and that this would encourage the old women to attend, or at least to take an interest in the project. But it was pure comedy.

There was one play about faith healers: people who would come and read verses from the Koran and then pronounce the patient cured, even if they had appendicitis. I think this kind of treatment may sometimes have a psychological effect but not, obviously, when there is a genuine case of malfunctioning of some organ. These people would do anything for money.

We were surprised to see how many people came to our plays. Of course, for the first play we gave away all the tickets free. But eventually around sixty people used to come to each performance. Once all the chairs were occupied and there were even people standing.

At that time we were very hot-blooded and politically-minded. Naturally, that landed us in trouble with the authorities. We didn't have much time for the club after that because it was a very important year for secondary-school students. I was at secondary school all during that time.

We were the first science group to finish secondary school. Our standard wasn't bad, and I can say that with confidence, because at the American universities I didn't find it difficult at all. During the three years at intermediate school, I used to be either first in the class or second. Then, of course, the foreigners came,

Mohammed—like any Western technocrat, almost . . .

The Qatar Fertilizer Company
Storage tanks where oil is kept until collection by tankers

and I think they were smarter than we were, so I went down to second, third or fourth place but having a better average by the way, because the competition was greater. Perhaps the Palestinians and Egyptians had a more solid educational foundation than we had in our new educational system because we were the guinea pigs, so to speak. I remember, I did my O-levels in England very easily. When I went in 1962 to Brighton, my English wasn't bad at all.

Going to England was an exciting experience, naturally. I had spent hours sitting trying to imagine what it would be like. At that time English people who came here had this colonial attitude, they were a different class, they didn't mix with people. I don't think you can blame us for thinking all English people were like that. These were the only English people we had come into direct contact with. When we began to meet the people we began to realise that the British people in Qatar at that time were not really a sample of the British back home. We soon realised that life in Britain was totally different.

About four of us were selected by the QPC to go to England on a scholarship which the oil company awarded at that time. I remember we were told by the representative here that all we had to do was spend a year in England, and then we could go to university. We were not told the whole story about the qualifica-tions we would need. We arrived and I studied English for six months. Then the school decided to put me through the O-level course. I passed. Then I was told that I couldn't go to university without sitting A-levels, which require at least two years. So then we knew we had really been taken for a ride, but there was no way out of it.

Apparently the muddle arose because the QPC man respon-sible in Qatar and the man in England were acting independently. Anyway after we had done the first year we immediately started writing to Sheikh Jassim at the Ministry of Education. He eventually said that those people who were doing final English could go to the States, and those who were not could be sent to Arab universities. So only two of us went to the States, myself and the man who is now the Qatari ambassador in Kuwait. We used to go and see Sheikh Jassim and tell him all our problems and get his advice, and he would give us a very nice dinner; we would starve ourselves for it for two days in advance. Two-inch thick steak after living on family food! We always looked forward to it. We would get some money from him, too. We always looked forward to seeing him.

So I went to America to continue my university studies: to Texas National College to get through the freshman require-ments, and then to the University of Colorado, in Boulder, where I finished my BSc in electrical engineering. After three-and-a-half years' education in England my English was reasonably good compared with other Arabs, so when I went to America the man who interviewed me said 'Well look, I suggest you go with the Americans and just be like an American student, you'll benefit more. There's no need for you to take the English-for-foreigners course.'

I attended two classes in American and English literature, Geoffrey Chaucer and what-have-you. I thought the English literature was very good. I had difficulty with the medieval English but anyway it was a good experience. I think literature is history also, isn't it, in many ways, and I enjoyed it very, very much. We studied Virginia Woolf and the stream of conscious-ness. I don't remember her novels now, this was more than twelve years ago. But I always remember the stream of consciousness, for some reason. I don't know why. Not only that, it stuck in my mind the first day. Kafka's *The Listener* was a very interesting story. It's all metaphoric. Somebody is knocking at the door, and people are talking and listening, and not opening the door. The professor was asking, 'Who is the listener?' I knew, and I wanted to speak but being an Arab. . . . The professor said 'Yes, Mohammed, what do you think?' I said, 'Well sir, the one who knocked at the door was Jesus Christ'. 'Very good, yes. And the listener?' 'The Jews' I said. Because it was meant that way. I don't know how I knew really. Because it was religion, and the period of history; it was a shot in the dark maybe. The professor said it was exactly what Kafka meant. I was very hesitant to say it, being an Arab. I don't remember the details of this course, but we did Joyce too. And Lord Byron. I liked him. Very romantic, I liked that. Sometimes when I get fed up I turn to an anthology I have. It relaxes me very much.

I brought back all my English books with me, every single one. I have a library upstairs, where I spend most of my time reading. *De Gaulle's Memoirs* and the *Encyclopaedia Britannica* in this sitting room are just for décor. We use the library a lot and the study.

I met my wife in America where she was doing her PhD. She was almost 70 per cent through it when we decided to get married so she had to stop there and take a Master's degree instead. Of course, at that time we thought it would make a difference of only a year or two, but we came back here and it wasn't as we had thought. Life went on and on. We had children, things became more and more complicated. But as far as I am concerned, being an engineer, if I look at what is most beneficial to my country, I think it's not so important to do higher studies, because we need engineers and engineers are practical people. You need the BScs to give you the guidelines, but the rest of it is experience, there's no question about it. Even in England you would rather have an experienced person than an academically qualified person. Of course, the academically qualified person has his own place in society and in life, but in our position, which do we need more? Just BSc holders, engineers. But in my wife's case it was different; she was involved in the academic sphere. In America, the person who taught me the first two electrical courses had only a BSc, I think, but he was a full-time professor in the university. But here, it is a must to have a PhD to teach at university or college. So my wife was teaching laboratory work and everything else at the college here, but because of her Master's degree she could not hold more than a lecturer's post. I thought that if she went on like this she would be in the same position indefinitely. She majored in nuclear physics for her BSc, and her Master's degree was also in nuclear physics, but for her PhD she changed from nuclear physics to thin film study, in which you study the properties of matter, of metals and alloys, their tensile strength, flexibility, their boiling point, how brittle they are, etc. Unfortunately it is a very involved subject and she needs a lot of modern equipment which is not available here or in Egypt, this is why she also goes to England from time to time.

Eventually it was I who told her that she would have to make up her mind. Being a woman with four children, it was difficult for her to leave the house. So we had to look for a university with the least residency requirements, which is why we chose Cairo. What happens is this; she carries on everything here until she is ready to do a specific experiment, then she goes off for two to three months to Cairo. I have encouraged her a lot, and at the last minute I appealed to her ego. 'You must decide, and if you don't go for your PhD you must be chicken'. She didn't accept that, she said 'No, I am determined to go', and now she's there.

Really I shouldn't be saying this myself about my own wife, I'd rather this came from somebody else, but she is very clever, I knew this from the beginning. She is very, very intelligent and I think it's really a pity to waste it. She loved her work, she wanted to go further, no question about it. The handicap was the house and the children. I told her that she shouldn't worry about that or feel guilty or anything: I'd take care of everything. And I think it's working fine, she is enjoying the work, that's for sure.

When my wife comes back she will teach at the college. But if she wanted to work in industry there wouldn't be any problem about her being a woman. Women do have difficulties about work—but sometimes we think there are difficulties where there might not be any. If she wanted to go and work, who's going to stop her? My influence wouldn't help her—if anything it might impede her. She will simply be accepted as Dr So-and-so. But the fact that women can work at college here is a very big step. Last year she taught not just girls, but also boys.

In general, Qatari women have developed a lot, I think. Sophisticated Qatari women are as up-to-date fashion-wise as English women. In the old days things were different. But the funny thing is that girls were freer then, in some ways. During official holidays like Eid, you would see girls dancing in the open, and just a couple of hundred yards away you would see men dancing. You couldn't imagine that happening now, could you? In scientific terms, I would say that the whole formula has changed and it will take time to reach a new equilibrium. Up-to-date technology has to be matched by up-to-date ideas and by an infrastructure. At present we are developing at a far faster pace than our infrastructure can cope with, i.e. the availability of accommodation, schools, teachers, etc.

Moreover, our mental infrastructure is also subjected to the same pressure. For instance, I still find out who will be present before I take my wife to a party. The problem is that some Europeans or expatriates don't pay any attention to whom they ask; they just invite anybody. But I wouldn't take my wife if somebody was there who wouldn't understand why she was accompanying me. He might be old-fashioned and prejudiced. Of course, I wouldn't dream of stopping my wife from going if she wanted to—but in general it's all a matter of time. If you take this into account then slowly very slowly, things do change. A very important person who three years ago wouldn't have dreamt of taking his wife to parties now does so. The intellectuals are loosening things up. In every society, the educated, the intelligentsia, take risks. But blunt confrontations can create difficulties that no one wanted. If you want to see things change, you've got to be really careful. I think my wife would agree with this. She wouldn't feel bad if I turned down an invitation to a party.

But let's not give Europe the whole credit for the changes. People also visited other places—don't forget Beirut, don't forget Egypt. Don't forget that Qatari girls go to Bahrain. I think the size of our society has a lot to do with conservatism. People know that such-and-such a girl is the daughter of so-and-so; her father works here, her brother there. It's a small community. When she goes out, somewhere else, she is no longer known and she can do what she likes. I have done this myself in the past; I don't know whether I was recognisable or not.

But in the last three or four years, Qataris have begun to travel and this has given them a lot of freedom to express themselves. Travelling helps them psychologically to adjust and to live more happily. Having seen more freedom they come back here and try to live the same way. OK. People will try to resist them; this always happens. But if they are really determined they will get their way eventually.

But there is another aspect of our society which I would criticise; this is the envy. If somebody works hard and builds himself up, then I'll say 'OK. Good for him.' He deserves it, he works for it. But you will hear a lot of Qataris say 'I am a Qatari. Why shouldn't I be rich?' But that doesn't necessarily follow, does it? Why should you be rich because your country is well off? I mean, in America there are people living in the gutters and people who have huge ranches, private aeroplanes and everything. Of course, we do have a fairly small population and a great deal of wealth, but do you think the government should give these people money just to sit at home? For the time being, we are doing very well! We are very wealthy, we have interesting jobs, highly paid jobs, people are coming in from the outside to work for us. But how do we know that everything in the future will continue in the same way; maybe we'll have to run our own country then. The way it is now we are totally dependent on foreigners. Why? Partly because we have no incentive to work hard. If you work hard it's just because your conscience tells you to. But if you don't you won't be fired. The unfortunate thing is that if you do work hard you'll be in no better a position than those who remain completely passive.

I think that Qataris should be encouraged at their jobs. The Qatarisation programme is going well. But there are sometimes two if not three people—maybe one or two Qataris with one expatriate—doing a job which could be done by one person. This is doing a lot of damage to the country. In a few years' time we'll regret it.

I'll tell you what happened to me. I came back from the States expecting, as normal, to be assigned to a job. I am an electrical engineer and I knew I was meant to work in the electricity department. I came back and I met this English chap. In a very typical English way he told me, 'You know, we don't have any posts open'. I felt ridiculous and laughed because he knew perfectly well that when graduates arrive, posts are created for them—which is wrong, of course. I thought they should really say, 'OK, here is a man, give him three months and he takes over—if he can.' If he can't, that's another matter.

I was assigned to one of the distribution engineers who was supposed to show me around and train me, so to speak. I used to sit and wait in my office. Sometimes he would call me and say: 'Would you like to come and look at this with me?'—but then would fail to turn up for days. I complained about it. Eventually I took a book and sat in the engineer's car, since he couldn't go anywhere without it. That was it, he had to accept it. It didn't always work. Sometimes the car wasn't there. I knew perfectly well that the man was trying to avoid me. Finally I went to the Englishman in charge. I said 'Please, I am not here to sit at a nice big desk in a comfortable office with an air conditioner over my head. I came here to learn and to gain experience. What can I do?' He said 'Why don't you do a systems study?' I thought it was a very ridiculous thing for him to suggest but I am glad he did. I am thankful now. It gave me an insight into the whole system. I had to learn every substation, every transformer, every transmission line, every distribution cable, the power stations, their quality and characteristics.

I remember I went to the power station and told the station superintendent I was doing a systems study. I kept asking him questions, and I asked 'What is the impedance of your generators?' He said 'Hm, er, well, OK, let me take down the manuals'. He took down the manuals and paged through. I said 'It's not there, just look at the nameplate on the generators and it will be there'. He said 'You're a graduate of where?' and I said 'I'm a graduate from the United States'. Then his whole attitude changed: he became very respectful.

Later on there was a vacancy at the power station and it was suggested to me that I should fill the vacancy. I went there and it was a very good thing. The management wanted to get me out of the way, and I'm glad they did. For the first three months that I worked there I was completely and absolutely ignored. I wasn't treated any differently from the chair I was sitting on. Sharing the office with me was my electrical foreman. When the phone rang I would take the call. The caller would say 'Could you get me Rafeeq' and I'd say to Rafeeq 'It's for you'. And he'd get information from the shift charge engineer that various things were wrong and needed attending to. I kept my cool, as the Americans say, for that period of three months. In the meantime I went round, concentrated and learnt about the plant. One morning I looked in the shaving mirror and said 'Mohammed, you are now ready'. I went to work that morning, had my cup of coffee, sat down in my office and said to this Pakistani chap 'Rafeeq, do you like your job?' He said 'Yes sir, I do'. 'Well then,' I said, 'you've got to listen to me and remember this very carefully. From this very moment, if you accept any instruction not through me you won't be kicked out of your job but I'll kick your bloody ass so hard you won't need the staircase. You'll land outside the fence of this power station.' He looked at me and said 'Yes sir, I understand'. I went on, 'If somebody asks you to change even a light bulb, you are not to authorise it without consulting me.' He said, 'Yes sir.' I said, 'But never mind, I'll back you up. On the other hand if you don't consult me then I'm not on your side.' He said, 'Very well sir, I understand sir, I shall abide by your instructions.' Then the phone rang. The caller said 'Can I have Rafeeq?' I said, 'Yes, gladly. Rafeeq, telephone.' Rafeeq said to the caller, 'Well sir, I'm sorry, I can't take instructions from you, you've got to go through my engineer.' The caller gave a cry of dismay and said, 'Can I have your engineer?' I took the receiver and said, 'Yes?' and I put the telephone down. The shift charge engineer then came storming into my office and said, 'Are you trying to create trouble?' I said, 'Yes'. I said, 'Look, I've been here now for three months. I've had enough'. He interrupted: 'Look, the turbine is about to stop.' I said, 'I don't give a damn if the whole station stops. Why have I done this? I insist on telling you why I've done it.' The superintendent came and the deputy superintendent. They apologised, they begged my pardon. I told them, 'Look, you've ignored me. If I was an Englishman, ignorant as I was, it would have been a different story. From now on if you give any of my electricians any instructions, not coming through me, I shall fire him. I'm very capable of creating a big row.' From then on things went very smoothly. These were Englishmen I was dealing with. There were one or two other Qataris there who were confronted with the same problem but it was too big for them. Eventually they just retreated into their shells.

I was promoted quickly. From being an electrical maintenance engineer, I became deputy superintendent of the power station. Eventually, the Minister gave me the posts of deputy engineer and manager as they became vacant. This was a big jump only two-and-a-half years after joining the department.

Then about four years ago I heard very strong rumours that I was to be made the engineer and manager—the post I occupy now. I said to myself: 'I'm not really ready for it.' I thought that as deputy engineer and manager I was doing a good job. But I knew I wasn't yet ready to take responsibility for the whole department. The rumours grew stronger and the Minister was very keen. I met His Highness once and told him: 'I have heard this rumour that I am to be promoted. I would like Your Highness to hold back that decision. I'm not ready for it yet. When I am ready I'll come and tell you.' I remember he laughed. He didn't comment at all; he just laughed. So I left it. Time went on and, I think it was two years later, I then felt ready. I went to the Minister and said: 'You wanted to promote me two years ago when I wasn't ready. Now I am.' So the Minister said 'OK'.

When I became manager the department was trying to deal with a much heavier work-load in the same way as it had done in the past when we were a very small community with few consumers.

I started by delegating responsibility—I believe firmly in that. I used to spend a lot of time just signing pieces of paper, rubber stamping without reading. If a letter involved finance, I decided that the accountant should really sign it. Then I can hold him responsible if anything goes wrong. I applied this principle right along the line—and I wish more people would.

In general, dealing with generators and cables is very much easier than dealing with people. But there are times when you get fed up with things that don't react, don't have life. You like to say to something 'Do this' and it will be done. But sometimes you like that 'thing'—be it a human being, a machine or anything—to say 'No, I can't do it' or 'I will not do it', just for the challenge. Take literature for instance. When you read, your thinking is not constrained by the limits of what you are reading: you feel closer to the earth or you soar heavenwards. But you are constantly moving on different levels—I find that relaxing. I am always reading a book. I try to read books once or twice a week. I have the *National Geographical Magazine*, that has a lot to read in it. Then I'm very keen on fishing. I used to go to one of the islands; I spent hours floating there wearing a snorkel, looking at sea life and the coral. It was beautiful there with the sun and the little fish. Sea life is really my relaxation.

Hammad—Ambitious, Within Reason

The features well-marked but fleshier than usual in a Qatari only in his mid-thirties; the mouth full. Humorous brown eyes that miss nothing. Liberal ideas contrast with conservative family life. Other men usually stay in the *majlis*, they don't come into the house. Ambitious but not much given to politicking, more likely to take refuge in his shell. Like most Qataris has powerful dislike of flowery sentiments and languages: 'If you go into a house in Egypt, people will tell you that you make it shine. I personally don't like this kind of thing. We Qataris consider it tasteless to say to their face how good and generous they are; it's an insult.'

Besides being director of a Government department, he also supervises a couple of successful business enterprises, a contracting and a general trading company. Not yet in the millionaire bracket, possibly never will be—likes spending his money and determined to enjoy life. 'Let's put it like this. If a man has the opportunity to make money and he doesn't take it, he's mad. Equally he shouldn't let money rule his life. I don't let it rule mine. I never talk business outside office hours.' The conversation takes place on his business premises and turns on those businessmen, a rapidly growing number apparently, who care only about making money and not about friendship. On the doorstep, just before leaving, he pauses: 'Do you know, I've been here just socialising for two hours—did no business.' He looks pleased with himself.

We lived in Wakra on the coast which was convenient for my father who was a pearl merchant. After some time we left to go to Doha. I don't remember much of Wakra except that there were a lot of ships there, also our house which was white and very nice. It's a ruin now and I've built a beach house there just to remind my father of old days; also the children like to go there on Fridays to fish.

When I first came to Doha there was no school here. So my father decided to take me with him pearling. I was only five at the time but my mother was dead and that's the reason he did it. He remarried a little later but since he was anxious that I should be educated he took me to Saudi Arabia, to Khobar, where he left me with family friends. I felt very homesick and I didn't study very much really. My father's reason for going to Saudi Arabia was first to have me educated and second to get rid of his slaves. At that time slaves were freed by the British if they reached Bahrain—this was just shortly before they were freed in Qatar itself—and since this would have meant a serious loss for my father, the loss of his livelihood in fact, he sold them in Saudi Arabia. I didn't like to see this happen to people of my own age. But as pearling was collapsing my father's hand was forced. He had no cash, no land—nothing. I think he made 20,000 *riyals* out of the deal which was a lot of money at the time. There were six of them altogether. But there was really no difference between them and us. If my father bought a *dishdasha* or any clothes for me he would buy the same for them.

This situation continued until the war was over and the oil companies started to operate again. At the same time, the Emir

of Qatar freed all the slaves and offered compensation to all slave
owners. This was in the late forties. Many slaves refused to be
freed because this would have left them without work and money.
The slaves here were never really slaves; when you went to a house
you felt the slave and the master's son were equal. They still carry
our names and are proud to be one of us. We still visit each other.
These slaves of ours I talked about earlier eventually came back
to Qatar from Saudi Arabia. My father helped them to get jobs
and Qatari nationality again. It was our duty to do this. Now they
are living near us, in the same area, because the local communities
or tribes always ask to be housed near each other.

With the 20,000 *riyals* he was paid, my father went back to sea
and changed his trade from pearling to transporting goods, such
as sugar, rice and tea. At this time governments used to buy these
things and distribute them free to the people. It wasn't traditional
for Arabs to engage in trade like this, but they just had to change
their ways: it was a matter of life and death. At the same time, they
didn't carry out their trading in Qatar. If they had, people would
have asked them what on earth they were doing, why they were
doing this nasty job. So they operated through Bahrain and
Dubai and other foreign places. In the old days it was shameful
for a Qatari to open a shop and sell goods, that's why most local
trade was in the hands of Iranians. The Qataris themselves
preferred to place their money in the hands of Iranians who would
then trade with it. Nor would they accept any interest because
interest is *haram*, or forbidden, in the Koran. A long time ago
if a Qatari opened a shop, people would come and laugh at him.
'Are you crazy?' they would ask. A change had to come. It has
come very fast when you think that even fishermen and carpenters
were looked down on for doing dirty jobs. People would not
marry the daughter of a fisherman or the daughter of a carpenter.
Pearling was different, because pearls were rare; people had to
risk their lives to find them. Going fishing was nothing special,
but to find an oyster you had to dive at least seven metres. It was
acceptable also to sell goats and camels and sheep. Don't ask me
why, because I'm not a historian. But I am a bedu by origin and

I know, for instance, that while it was all right to sell sheep and camels and goats, it was not good to keep a cow. Bedus didn't eat beef. Maybe a modernised bedu could explain why. People preferred camels to cows. They always addressed their poetry to the camels.

After nearly a year in Saudi Arabia, I went to the newly started elementary school in Qatar. I did well because I am technically-minded. When I was eleven I started at the new Technical School. They wanted to encourage people to attend so they didnt take any account of age. My father was very dis-appointed; he didn't want me to go to the school. He said, 'You are going to wear trousers and you will end up as either a black-smith or a carpenter, and this has never happened to anyone in our family before.' He wanted me to go to the religious school. But I wanted to stay where I was because I liked technical work: I used to take my bicycle to pieces. Anyway, when he saw how determined I was, he allowed me to go on with the school. I came top of my class—at least I was the first among the Qataris in my class, but in front of me there was one Palestinian. This meant that I could go abroad to study at government expense. But my father said, 'You're not going to England You will be trained in a profession which is not in our tradition.' But in the end he was persuaded, and allowed me to go. When he said 'Go', he was crying.

Anyway I went. I was seventeen. I think my father eventually agreed because other people convinced him. He had wanted me to go to Saudi Arabia or Cairo. He thought that if I went to England I wouldn't come back.

While I was there I always wrote him. I wrote him that I was happy, that I was staying with a nice family. My landlady in Shrewsbury once wrote to my father saying, 'Your son is a good boy, we like him' and she also sent him a book of pictures of castles in England. She thought this was the kind of thing that might interest a bedu like my father. He wrote to her—or at least got someone else to write, 'Thank you very much, Mrs Eden. I am very glad my son is living with you.' She started to laugh as she read it, so I said, 'Why are you laughing? It's true that I'm living with you.' She said, 'No, you're not *living* with me. You are *staying* with me.' In Arabic we don't have such a distinction.

Before Shrewsbury I had been in Cambridge attending an English-language school. It was all very strange to me. It gradually became clear that we sometimes said the wrong thing because we were ignorant of British habits. For instance, we would repeat our greetings over and over again in Arab fashion, saying, 'How are you, how are you, how are you? . . .' and shaking hands. How were we to know that people got fed up with us going on and on saying, 'How are you, how are you?' We also thought it was wrong for young boys and girls to walk together in the street— but, of course, there was nothing wrong with it. We used to think they were off their heads, to act like this in front of other people, as Qataris then didn't see many females at home.

The way women behaved was strange too, but then we had already seen European women in Qatar wearing trousers and white hats. When we saw this as children we wondered at it. We said to each other, 'Their ladies are men!' This was also because they walked with their men, while our women didn't walk with men in the streets, and they didn't wear trousers like men. At that time I thought European women were wrong and our women were right. I was very nationalistic.

After four years at Shrewsbury Technical College I came back here at the age of twenty-two to become distribution engineer in the water department. I was responsible for the distribution of piped water and water delivered by tankers and for extending the piped water supply throughout Doha. Then I became planning engineer and after four years I moved up further to become deputy water engineer. Three years later when I was thirty I became director of the Water Department.

In the old days, the water came from wells not far from Doha. The population was very small and the water was good for drinking. It was brought either by donkeys or by camels and distributed to the villages and Doha. Later it was brought by truck. Donkeys were used up till about 1945 or 1946, I remember.

Trucks started to be used in 1948 or 1950. In the 1950s the government took over the distribution of water. It came from a small distillation plant and was mixed with well water.

When I was a child, drinking water was stored in a big drum: it served about twelve people for drinking and cooking. This water had sometimes to be bought. But everybody had a well, either in the house or nearby which provided water for washing and bathing.

Neighbours would share a well. We didn't really notice water being scarce, we managed on what we had. Mostly people were at sea. A small or medium vessel carrying about fifteen people to go pearl-diving, would take with it about 300 gallons of water. They would go as long as a month before refilling. They were desert people and were used to not having much water. I think my father still has only one glass of water a day.

When I came back, the Department's main problem was the shortage of water. We had to convince the authorities that we did not have enough water underground to meet our needs and that we should have to resort to desalinisation. They had hoped that more water would be found but our study showed conclusively that our own resources were insufficient to satisfy domestic and industrial demand. We are still researching to find the cheapest method of getting water. We, in the Gulf, have by now the widest experience of desalinisation. In 1952 we produced 200,000 gallons of water per day. Our plant was the biggest in the world. Then, in 1958, we were producing 600,000 gallons. Now our production has risen to 8 million gallons per day.

In general, a family with a garden consumes 600 gallons of water a day. Every Qatari has a garden; no Qataris live in flats because the Government provides us with free land and they prefer to build a villa. Since they don't pay for water—or for electricity—this costs the State a lot of money. But when they have to pay, I think they will reduce their consumption.

But our main problem is not the cost. It is the rate of expansion of this country. Buildings, people, traffic—they are increasing all the time. You don't see this in England. I worked for the Water

Board in Spalding in Shropshire as a trainee with the resident engineer. Water work there was easy because there was no building: we just had to check extension pipes, whether the hospital supply was adequate. It was an easy life. While here we are always expanding. Because of all these difficulties some people in Doha still only have piped water for a few hours a day; their main supply is provided by water tankers. But by the end of 1977 we should have a round-the-clock service.

At the moment there is no actual shortage of water supplies here. But we are setting up a water resources section to investigate alternatives for the future; we may have to recycle sewage effluent for agricultural and industrial purposes. If the flow of oil is reduced, then the Government will have to turn to other industries, such as steel and petrochemicals to finance desalinisation. Our industries will have to pay for our water. Every country should think about the long-term depletion of its resources, whether water or anything else. Since we have no rivers we are specially aware of the problem.

My normal working day is from 7 a.m. till 1 p.m. I don't spend all my time in the Water Department because I am also a member of the Board of Directors of Qatar Petrochemical Co., and for the last three months the management team has been opening parts of an ethylene plant for making plastics, so there have been a lot of meetings and discussions. It's a very big complex, an investment of about 2,000 million *riyals*. The directors of various departments and organisations also discuss and co-ordinate the water and electricity requirements for industries, for this year and for next year.

I don't sit idle in the afternoons, I usually have some work to do, such as site meetings to discuss things with the engineers. I also attend to my business. We have Fridays off. But I don't feel that I am tired and need a day off. I have a long leave in the summer, six weeks. Then I forget about the telephone ringing and the complaints and the meetings. I get up late and read newspapers and books. I used to take the family to Beirut on holiday, before the trouble started there. This summer we went to

Britain. We are always planning to go to Tunisia or somewhere else, but communications aren't easy—while you can get a direct flight from here to London. That's why many people from Doha choose London. Also you don't need a visa for London. And we enjoy England because it's different, it's not the usual routine.

I know that life here is boring for foreigners. But it's not for us Qataris. This is where we were born, this is where we have our families and our friends. Of course we like to get out and enjoy ourselves sometimes, but we soon get homesick. I feel homesick when I'm away from the Gulf. I miss the sun and the desert and even the hot weather.

Abdulrahman—Down-to-Earth

The director, like most Qatari directors, is quite young, only in his early thirties. His nose is short, sharp and unhooked; his hair longish and curling under the Arab headdress. He wears horn-rimmed glasses. He is friendly but businesslike and clearly harassed by overwork. 'You were five minutes late', he says, obviously quite pleased of the opportunity to scold a European for unpunctuality, to judge by the glint in his eye. He likes to tease but he also really is a stickler for punctuality and efficiency and a great supporter of rationalism versus emotionalism—clearly in reaction to his own environment. He is a moderniser, though socially he is something of a conservative, possibly because he was brought up by a very religious father and educated in an Arab and not a Western university. Tradition and family ties are very important to him. He looks happiest when speaking of the spring days he spends with his and other families out in the desert living in tents. But such distractions are rare, for he is one of the hardest workers in Doha, totally devoted to his profession. 'Why do you have to work so hard?' ask his friends with concern, 'you'll drop dead one day and they will build you a monument on the roundabout. Where will that get you?'

I was born in a Qatari village called Semaisima where I spent part of my childhood. This was during and after the Second World War. It was a poverty-stricken area. Many of the tribes there moved to Bahrain and our family was among them. Bahrain was flourishing in those days. Oil hadn't yet been discovered in Qatar and the economy there was also affected by the war. In Bahrain, I went to school until I was about ten, but I don't remember much about it.

Later on things improved in Qatar and we returned to our country. But we didn't go back to the district where we lived before. We returned to Doha round about 1958. It was a small town then. I finished elementary school there and I used to spend my spring and summer holidays in our village on the coast. There I stayed with my grandmother and my cousins. We had a wonderful time, especially in the spring. I remember in '59, '60 and '61, the rain was heavy in Qatar. And the pastures were beautiful. Once I was coming back by car and the car broke down, so we walked to the village. I was then about four feet tall, and the plants were so high that I could not be seen among them. These were beautiful things. Now they do not exist any more. After the rain we used to go on trips looking for truffles. We used to go hunting for hares and the like. We had no responsibilities, except for studying. Problems had not yet come into one's life, and one was happy with one's childhood. Sometimes when I'm alone, I recall my childhood, how I lived. I felt the whole universe belonged to me. These things may seem insignificant, but they are important to me. A beautiful childhood may have a positive influence on one's future. I lived a good life indeed. My parents loved me and so did the rest of the family. I wish my children could have a childhood like mine. I try to give them something of what I had, although I cannot provide them with everything. Once people led a simple life, it was easier to relax. This is what I remember of that time. Then I finished secondary school, went to university and started to work.

My father used to tell me that when we went to Bahrain, life was difficult. The oil companies had just started operating there, and he worked for one of them. The work was very hard. Men worked like machines. They carried sacks of cement on their backs. There was strong pressure from the company on the workers. Wages were very low then, but life was also cheap. They had a distance of more than 20 km. to walk each way because the companies did not provide transport. People were in need; they had to accept these conditions so as to support their families. They were depressed by what was happening to them. In those days there was no government in the real sense. This affected people psychologically and they couldn't forget what they went through.

After we returned, life in Qatar was not bad. The British were more flexible in Qatar than they were in Bahrain. The workers and the civil servants were granted some kind of rights. Indeed life was much easier here.

When we came back my father worked as the *imam* of a mosque. He also worked in taxis and had other jobs. He died about nine months ago. My father was also a pearl diver and when I was small he wanted to take me to sea with him. He would go diving in between jobs, because there were no permanent jobs—that's how things were then. But my mother refused to let me go. She was afraid of the risks. I never went even though I was curious to see what the life of the divers was all about.

I respect my mother and father because they brought me into this world and took care of me. But I am not the sentimental type. I do not let my heart rule my mind. I try to bring up my children in the same way. But that does not mean I am without feelings. In my view, sentimentality has a bad effect on one's work, one's life and one's future. Let us suppose that my parents were still alive and they had an accident. If I were sentimental I might not have the strength to bear the shock.

Also I say what I think. I am straightforward. I don't like to talk behind anybody's back. We have a saying that goes: 'Telling lies will get you nowhere, only the truth will save you'. This proverb is my motto. I don't like telling lies, even if telling the truth is to my disadvantage. Being nice or hypocritical is not good for our future as a developing nation in the Arab world. Honesty is the basis for work and success. I believe in God and in his Message. The Message of Islam inspires us to do this. What I am saying is nothing new. The Prophet, peace be upon Him, was frank.

My mother and father had great respect for each other. I consider this a good thing. But they never spoilt the children. I do not like excessive affection in bringing up children. I think rational love does not spoil children.

My family led a normal life. The women took care of the children, washed, cooked, fetched water and sometimes even collected firewood. The men used to go diving in the summer. In winter, if they were not working for the oil companies, sometimes they would go hunting. Their life was beautiful indeed. There were strong family ties then. Later life became more complex and urbanised, life changed and there were more facilities. In the past they cooked with firewood, now they use ovens, fridges, electricity and air conditioners. In the past these things were not available. People lived in houses made of stones and mud bricks; now they live in houses made of concrete. But among the old people social ties remain strong.

My generation was caught between the old generation and the new one. We took more from the old. Life has changed a lot, but women still stay at home, this has not changed. Relatives still respect one another and exchange visits. In the past one was encouraged to marry from his relations, now one doesn't have to do so.

Our traditions have changed but I'm glad we don't yet have the freedom of manners people in Europe have. This may seem natural to them but we are not accustomed to it: the freedom of the individual is a little excessive from our point of view, this is due to our Eastern nature. Of course, everybody wants freedom of the press and freedom of expression. That is normal, for them and for us. But I am referring to the freedom which involves the individual. This doesn't go with me, because of my Eastern background. A girl in Britain has complete freedom to choose a boyfriend, stay with him, come and go with him. In our Eastern society such things are not allowed. I do not know what will happen in the future. Personally I will not allow my children to do this. Here we may allow the man to do this, but not the girl. . . . If you ask whether it is fair to allow a boy what may not be allowed a girl, I would say it is not fair. The boy shouldn't have complete freedom. We also have the restrictions of the Muslim religion. Things may change in a few years' time. But as long as I live I will not allow these things. I will not allow my daughter to go out with a stranger. Nevertheless she will have her say about the man she will marry. After we've made inquiries about the person. It would be difficult for me to allow her to go out with her *fiancé*. For a girl it doesn't mean she will not see anybody at all before she gets married. Indeed, her family may know other families who have sons. And through exchange of visits the boys may get to know the girls.

Britain is known for holding on to her traditions. There are old families here that still cling to the past. There is a bigger difference between my generation and the new one than between us and the older generation. We are more aware of our responsibilities.

Nowadays anybody can get whatever he wants because life is easy and there is plenty of money. Now we can change our cars once or twice a year. In the past we couldn't even get a bicycle. Nevertheless financial problems sharpen one's character. When everything is within easy reach, one tends to take things for granted. The new generation is not as concerned about work as my generation. But perhaps they will take on greater responsibility in the future for there are certainly some good people among them.

I'll tell you something about myself. During the summer holidays I worked as a porter and as a telephone operator. I also worked for the electricity board. I worked, studied and worked again, until I became the head of a department at the Ministry of Agriculture. The difficulties I went through sharpened my sense of awareness. Nowadays the majority of young people don't work in the summer holidays. They want to have holidays and go on trips.

When I finished secondary school I went to Cairo on a scholar-ship to study agriculture at Azhar University, where I spent four years. I graduated in June 1968 and returned to Doha. I joined the Ministry of Agriculture, which was then called the Department of Agriculture, as Head of Agricultural Expansion; four years later I became the Director of the Department of Agricultural Affairs and have held this post since.

I chose agriculture because it appealed to my practical nature. In the East, agriculture is not as highly regarded as other professions. Instinctively I felt that agriculture would be useful to the country. In agricultural work you feel you are taking an active part in life. In nature you see the power of God at work. Agriculture involves work in the field and in the office. Personally I like working in contact with nature in the field. The results are more tangible than those of office work.

When I went to university I had no background knowledge of agriculture, because in the past there was no agriculture in Qatar in the accepted sense of the word: people just worked in their own small fields. Still, studying is not everything. At university they teach you practical things like field work, but experience is gained when one starts work. The theoretical side complements the practical. I chose agriculture without my family influencing me. After I returned, I heard people say 'So-and-so is a peasant', or: 'So-and-so is a farmer'. This derogatory attitude is quite common throughout the East, but it had no influence on me whatsoever, although I knew well enough what people were saying about me. On the contrary it made me all the more determined to show people that agriculture was not inferior to any other profession. The number of Qataris who took up agriculture is limited. We are still only three: I was the first, then two more followed. Only three Qataris have BScs in agriculture. There are also five or six who completed a secondary agricultural course. This was done after discussing the matter with the Ministry of Education. In the long run we hope to get more people interested in agriculture.

The Department of Agriculture was established in 1954. It was then a small department with a limited staff. It offered assistance to farmers so as to encourage them with their work. In those days there were about two hundred nurseries. Later the department became a ministry. We enlarged the specialisation sectors and increased our staff. We also increased our assistance to the farmers and are trying to provide more help. The number of farms has reached four hundred. When our population was small we exported vegetables. We still produce vegetables and new varieties have recently been introduced so as to create a balance between quality and quantity. We tried to increase the area allocated for fruit and experiments have been carried out on palm trees, oranges, lemons, grapes, pomegranates, figs and guava, in order to find the kinds which could be successfully grown here. We have special nurseries for experiments in the north which produce a large number of plants, especially fruit seedlings which are given free to the farmers. In addition to the vegetables other new ideas have been introduced to agriculture.

When you come back to your country after an absence of four years, you feel apprehensive at first. Any work you start for the first time carries an element of fear, which is dispelled after you settle down to the job. When I was studying I used to feel that after graduation the responsibility for developing agricultural plans would fall on me. But I never thought that one day I would be the number one man responsible for agriculture. I would not have worked less, whether or not I was a director or a head of department. Indeed, I consider myself a worker in the service of my country regardless of the position I hold. I worked very hard so my promotion was based on merit. When I returned all I wanted was to serve my country. Our Arab brothers and the non-Arabs who work here are also helping us. But the natives have a greater responsibility towards Qatar than the foreigners: they feel this generation must work harder so that the next generation will be proud of it, because it paved the way for them.

I had many things on my mind. The country grew nothing but vegetables. I thought we should at least rely on ourselves for the breeding of poultry and for producing milk, instead of using imported milk or milk powder. In some countries progress is measured by the quantity of milk consumed. Also we are now working on plans for breeding livestock for meat production. In one, the houses for the project are almost ready and the whole project will be ready in a few months. The area so far is about 100 hectares for growing mostly clover, barley and possibly palm trees.

Qatar is, of course, a desert country with very limited agricultural potential. It is divided into three agricultural regions. The northern region is muddy, with a high percentage of silt. It is a low-lying land; with time floods accumulated layers of silt. These layers vary from 3 ft to 8 ft. The lands which are now being exploited for agriculture are in different areas. Water from wells is used, because rain is limited and seasonal and falls in the winter. There are no rivers. For agriculture we depend on underground water with a varying mineral content. We use these waters for growing vegetables, fruit and fodder. The midland region is also low-lying. The earth is composed of silt and sand and is lighter than the soil in the north. It grows vegetables, some citrus trees and fodder. It relies largely on well water. The southern region is mostly sand with some silt and light soil. Also the percentage of mineral deposits in the water of wells there is a little higher than elsewhere which makes it not so good for vegetables. So most of this region is exploited for growing fodder and palm trees. There are artesian wells in this southern region in the Salwa and Abu Samra regions which we discovered recently.

FAO (Food and Agriculture Organisation) and the United Nations Development Programme are helping us to set up a project to survey the soil and water. We have a plan for the conservation of underground water. We have to be careful about the amount of water pumped from wells for agricultural use. We are also studying the 'Use of Land and Water' plan which ties up with the other project. In general we have to be very careful in the use of water. The expansion of the agricultural area should be thoroughly studied so that we do not build something at the expense of other things. Experiments are being carried out so as to get the maximum benefit from as large an area as possible with as little water as possible. There are also plans for the use of distilled water in agriculture and for modern methods of irrigation like the drip-irrigation system which is already being used for certain tree plantings and has given good results.

Regarding the agricultural future of Qatar, one should be hopeful—but realistic. Oil has a limited life. The same applies to water. The water stored underground will decrease if not carefully used. In the meantime, the problems in agriculture here are many. The most important is the scarcity and high cost of labour. The landowners are Qataris but few of them cultivate their own land. They employ labourers to work on the farms. Many let their land to farmers, to Arabs and non-Arabs who are resident in the country and who have experience in agriculture. The most important agricultural problem they face here is the scarcity of labour and the cost of labour which has soared up over the past five years.

One day, according to all the reports, the oil will dry up. The result will be the same for Qatar and for the rest of the world. There are other countries which have water they could use for agriculture, but there are also countries which have no water. There are other forms of energy, such as solar and nuclear energy. There are also projects the Arabs could think about. For example, we have rivers like the Tigris and Euphrates, which run into the Shatt al-Arab. The States of this region should think about the possibility of exploiting these rivers instead of letting them run into the sea. The rivers could be re-channelled to places like Kuwait, Saudi Arabia, and from there they could be re-channelled to other parts. We should think of this very seriously. This is going to cost a lot of money, but the money is available. If this is not done now, it will be difficult to do it in the future, when there may not be any money. We should produce at least some of the food we need. We could also build dams for exploiting heavy rains, lke those which fall in Saudi Arabia, Yemen and elsewhere. In this respect I do not take Qatar as being isolated from the rest of the Arab world. I take into account that one day there will be a United Arab State. I do not know if this will happen in a year, a hundred years or a thousand years. Nobody knows. This is the aspiration of all the Arabs. What Saudi

Arabia has belongs to all the Arabs, and what Egypt has belongs to all the Arabs, and this goes also for the Sudan. You have great wealth in the Sudan. The Sudanese don't say that their wealth belongs to them only. The Arabs are all brothers, from the Mashriq to the Maghrib. But this is too broad a subject to be dealt with now.

Khalife—A Man of Quality

The director's office, behind a great lorry yard, is plain and functional. Behind the desk sits a slim man in his late thirties with fine-boned features, a rather darker complexion than most Qataris and striking pale brown eyes that immediately betray the kind of anxious honesty and heightened sensitivity that rarely go with a perfect peace of mind. A self-proclaimed plain man, full of complexities, on whom the strains of this transitional period tell more than on most, possibly because he is acutely aware of other people's feelings. He is one of those who have had only a technical and not a university training, since the educational system in Qatar was still in its infancy when he was a boy. Like most Qataris he is unpretentious and despite his position he still likes to crawl under machines, so he dresses Western style, one of the few Qataris to do so, particularly in his generation. He is wearing a crisp blue and white striped shirt that neatly underscores the military strain in him. He is the kind of man one might elsewhere expect to find among the modernising officer class: keen on organisation and discipline, disinterested, patriotic and with a sense of vocation beyond mere professional pride. There are other directors in Qatar who enjoy their work, but most of them would be equally happy to move on: upwards, sideways or out into business. In Khalife's case it is impossible to think of him in business, impossible in fact to think of him elsewhere than in this department which he joined as little more than a child, which he grew up with and which grew up with him. A rare individual who can speak of a desire to serve his country 'to the best of his ability' as he always puts it, without either causing or feeling embarrassment. From a file on his desk, which, as the most conscientious of men, he has carefully prepared for inspection in advance, he produces a document which is important to him. They are a justification of his life in many ways, these few typewritten lines from a UN agency affirming that the department is working well and has no need for external assistance or advice.

Near the department where he spends much of his time, Khalife lives in a medium-sized villa with a pleasant tree-filled garden. The *majlis* is smaller and more homely than many; there is room for only eleven people to sit. The cream-coloured matching sofas and chairs are arranged round the wall in traditional style. Khalife's wife would like a bigger room because everybody has bigger *majlis* these days. But having no external business activities and with only the rent of a couple of houses as extra income—they let them out at a remarkably reasonable rent by Qatari standards—the family cannot afford it. Obviously anyone with a director's salary is well-off, but the cost of land and building is so colossally high in Qatar today that only a Government subsidy or a substantial private income can cover it. Besides, they have just bought a small farm in the desert which is not yet self-supporting. On Fridays they often spend the day there, either by themselves or with friends.

This Friday the guests are mixed, foreigners and Qataris. There is a young Qatari who works in the Petroleum Department and his lively Bahraini wife. There is a vivid, red-haired Syrian girl with a Palestinian husband who has lived in Qatar since childhood. Both men are wearing Western dress, both women wear jeans. Khalife is in the Qatari *thaub*, which he claims is more relaxing, while the Qatari women all wear long dresses. Khalife's wife is in her mid-twenties, a girl with strong, handsome Arab-style features and almost waist-length hair which she would cut if he would let her; she is pregnant with her third child and wearing a long red maternity pinafore from Harrods. She impresses as being intelligent but not intellectual, determined and possibly more down-to-earth and less high minded than her husband. In the car she brings along her English language book, having not quite finished the lesson of the previous day on the sinking of the Titanic. Married at sixteen, she is now completing her education, with her husband's active encouragement, ten years and two children later. But in Qatar this can be an expensive business. Having his wife tutored by Egyptian school teachers making money during their afternoons off for two hours a week in both English and modern mathematics—so she can also help the children with the latter, the curse of all Qatari parents—costs Khalife almost £200 per month. This is a considerable drain on the family income but it is clear that Khalife regrets it far less than he would seeing her reduced to gossiping with her friends. Besides, his wife's education is probably also an ingredient essential to the success of his marriage. Many of the first generation of educated Qataris now in their thirties have the same problem as men frequently had in the Fifties in England: they have left their wives intellectually behind.

The farm, half an hour's drive away from Doha, turns out to be several fields of unpromising sand, surrounded by tall sugar cane to prevent the desert from encroaching on the irrigated land. It is November and the wind is blowing lustily, but the sun is still quite hot. Small, wilting lemon trees stand in pools of water; they look miserable for the moment but eventually they will grow well. There are also aubergines and strong-tasting radishes. There are sheep and hens and turkeys. But the eye is drawn irresistibly to rest on some small vivid emerald patches of cattle fodder; they rouse something of the same feeling of reverence amidst the harsh glare of the surrounding desert as the first shoots that push through the hard ground in Europe after winter. The farm is run by two Baluchis from across the Gulf, for few Qataris have agricultural skills and anyway would never accept such a low-paid, low-status job.

In the midst of the irrigated land stands a small, unpretentious prefabricated one-room house. It is carpeted, wall-papered, there are cushions round the wall and it boasts a big fridge and an air-conditioning unit. The cooking and other facilities are in outhouses. There is also an elevated swimming pool, half-covered by a roof as a protection against the glare of the summer sun. It is an expensive installation but without it the women in the family would find it hard to bathe; it is still not accepted for Qatari women to expose themselves in swim-suits on beaches, although foreign women do so quite unconcernedly.

The picnic proceeds at much the same desultory pace as picnics anywhere. The car is unloaded. Some people eat a breakfast of hard-boiled eggs. Others wander off to view the estate and munch a few radishes. Husband and wife begin to prepare the food for lunch. The Bahraini and Syrian ladies remain indoors extended on the cushions drinking Arab coffee with cardamom, while their husbands play ball outside and pretend to look after two three-year-olds who soon potter off into the desert by themselves.

More people arrive. The wife's sister and somebody's mother, a self-effacing old lady in black without a *batula* who dedicates herself to the salad. One of the sisters, a jolly, bouncy schoolgirl of sixteen, wants to practise her English. She soon asks the inevitable question, 'How do you like Qatar?' Then, with all the solemnity of someone imparting a sensational piece of information, she discloses that she is going to a party with 'boys'. This is indeed sensational. Boys? 'Well . . . one boy.' 'Your brother?' Gales of giggles.

Lunch-time arrives and it becomes fully apparent that this is Arabia. Not by the nature of the food, but by its sheer quantity. This is full-blooded traditional desert hospitality. Besides Arab bread and salad, a huge pile of fresh Australian steaks (at £8 a pound), mounds of veal kebab and chicken. Khalife prepares the barbecue, evidently totally absorbed and oblivious to the irony, which must strike a stranger, that it should be here, in this desert, whose harsh barrenness drove generations of his forefathers to a dangerous life at sea that he—like so many other Qataris—should find peace and contentment.

Apart from the new developments you see now, Doha will remain Doha for a Qatari. What we notice here is the rapid change, the building of roads, ports, schools. If you have no cars you don't need roads; we just had footpaths in the old days.

I can remember back to when I was eight and ten years old. There was no modern-style school, just Koranic schools. I never had the chance to go even to Koranic school. Schooling wasn't compulsory. I lost my father when I was ten years old and none of the family appreciated the need to send me to school. Nobody really thought of it at that time. Of course you had to pay too and my mother was a widow.

In those days, widows like my mother were looked after by their grown-up children—and I had older brothers and sisters. I'm the spoiled youngest. My brothers were working: fishing, pearl diving. Then they joined the QPC. If a woman had no other relatives than her daughter, who was probably married, she would have to stick to her. She wouldn't starve. She would go to her daughter's husband and she would be welcomed, because in those days family ties were stronger than now. Nowadays people have to depend on themselves; they don't care so much for others. But even now a woman could go even to very distant relatives and they would welcome her. In this the Arab world is different from the West. If I had relatives who had fallen on hard times I would support them for as long as I could. I admit that this is something which is slightly decreasing because of people being widely scattered. If the attitude of the younger generation has not already changed, it will change, and that is a pity. Now the State provides for widows through the social welfare department. And the widow doesn't, of course, want to go to her sister or anybody if the State will pay.

I began going to night classes while I was working at the mechanical equipment department. I was thirteen years old and working as a labourer. I remember feeling under great strain at this time. I wanted to achieve something without knowing how to do it; I didn't really know where I was going. The people who used to run this department arranged for me to move from section to section: to spend four months in a machine shop where I learnt to use the various measuring instruments—caliper gauges etc.; three months in the gearbox shop; a few months in the engine shop, stripping and rebuilding engines. But because I had no educational background whatsoever it was all very difficult. Luckily, the department organised some private tuition for me. I was interested in maths and if I had a difficult problem I sought the help of the office manager. Then the Artisan Training School opened in 1954. I joined and soon I was studying full-time, sleeping at a boarding school which was financed by the State and run by the Education Department. I spent three years at the Artisan Training School and finished there in 1958 when I was eighteen. I came back to the Mechanical Equipment Department as an employee and was sent to work in the machine shop. I liked that particular section because you can invent: you design something and you make it, you make bolts, nuts, you regrind a crankshaft or rebore a cylinder block. I like practical work that also makes my mind work.

As before, friends helped me to go on training. Mr Glue, an Englishman who was head of department, and his assistant Mr Gray, recommended me, the education authority okayed the recommendation and I went to the UK at the beginning of 1959. I had never been outside Qatar before. I went to learn English in an obscure village in Devon called Cheriton Fitzpaine. The family was called Woodward. Mr Woodward was a vicar, retired from London and now preaching in the village. They looked after me very well. Mr Woodward used to take me for private tuition in English; then in the evening when he went on his rounds he used to take me with him and introduce me to the people; I really liked that. We arranged with his friend, another vicar, to give me private tuition in maths at Exeter Cathedral. The Woodwards never interfered with my religious beliefs and they were quite interested to learn about Islam.

I was quite happy although some things were strange or difficult. I realised that I could not necessarily have all I wanted. For example, when I went to my room I knew I could only have the electric fire on for a certain time. I couldn't have the lights on all night. I had a small tape recorder and sometimes wanted to listen to some Arabic music. I could listen to music, but using electricity was expensive, people had to pay the bill. I had to respect their feelings. This applied not during the period I was living with the vicar—they were quite well off and didn't need students to augment their income—but especially when I was living with Mrs M in Shrewsbury I had to be careful. I mean they really needed extra money so I had to be careful and couldn't have the heaters on for twenty-four hours. The cold was the worst thing. After a few hours in bed I felt warm, but in the morning when I got up the whole place was freezing. I suppose if you are in Rome then do as the Romans. That notion helped me. I never wanted to be different. I just felt I had to be like the English, while preserving my own ideas and identity of course.

The greenery of the countryside was a very nice change for anybody coming from here. When I'm in Devon, watching the farmers, smelling the fresh air, seeing the green, it really makes me feel different, I feel healthy. Here there are some places where I get this feeling. For example, when I go fishing—which is one of my hobbies. Greenery makes you less tense than staring at the sun and the sand as Arabs have to do. That's why the first thing the ordinary Qatari wants is a garden. It brings life to the house, it makes you relax, it's good for the kids and for the old people. It's relaxing to sit on a chair under a tree.

After Devon I went to Shrewsbury where I went to the Rolls Royce Sentinel Works, Diesel Division. They started me from scratch on really basic work, like making bolts. It was a school for apprentices. You have to go through this so you don't get muddled when you join the assembly line. I stayed there for three years. During that time I went to Shrewsbury Technical College on block release for six months. They teach you maths and English, drawing, geometry. I went also to Derby and Birmingham in short courses. I finally came back to Qatar in 1963.

In all I spent five years in England with only a couple of weeks back in Doha in between. But I don't think England changed me that much. As a Qatari I remain a Qatari. My purpose was really to achieve something; to work abroad, then to come back and serve my country by implementing what I had learned. So if I was feeling upset and puzzled by people or my pocket money was not enough and I was stuck in my bedroom and couldn't go to the pictures or something with others, I set all these small worries and irritations against what I had come for; I began to see them in proportion.

I was never really surprised by anyone in England. Why, I don't know. Maybe it was because I wasn't trying to be different from other people. Staying with a family also helped: there is a big difference between families and digs. If you are treated as part of the family it makes life easier and study easier. You know you're accepted. Also you try yourself to become part of them. In Shrewsbury on Sunday, for instance, I never went out. I had to help Mrs M, I called her 'Ma' and she called me 'son'. I felt sorry for them, they were so old. I used to go to the back garden to the greenhouse and pick the tomatoes, potatoes and cabbages, wash them and help washing the dishes. I didn't do this in Qatar, of course, but it seems natural in England because everybody does it. The husband puts on an apron while the wife is busy doing something else or feeding the kids, so it's a matter of cooperating. It was very nice and I enjoyed it. I don't do it here, unfortunately, because I don't have the time and my family is not really in need of my assistance because we have a nanny and things. Besides, my wife would think I would mess everything up if I came into the kitchen.

When I came back from England at the beginning of 1963 I

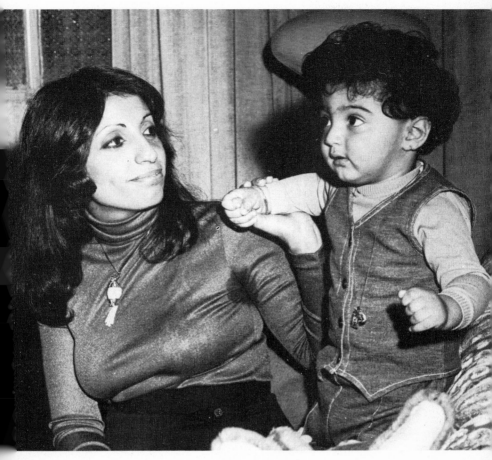

Atiqa, the doctor, with her small son

Aisha, the radio announcer

worked as a workshop superintendent. I spent a lot of time on the shopfloor trying to put into practice all that I had learned during my training in the UK and acquiring more technical experience. I wanted to spend a few years sorting things out. Then, as a qualified Qatari, I had to feel my way slowly, gradually establish my position, in relation to the many foreigners in the department.

I worked in the repair workshop which was part of the Ministry of Public Works. The mechanical equipment department in which I then worked, now looks after more than 1,150 vehicles. Then we had between 70 and 100. Part of the job of this department is to acquire and service new vehicles and plant. It is fully responsible for the maintenance and repair of all Government vehicles. Today we deal with thirty-six Government departments. Less than half the people working in the department at the time were Qataris: now more than half are. The total number working in the department now is 800. You appreciate that when you start a department like this you need a lot of highly qualified technical people which, inevitably, we didn't have at the time. We had only drivers, foremen, assistant mechanics. But in the long run we managed to find enough Qataris up to the standard of the non-Qataris working here. Our aim has always been to achieve this because, ultimately, a country can only be run by its own people.

The policy here is to Qatarise all departments as far as possible. But our problem is that the pace of development is outstripping our capacity to produce trained and educated people. After all, you've got to have engineers and supervisors and so many other categories, and even if we create a sufficient number of graduates we still won't have enough skilled technical staff at lower levels: welders, fitters, etc.

When I came back I had to face the kind of problem that anybody faces when the move into a new house. It takes a bit of time to get it organised, you know. Also I had to face the problem of how to create a disciplined work force.

My attitude was this. While I may be a Qatari, I can't prove myself by simply wearing a *thaub* or *agal* or having a Qatari passport: that's not enough. You have to work better and harder than non-Qataris. Some of the work-people at that time were illiterate. They had no experience of modern industrial discipline because the life we led in the past was so very different. I felt that they couldn't be blamed for their shortcomings, but that it was my duty to guide them on the right road. I knew I could only achieve this slowly, by a process of give and take. Nowadays my fellow Qataris who work in this department are punctual: they do come on time. I think this is a great achievement, because this department has its own very particular organisational problems since it is linked to so many different Ministries. To maintain its efficiency you simply must have discipline, you must have your people co-operating. The main point to remember, I think, is that you yourself have to set the right example.

One of the things I am happy about is that I have succeeded in making people return to the department to work overtime, not just because they want to collect extra money for working more hours, but because they actually want to finish off a job or clear up a problem—which is what overtime is really intended for. Sometimes one man can do the job of ten, if he's really interested in his work.

As far as my professional ambition is concerned, I suppose my attitude is that there is no end to what human beings can achieve. I enjoy my work because it's tough work, I mean, it's not a routine job: you meet new problems every day. Engineering itself is an interesting line and then there's also my administrative work where new subjects are constantly cropping up. I'm always learning.

We have lived through big changes in Qatar. But for us, these changes appeared slowly, day by day. I mean, they do not shock people except for those who have been out of the country for three or four years. They notice the tremendous transformation. It is usually the older people who find change hardest to digest, which is natural. Take my mother. When I came back from England in 1963 after five years, I had to go and live with her.

Knowing that she was old and sick, I couldn't very well abandon her. So I lived for six months or so with her and with my brothers. I had to accept her way of life. I couldn't be fussy about decorating the house or installing hi-fi stereo. It would have been wrong for me to have come back and given her a sudden shock. I think if you start off with this attitude you can get along with the older people, like my mother, quite well because there is mutual understanding. Later she has to learn to appreciate your way of life and accept your freedom of action although, of course, you always owe her particular respect because she's your mother. It might be difficult for some people, I expect: in fact, quite a restriction for someone who is young and wants to develop their own life-style. But you have to compromise, especially with your own family. Later, when I moved to my own house, I still went back to have meals with her. I couldn't make myself completely independent; it would have been too hard on her. I would go and fetch what she needed and chat endlessly. With any old person, you have to give them plenty of time to do all the talking while you just listen. In between you have to think of something to tell them which is not too modern and not too far removed from their familiar world. If you're staying in the same house, even you are married, your mother will stay awake and wait for you to come back, listening for the noise of the gate as you bring the car in. Even if you are married, she will be thinking about you, not accusing you of doing anything wrong: she will just say, 'You work hard and you get up very early in the morning, you've hardly had enough sleep,' such things, you see? Purely motherly concern. I think it's a great thing that children are loved and protected like this.

Life is changing; you've got to change with it. Still, there are aspects of our old life that we miss; we miss nature. When you hear the pearl-diving songs and drums on television sometimes, happy memories surge back. I find great enjoyment listening to the old diving songs. There's something in them which saddens you and makes you regret that this world has passed away, and that all that is left are the songs. When you listen to them you feel for the people who once died at sea, who were eaten by sharks, or who became sick and had to be dropped overboard.

But the old people who were once divers, who lived a hard life, tend to say, 'I hope those days won't come back again.' We should bear this in mind. The old days were no joke.

PART THREE

Between Two Worlds—
The Women

Introduction—Who Will Bell the Cat?

'The Europeans are mistaken in thinking the state of marriage so different among the Muslims from what it is with Christian nations. I could not discern any such difference in Arabia.

'Polygamy is permitted, indeed, among Mahomedans, and the delicacy of our ladies is shocked at this idea; but the Arabians rarely avail themselves of the privilege of marrying four lawful wives, and entertaining at the same time any number of female slaves. None but rich voluptuaries marry so many wives, and their conduct is blamed by all sober men. Men of sense, indeed, think this privilege rather troublesome than convenient. A husband is, by law, obliged to treat his wives suitable to their condition, and to dispense his favours among them with perfect equality: but these are duties not a little disagreeable to most Muslims; and such modes of luxury are too expensive to the Arabians, who are seldom in easy circumstances.'

from Carsten Niebuhr's
Travels In Arabia (1772)

When the first oil flares light up the dark desert, passengers on the London to Doha flight lean over to look out of the window; so contact is established. The young man sitting by the window has been twitching his leg compulsively, a sure sign of nervous tension in a Qatari. Now it emerges that he has not brought back the half-petticoats his wife requested; as a matter of fact, the salesgirl at Harrods even denied the existence of such things. 'Do they or do they not exist?' he asks anxiously. It would, of course, have saved a lot of bother if his wife had come with him to London and bought them herself. The trouble is that she doesn't like flying. Actually, she's terrified in an aeroplane; she sits paralysed with fear, clutching the sides of her seat and staring straight ahead. But doesn't he know that such phobias can be treated? Yes. He leans back comfortably in his seat, stretches his legs and gazes dreamily out at the oil flares. It's not that he's indifferent to her problem, but—well—that's the only time he's boss, when she's paralysed several hundred feet above ground level. As soon as the plane lands and comes to a halt, it's back to normal: do this, do that, take the hand luggage, hold the baby etc. etc.

The point of this anecdote is not that women in Qatar really wear the trousers, or rather the *thaub*, but merely to emphasise Niebuhr's sensible observation of two centuries ago—that marriage is not so very different among Muslims and Christians, and that Muslim women are by no means the downtrodden slaves that Westerners imagine them to be.

Of course Qatar is a male-oriented society. Men are economically, socially and legally dominant—as they are in the West and even more so, since the country is only at the beginning of its development and has not had the advantage of several hundred years of economic growth and education. At worst, a woman might be divorced, while she herself could not easily divorce her husband. Her children might be taken from her after the age of seven or nine. The family could take the dowry rather than let her keep it. She inherits half as much as a man; her legal testimony is worth half as much. If her husband felt so inclined, he might keep her a virtual prisoner in the home. When guests came, she would be expected to disappear, unless they were members of the family.

It is equally true that in the majority of cases, one man and one woman live together. They love each other or are indifferent just like Westerners. Sometimes, if hers is the stronger personality, the woman dominates the man. A European woman still living in Qatar was astonished one day at the beginning of her life there, over twenty years ago, to see a woman, complete with *batula*, chasing her husband down the street with a stick. Of course the social disabilities suffered by Qatari women have been and, to some extent, still are considerable. But she is no more a slave and chattel on account of this, than a Western woman who may easily be abandoned and left destitute by her husband. The Qatari woman at least can rely on her family to look after her; the Western woman usually cannot. This is an area where there is no black and no white—only different shades of grey.

If it seems necessary to begin any discussion on women's position in Qatari and Arabian society with some banal pieces of common sense, this is because the whole question has always been obscured and confused by stereotypes, in this century particularly by Hollywood's versions of the Arabian Nights. From these it is well known to all Westerners that Arab men—especially 'sheikhs'—kidnap women and take them against their will, while the women themselves fall into two categories: the veiled downtrodden drudge or the sensual harem concubine. Such images say more about Western fantasies and forms of psychological escapism than about daily life in Arabian society.

On a more rational level, there is one genuine obstacle which faces Westerners who try to come to grips with Arab society. This is the legality of male polygamy. In fact, as Niebuhr pointed out, men rarely avail themselves of the privilege: this is either because they cannot afford to, or because they realise that they can only be happy with one woman. As he observed in his usual sane way: 'It would be unfair to judge of the manners of a whole people by the fastidious luxury of the great.'

The older men in Qatar who have married two wives or more have done so often—but not always—for practical reasons: because their first wife was childless or sick and could no longer be a wife to them. The overwhelming majority of young men simply would not consider marrying a second wife today, while the young women themselves would no longer accept it. The threat of a second marriage uttered by men in a playful way, when they want to apply pressure in some direction—say they want their wife to have more children—is not pleasant for the women who immediately rail at it. But it hardly constitutes a major social problem such as the large dowries that are being demanded by some fathers, for the practice is gradually dying out by itself.

Still, male polygamy is sanctioned by Islam and this contributes to the deep-seated belief in the West that the Muslim religion is primarily responsible for women's low status in Arab society. In fact, the emergence of Islam greatly improved women's condition at the time.

In pre-Islamic times, it was believed that men who could hunt, fight, defend themselves and collect food were much more useful to a society of desert tribes living at starvation level than women who could be carried off and disgrace the tribe. Before the coming of Islam, it was common practice to kill baby girls at birth. Women had become little more than slaves and chattels.

Islam changed this situation. Like Christianity, it set women on an equal spiritual level to men: both women and men have equal opportunity to go to paradise. Islam made it a duty for both sexes to educate themselves 'from the cradle to the grave'. On an economic legal level, Islam gave women two valuable new rights: the right to inherit and to dispose of their own wealth as well as to receive and retain their own dowry. However, when it came to the question of marriage, women's status unquestionably suffered as a result of the implicit assumption made by Islam that the primary purpose of marriage is the propagation of children. Partly for this reason, a man is allowed four wives at a time and an unlimited number of concubines. Moreover, the number of women and children left by Muslim men who died in battle and who needed protection in the anarchic society of the desert made it difficult to outlaw polygamy entirely. But the Koran lays down stringent conditions for multiple marriage: the man must treat his wives with absolute equal fairness and if he cannot do so, then he should have only one. In another section, the Koran states that it is impossible to be equally just to two women. It is true that there is a *sura* or verse in the Koran to the effect that men have authority over women since they are financially responsible for them; but then the Christian marriage ceremony has for centuries enjoined women to 'obey'.

During the high noon of Arab culture, there were many famous women mystics and scholars. Then, as the culture declined, the position of women declined too. Also Islam had its misogynists like St Paul, who interpreted parts of the Koran in such a way as to undermine women's status. But by far the most important factor in this decline was the perpetuation—in the lands overrun by the Arabs—of social customs common in pre-Islamic times. Veiling and seclusion, for instance, were practised in the Byzantine Empire and in Persian long before Islam. Just as Christianity absorbed many pre-Christian feasts and customs, so Islam was infiltrated by the ancient social practices of the East. The problem for women was that these customs gradually became identified with Islam and so came to be regarded as sacrosanct. Many Muslims came to believe quite genuinely that veiling women was a religious duty, as many Christians have believed and still believe—with as little justification—that women are excluded by the Bible from the priesthood.

The position of women in Arab countries differs as widely as the position of women in European countries and to deal with this whole question is outside the scope of this chapter. But one point might be made. While the seclusion of women and the curtailment of their liberty generally was carried to far greater lengths in Arabian society than in the West—no doubt partly because the conditions of Arabian society itself were generally harsher—the assumptions about women that lay behind this kind of treatment were virtually identical in Western and in Arabian society. Both started from the same fundamental premise: that a woman is dishonoured by any sexual involvement with a man outside marriage—while the man, of course, is not. By trans-gressing this code, a bedu woman, if she was unlucky, might be done away with by a member of her family. A Victorian woman could be and often was thrown out by her family and so forced either to prostitute herself or to enter an almshouse. Given that the price women had to pay to society was so great, there was a great deal of logic in the bedu habit of separating the sexes as much as possible (except within the family itself).

As is evident from the above, the parallel should not be carried too far, but Qatari girls frequently strike outsiders as very Victorian in behaviour and attitude. (It is probably no accident that even when they speak English, Qataris both male and female never speak of 'women', but always of 'ladies'.) Qatar, as has been said, has made an astonishing journey through time and this fact is responsible for some strange incongruities in the society. Moving through Qatar meeting the women there, is rather like leafing at random through the pages of a history book. There are women who are firmly based in the fourth quarter of the twentieth century: they write PhDs, have interesting jobs, earn the same as men and more, and have their babies spaced out to suit their career. On the other end of the scale, there is the quasi-medieval situation where one bedu girl is virtually a prisoner in her house despite the fact that she is married. However, by and large, the majority of Qatari girls seem to have been parachuted into the Victorian era.

The long dresses and the long tresses partly explain this impression. But the general framework of their lives and ideas are far more important. Like Victorian women, Qatari girls are very closely enmeshed in a tight family web, and few—if any—would carry the struggle for their personal freedom to the point of breaking away from the family unit. They want more breathing space, more freedom to come and go, more school outings and women's societies, more opportunity to meet young men. But at most they want to have their corset only less tightly laced; they do not, at this stage, want to do away with it. The more daring are debating whether to bob their hair. Moreover, it is probable that the young men also suffer from the situation. Many have been abroad to study and had foreign girl friends, so when they come home they have more difficulty in adjusting.

Even the most independently minded among the young women, with aggressive ideas on women's position in society, will often confound expectations and remain within a very traditional frame of thought by Western standards. Leilah, possibly the most outspokenly radical woman in Qatar on this issue, is a case in point. One reason for this is the strength of family ties. Another reason is Arab nationalist sentiments. Many of the most sophisticated among Qatari women who are educated and travel abroad will advocate the wearing of long coveredup dresses, modest behaviour in mixed company and even on occasion the retention of the *abbaya* because they feel that they are Arab and fear the swamping of Arab by Western culture.

The young women in Qatar today are of rare quality. Paradoxically, this is partly because of the very social disadvantages they suffer, which seem to make them all the more determined to work hard, study, prove and improve themselves. When one compares their lives with those of their veiled middleaged mothers, they have already come a long way. Not that the older women with their facemasks are the anonymous downtrodden drudges that Westerners imagine them to be; when they remove their masks these older women often have strong, powerful faces and, besides, are generally mistress of their own homes. Still, their experience is limited and their minds are undeveloped. The lives of their daughters have been completely transformed by two factors: education and money.

The story of women's education in Qatar is remarkable in many ways. It began in 1956, just two years after the first boys' nonreligious primary school opened. Of course, there was resistance at first. But the really striking aspect of the young women's stories, as told here, is how fast these resistances faded, even parental opposition to the girls leaving the country to study abroad, a development which strikes at the root of the whole traditional social system. Now within just two decades of the creation of the first primary school, girls are studying to be doctors, journalists, biologists, even engineers. When one remembers how the first women doctors in the West were scorned and ridiculed in the late nineteenth century by institutions of learning that had existed for around seven hundred years and until how recently fathers were telling their daughters that it was a waste for them to study since they would only marry anyway, one comes to realise that the introduction of education for women is really a very extraordinary achievement for which countries like Qatar are all too rarely given credit.

Money is the other great liberating factor, particularly for women. The fact that education is free and universal, up to university level and beyond, for anyone reaching a basic academic standard, is vital to women. Since the State pays it means that no family need be called on to 'waste' its money on educating its daughters. Then money enables girls to travel, to see different societies and to develop their personalities. Ironically, money is what enables Qatari women, in some circumstances, to do what many of the most liberated, progressive women in the West still cannot do because they do not have the means. Qatari women can and do continue working even when they have small children. They can study at home or abroad after marriage, because the money is there to pay for the nannies, cooks, the air fares, the university fees and the long-distance telephone calls to the children.

For women who want to get somewhere and whose husbands back them up—and this is obviously a vital factor—money is what enables them, in one move, to by-pass centuries of historical development in a game of social snakes and ladders. The risk for such women is, however, that having moved fast up the educational ladder, they may slide equally fast down the social snake when they come back to look for a job commensurate with their abilities and training. Jobs are opening up for women, but slowly.

To challenge the sexual *mores* and the family structure is always a revolutionary undertaking in any society. And women's changing status is unquestionably the major social problem in the Gulf countries today. In Qatar, society has given in to women's pressure completely on the educational front and partially on the job front. It is trying to keep its balance by maintaining, up to a point anyway, the traditional segregation of the sexes on a social level. (Curiously, the situation is almost exactly the reverse of the position in the West until very recently.) In the long run, this is an untenable position, particularly since the capitulation on education has been so far-reaching. But then, apart from the old, nobody really sees it as anything other than a temporary holding operation. The point, as put by one technocrat, whose wife complains ritually every six months, is to allow the old people to die in peace, without being too upset. 'I try to make it up to my wife by taking her abroad once every year,' he explained.

In the final analysis, there is none, or at least very little of the anger (as opposed to frustration) about women's position in society that a Westerner might expect to find in Qatar; certainly women there are less angry than in the West. And the fact that Qatar is less developed is not the only reason. Anger is an apposite emotion in a position of stalemate, but in a rapidly changing situation it is a waste of valuable energy. Like a lot of moles, Qatari women are burrowing away underground gaining degrees and diplomas and doctorates on the basis that one of these days society will simply find the ground giving way under its feet. Moreover, they know that if progress is slow (to their mind), it is because everyone is a little frightened of what the neighbours will say or is afraid of shocking the old people—of being the first to stand out, the one to bell the cat, so to speak— rather than because society is upholding tradition on ideological grounds. This also makes a difference.

In reality, women's problem in Qatar is less lack of progress than the danger of a backlash as society begins to realise fully what has already happened. This is why the most intelligent reformers in Qatar and in other parts of Arabia advocate a course of action which may seem exceedingly strange to Western women whose problems are at once so similar and so different. Keep your head down, they say, don't make too much of an issue of the veil or the *abbaya*, and above all, keep burrowing—keep studying. It is probable that only the next generation will reap the rewards. Even so, unless something totally unforeseen happens, there will be more difference between grandmother and granddaughter in countries like Qatar than there has ever been anywhere on the face of the globe.

1. WOMEN VEILED—
THE MIDDLE-AGED AND THE OLD

Zalikha, Who Knows the Old Days Were Better

But for the *batula* which she wears as another woman might wear an expensive necklace, with underlying pride, Zalikha belongs to a breed of middle-aged women you might meet anywhere: powerfully built, plain-spoken, busy and quite unapologetically reactionary. The old days, in her eyes, were a kind of golden age, although she herself is black and was a slave then. For the present day and the present generation she feels a kind of pity, tinged at the edges with disdain.

She lives with her husband in a very modest concrete house, a collection of small rooms opening onto a spotless, high-walled courtyard presided over by a single tree. Above the house looms a very long pole, for she has an idiosyncrasy: she likes, on occasion, to run up the Qatar flag. Something of a professional at interviews—she is interviewed about the past on the radio sometimes, being one of the few women of her age, neither too shy to speak publicly nor too concerned for her social status—Zalikha takes immediate command of the situation. You are conducted to her bedroom—Qatari women sometimes use their bedrooms, like some European women use their kitchens, as a living-room. It is a small room, containing a bedroom suite, matching bed, wardrobe and chest of drawers; sober and somewhat similar in style to those English suites of the Fifties, only considerably more expensive. The only picture on the wall is a photograph of her eldest son; it is hung very high up, above the wardrobe. The carpet is thick and comfortable and that is where you sit, although a chair is produced from somewhere out of polite regard for Western habits. The toddlers who habitually hang round Zalikha's skirts are firmly locked out.

She is talkative and quite unselfconscious. She is also touchingly considerate of your potential areas of ignorance. 'Salt' she enunciates slowly. 'Salt, you know what I mean?' You do know what she means, of course; but this is not really the point. What she is revealing is an underlying assumption that there is little, if anything, in common between your world and hers. While she is prepared, in line with Arab tradition, to extend infinite kindness and tolerance towards you as a stranger and a guest, she does not doubt for a minute that her ways and her habits are far superior to yours.

In the past, when our husbands were away at sea, we women used to look after our homes and children. There were no nurses or anything of that sort then. We respected the other members of our family: fathers-in-law, brothers, etc. While the men were away we stayed at home, of course; but although we were women we were even more responsible than the men.

Before pearling crews left, we were kept busy with preparations. Different members of the crew had different needs, according to their job. My husband was a diver and he had to have a 'stone'— the metal weight he tied to his foot—a nose mask and diving trousers. These trousers were to protect the divers from dangerous fish. They were made by a tailor but the other things were bought ready-made.

When the ships were sighted at sea after four months' absence, we women took cats and palm leaves with us and made for the beach. As soon as the sails were clearly visible we would call out:

> *Away! Away!*
> *We drive you away oh sea. . . .*
> *Oh our big sea, bring us happiness!*

We would beat the sea with the palm leaves and squeeze the cats until they wailed: 'Waw.' This sounded like *raja'oon*— meaning 'they came back' in Arabic. Then we tied pieces of cloth to the palm leaves, dipped them in kerosene and set them on fire. We wanted to burn the sea so that the divers could never go back to it. We dipped the cats in the sea, saying; 'the ships have come' 'come' in this context being *ja'oon* in Arabic. The cats cried: 'Yaw, yaw.' We didn't drown the cats, we just dipped them in the water.

The return of the ships was an important occasion for the women, because we could go to the shore to watch them come in. Children and girls were there; everybody was there. In those days we had no gardens or public places for recreation. So when the pearling ships appeared we were happy. The shore was the only place we could go to enjoy ourselves. But we didn't celebrate when the boats actually arrived at the beach: only when they appeared on the horizon. When the boats came close to the land, we women returned home.

The women did not even look at men who were not related to them in those days. They even waited to receive their husbands in the way I receive guests: I meet them outside at the door, don't I? Women met their sons and their brothers off the boats, but not their husbands. A mother, for instance, would welcome her son on the beach calling out: 'God bless you; God greet you; God give you health, my son; God bless my beloved son.' But a husband was never received outside the house; no, he was received inside. Even today, if my husband goes on a trip to Mecca or Saudi Arabia or Beirut, I don't say good-bye to him at the airport. I walk with him to the door and come back. When I know he is returning I don't go and meet him. These are our traditions. But if my son travels I see him off at the airport. In our tradition, we consider it shameful to meet a husband at the airport. I go with my son and watch until I see him get on board the plane; that isn't shameful. And it isn't wrong to see my mother and father off. But my husband—no, I wouldn't see him off. The girls of today see nothing wrong in doing it; a girl will go with her husband to the airport and to the market. She even drives the car and he sits beside her like a calf.

In the past, we lived in the desert with the sheikhs. We had no doctors. But there was a woman who helped other women to give birth: she was like a doctor or midwife today. After the birth we rubbed our stomachs with hot salt from Persia: this tightened the stomach muscles. We boiled fenugreek and other spices and drank this mixture, we also had milk—this was enough to see us through our maternity safely. We did not depend on wet-nurses then, but fed our own children. When the babies were fed, we left them in deep sleep and carried on with our work: milking cows and doing the household chores. If the baby woke up, we gave it cow-milk too.

Our way of having babies was different from what it is today. Now the woman is taken to see a doctor; the baby is bathed the first day. Then a woman would complete her maternity period only after forty days. In my own case, I had just my mother to help me. Nowadays women are given more help. It's better now; but in the past we relied on God.

In the desert I used to milk the camels. I could also put up the big woollen tents; it was the women who did that. Tents were made of lamb's wool and dyed in different colours. First, we spun the wool on a simple hand-loom made of wood and nails. No! I remember now—first we washed it in the sea, then we dried it, dyed it and combed it with the horn of a small gazelle. Sometimes we used camel wool, but that we didn't dye. We also bought wool from abroad, from Shiraz in Persia. I can't say exactly whether it was also imported from India or London; God knows. You can see the kind of carpets we made in the Bedouin Corner —that's a television programme.

We used to live with the sheikhs. Our main food was meat. We drank curdled milk which we prepared ourselves in big goatskins; they call it yoghurt now. We boiled it in large pots and added ghee and dates. We also baked our own bread. The staple diet in those days was milk, meat, ghee and dates. Now people eat different things. We didn't have the vegetables we have now. I don't know what the ordinary people ate, but the sheikhs certainly ate well. We had onions, oils and Arab chickens. Have you heard of Arab chickens? I mean real live chickens that lay eggs. Then we didn't eat the kind of chickens we eat today: nowadays they might have been killed twenty years ago and God knows if they were killed as they should be—killed with a knife, according to Islamic law. In the old days, we also ate desert rabbits, bustards, gazelles, karawan. In places like Doha, people did eat meat then, but it wasn't as plentiful as it is now. We had chickens in coops next to our houses. During Ramadan we didn't eat cattle meat but lived mainly on our own chickens and fish. Nobody *bought* fish. Every family went out fishing. If I had fish my neighbour also had fish: neighbours used to give each other fish, not like it is now. I still cook fish in the same way I used to: fry it, roast it or boil it. Except that now I fry it in oil, while then I fried it in fat. Then we made good puddings out of ground wheat. But the young men of today—just look at them! What do they eat? Sandwiches! The present generation is a generation of sandwich eaters.

During the hot season or during Ramadan, we used to prepare everything that might be needed in the household throughout the rest of the year. It wasn't like nowadays when a woman asks her husband: 'Go, bring me this and get me that.' The man would find everything ready when he came back in the winter. The woman never asked him to get this and that; no, indeed, she did everything by herself. The husband just handed over the money for the household expenses and she did the rest—without giving everybody a headache as they do today.

First, the woman would grind the grain and the spices, then the henna and perfumes. She never demanded to have a servant or wanted to be with her mother and father. Certainly not; she lived an exemplary married life. When her husband came back at the end of the diving season with his crew and friends, he would find that his wife had been behaving exactly as she should, not as they behave now. Now everything is upside down; when a woman is asked to provide anything, she claims she doesn't have it. Now, a man works hard and isn't even properly looked after. However much he pays towards the household, his wife is never satisfied.

Women here have changed a lot. Do you think that the women of the past were like those of the present? Not in the least; there's a great difference. Today if a man forbids his wife to visit her parents' house, she will probably say: 'Divorce me this minute. I will go to my father's house if I want to.' In the past, a woman used to visit her family only after being married for a year. In the old days we valued our reputation and our dignity.

I mean, when we were newly married, we wouldn't trail off to see our family every day. That would have been shameful. Whenever our parents wanted to visit us they were welcome, but we would visit them only one year after marriage, or even longer. When we had conceived for the first time, we gave birth to our first child at our parents' house and remained there until the fortieth day after delivery. We then came back to our husband's house. After that, any child we had was delivered at our husband's home, not in our parents' house or in the hospital.

Another thing that has changed is that people have become rich and everybody does as they please. In the past when we were poor, we women were careful not to spend more than our husband gave us. If our husband was away, we went to our guardian, some male relative, gave him the money and told him what we needed. There were also women who were like men, dependable. They were always old, never young. The younger women gave them money and they bought everything. In each lane or district there was such an old woman.

In the past some people also had servants who were slaves. I personally had an aunt, as we used to call our mistress. We were not free as we are now; we were *mamlouks*, slaves. When I gave birth my mother came to serve my aunt.

My navel cord was cut at Salata. I wasn't a slave then, but my mother's favourite daughter. When pearling began to decline my mother's brother fell into debt to the merchants and couldn't pay the money back. He was a captain so he was taken to prison. One day, while we were having our lunch, they came to the house and took us away, myself and my brothers, in settlement of the pearling debt. My uncle's creditors were given the money paid for us. People who gave loans in those days did the same work banks do today. On the same day my uncle was released from prison. If you get a loan from the bank, doesn't it take its money back? These debts were exactly the same as a loan from the bank.

I was a virgin then. My new masters found me a husband from their own household and I gave birth to my children there. When they decided I should be married, they never asked me. Nor did they ask my mother or my father or my brother. They chose a man for me and I married him. He was a slave but they loved him as if he had been their own son. It was not like nowadays when a woman is asked whether she wants the man or not; then she had no choice. There was no real dowry, only fifty *riyals* which I put in my pocket. This was paid to legalise the marriage. I was a slave and I had no say. But I would not have hoped to marry a different person and I am still his wife today. Today my sons are men—thank God.

Marriage now is different. A husband has to go to the market to buy bedroom furniture, tables and perfumes; the wedding lasts only for one day. In the past we celebrated weddings for seven days. We used to decorate the bridal room, first by painting the walls different colours. Then the sewing started. When we had finished we put cushions, pillows and mattresses covered in red, black, green and yellow broadcloth round the room. The pillows were covered with ten *riyals* worth of cloth, not like now. Then a curtain was hung across the corner of the room where the bride and bridegroom were to sleep: this was to hide them from people who might enter the room, for it is shameful to be seen. We bought different materials—satin and velvet—and embroidered them all, including our own wide gowns, and we covered the floors with carpets. The sewing was done by female slaves; each one had a needle clipped in her hair. On the wedding night we sprinkled the room with perfumes and scattered aromatic plants around. Then the bridegroom came in. The bride was brought in wrapped up in a carpet and carried by four strong female slaves like myself. She was put into the man's arms still wrapped in the carpet.

Brides had to cry. It was dishonourable to smile and laugh. If a bride did not weep, others would sometimes make her. And when she wept those waiting outside would laugh. If she cried, this meant that there was nothing wrong with her: she was intact. Then she could live happily with her husband. Brides who didn't cry were gossiped about; people would criticise her and insinuate that something was wrong until her husband came to hate her.

Now things are different. If you go to a mother to ask if you can marry her daughter, she will first ask whether you have 70,000 *riyals*, a house and a car. If you say you don't have a house and car, she will say she is not interested.

For example, if you come to ask if you can marry my daughter, I will say to you 'I have no objection, but let me talk to her'. When I consult her she will say: 'Why don't you marry him yourself?' Or else she may come to me and say: 'Mother, I want to marry this other man.' If I ask her how she could think of such a thing without the knowledge of her father and brother, she will reply: 'Sucks to you. Who's going to marry him? My father, my brother, or me? *I* want this man.' I will say: 'But, my dear, he has nothing.' She will just answer 'It's none of your business. I want him. I love him'. Then there's absolutely nothing I can do. Let her marry whom she wants.

These habits are new. The change took place some fifteen years ago. These days boys and girls make their marriage arrangements without consulting their parents.

Amina, Who Thinks Women Are Better Off Now

Amina is a frail elderly lady in her sixties with strong character.
Well-known in Qatar as being the first person to open a school for girls in the early nineteen fifties.

When I was young this was a small country and Sheikh Ali bin Abdullah was the Ruler. There were Koranic schools and religious teachers—*mutawwas*—taught in them. I myself studied with Sheikh Hamid Ahmed Abderrahim Darghaam and Sheikh Mohammed Jabir. I grew up learning the noble Koran. The building was not unlike this one, except that it was built of stones and clay, not bricks. The stone was covered with gypsum, the roof was made of wood and it had a large courtyard. We had no water.

Our house was in al-Jesra. We all lived together, but there was a room we called the *majlis* reserved for guests and the men. We didn't eat together. First the men would have lunch—then the women. In some families the men and the women sat together, but not in many. A husband might eat together with his wife and children. But not if the family was a large one where there were many brothers and children. In that case, the men and women each kept to themselves.

Boys and girls would study together. But the boys would sit on one side of the room and the girls on the other. The teacher placed himself in the middle, between them. There were usually about thirty to forty pupils. I went to school for three years and memorised the Koran, then stayed on for one further year to revise. Then when I was fifteen or thereabouts I myself taught. I taught boys and girls. I taught them the noble Koran and prayer duties—how Allah, glory be to Him most High, laid down duties of prayer and fasting and reciting the Koran. Then the sayings of the Prophet, may Allah pray for Him and preserve Him. Anyone who had learnt the Koran would leave and another pupil would take his place. Schools in the past were not like nowadays, that's to say with chairs and I don't know what. We used to sit on the ground, each child studying a *sura*, a verse of the Koran. I taught in my own house. At first I just used to teach the children to memorise the Koran and recite it, but not to write. Each child would take its turn to come up to me and read the Koran while I listened. Then I would read and the child would listen. That was our method. We would approach the Koran in parts; it consists of thirty parts. In those days we used to charge two *riyals* per part. It cost sixty *riyals* to learn the whole book.

When one child had finished the Koran, all the children would get together and go round the town. Their teacher recited these lines: 'Praise be to Allah who has guided us' and the children would reply 'Amen'. The teacher would say 'In the name of religion and Islam, he has chosen us'. They would reply 'Amen' again. 'Glory be to Him, the Creator, Glory be to Him.' This would carry on for a couple of days. The child that had learnt the Koran would be given money by his or her parents and neighbours. On the third day a party was held at their house for other pupils. All this was in the old days.

I wasn't the only woman teacher; there were others. I don't remember the year I began to teach the Koran, but I remember when I was employed by the Government in the early Fifties to teach girls. The girls came to my house; I taught them downstairs in my own home. Some of the parents and guardians were fanatics. They didn't want the girls to study in the Government schools. I used to have to go to their houses to persuade them. I would explain the sayings of the Prophet to them, may Allah pray for Him and preserve Him, that God has ordained education for girls and boys equally, and that to gain knowledge is a duty for all—male and female alike, and that we shouldn't just teach the boys and leave the girls. The fathers didn't object to the boys studying. They were only fanatical about girls' education. They didn't want the girls to be educated because they thought that religion forbade it. I had to persuade them that education is a duty for every Muslim, male or female. Then they gradually saw that girls' education was not sinful

We taught reading and writing—also the Koran and other religious books. The reason I opened the school was that I read the Koran and all the religious books myself and I knew that knowledge is light. And I had heard that there were girls' schools in other countries: I had not read of them, I had just heard people speak of them. So I thought: 'Why doesn't our country open a school?' So I went to Sheikh Khalifa who was heir to the Emir, and he granted my request. They opened the school. They paid for the books and the chairs and everything.

At the beginning of the first year, there were sixty girls, and at the end, one hundred and twenty. I divided them up into three groups and they gave me teachers from the Ministry of Education. In the first year I had two teachers, in the second year I had five. The girls were happy; they wanted to learn. They would come to the classes because they wanted to and not because they had to. Their mentality didn't change at once. But gradually as they came to know more, there was a change for the better in them. They enjoyed the school and never played truant. Even if a girl fell sick, she would not stay away from school. We taught them the Koran at first, then reading, writing, spelling, arithmetic and Arabic.

At home there was no favouritism; girls and boys were treated the same way, given the same food from the same dish. But, of course, if her father or brother ordered a girl to do something, she had to obey the order. She must serve the food. She must work in the house and help her mother. A girl must serve her brother, musn't she? He doesn't help with the housework. He is out of the house. The important thing is that when he comes back, if he wants something, it must be ready for him.

In the past, the girls wore long clothes, the *batula* and the *abbaya*. No girl would go out without her *abbaya*. At the age of about fifteen, when she became a woman, they would make her wear the *batula*. This was the custom in the past. But Qatar has progressed, although we still keep our traditions. They still wear long dresses, and a few wear the *batula*. But the *batula* is not ordained by Islam and if I were of this generation I would not wear it. There are a lot of people who still wore it two or three years ago but now have thrown it away. It's not a duty for a *Sunni*. A woman does not abide by her religion and safeguard her reputation by wearing the *batula*.

I've got used to it. At first I refused to wear the *batula*, but my family forced me to because at that time women all wore it. It was thought shameful not to. But now, because I'm used to it, I feel shy about taking it off. The fact that I wear it has nothing to do with what people say.

When I first started to teach, I never imagined that Qatar would change as much as it has. By Allah, every year Qatar develops more. Every year, praise be to Allah, there is more prosperity and knowledge. I would never have believed it. May the country grow and develop and may education and prosperity increase, *insh'Allah*.

Girls have started to go out and we can't say to them: 'No. You can't go out.' They can see for themselves that the country and the people have changed and started to develop. The girls' own attitudes have developed. There are parties and banquets and so on. A girl may travel abroad with her husband. We can't say no, even though we might think: 'By Allah. I don't like her going out with her husband, going to parties with him.' But in spite of what people may think, it is happening. Things have gone on changing until now she does actually go with him.

In the past, a man didn't see his betrothed until the wedding night. Now he gets engaged to her and she goes out with him. He has the right to see her. The noble Prophet, may Allah pray for Him and preserve Him, got engaged to Aisha, the daughter of Abu Bakr, may Allah be pleased with her. He got engaged to her and said 'I must see her'. So her father sent her with some dates and said to her: 'Oh, daughter Aisha. Go to the Prophet and find whether they are alright or not.' So she took the dates and said: 'Oh Prophet of Allah. My father sends you his greetings and says are the dates all right or not?' He said: 'Allah's blessing be upon you. They are all right.' Aisha was allowed to do this so that the Prophet could see her. But she didn't know about the marriage. Only an orphan girl, without a father, has the right to decide for herself about marriage. If her father is alive, he is responsible for her. Of course, now they ask the girl if she wants to marry. If she doesn't want the man, she says: 'I don't want him. Don't force him on me.' If she wants him she says 'Yes. I like him.'

But praise be to Allah, Allah has granted me what I hoped for the girls. One of my girls, whom I taught first, Nura Darwish, is now a school inspector. They are becoming inspectors, head-mistresses, doctors, teachers, employees in the Ministry of Cultural Affairs, in the Ministry of Social Affairs, in the Ministry of Information. If they like they can study engineering. I've seen them with my own eyes.

I'm happy for them, because they are my girls—the girls of my country. They serve their nation and so do I and *Insh'Allah*, we shall continue to develop. Life here has improved for the women; it isn't what it used to be. We were blind and couldn't find the path. Now we have light. Knowledge is light. They have been educated and the country has improved.

Some of the older women feel like I do, some don't. They don't like the change. No one opposes education now, but some don't like a girl being with her fiancé. When they see this they say: 'This is one of the signs of the end of the world.' But the Prophet, may Allah preserve Him, said, 'A time will come when men will resemble women and women resemble men and a woman will walk in the street with a man.' This started some time ago and we've seen it and these women say 'This is the time referred to by the Prophet.' But we say, it's evolution.

2. WOMEN UNVEILED— THE UNDER-THIRTIES

Atiqa, the Doctor

I wanted to be a doctor from the time I was in kindergarten. I just wanted to—there was no real reason. But at that time I knew that my family wouldn't let me go abroad on my own to study. So I prepared to be a teacher. In fact, I even taught for six months and after that my father gave in. I had no training to be a teacher; I went to teach straight from school. I taught here in Doha although I myself went to school in Bahrain. At that time schools were just beginning here. There was only a secondary school for the boys, none for the girls.

My brother who was younger than me was at the boys' school. Then he went off to study medicine in Cairo. My family had let me go to Bahrain because I had relations there—I stayed with an aunt. But in Cairo I had no relations, only my brother, and he was very young, like me. We were just about seventeen or eighteen. My family said: 'No, you can't go. It's a big city. Life there is too different from our life here.' But then my brother wrote my father a letter saying: 'Why don't you send her here? Why keep her there as a teacher if she doesn't want to be one?' You see, I hated being a teacher. I really couldn't stand it. My father saw that I was unhappy so he said: 'Well, alright then, if your brother looks after you . . .'. So I just sent my papers and went.

I don't know why my father changed his mind; I never really asked him. He was a very fair man, but he was afraid of what people might say: sending off his seventeen-year-old daughter all by herself and things like that. My mother never said very much beyond: 'Do what you like.' She didn't interfere.

When I first went to Cairo it was summer, so I went with my whole family. They stayed with me for three months and they found a girls' hostel where I could stay. There were a lot of my friends from Bahrain there; I liked that, being together with my friends. We had to be back in the hostel by eight o'clock. If I wanted to be out after that time, I had to have a letter from my father or brother or someone. Also my brother had to collect me. I used to have to write all this in a letter, including at what time I would return (*she laughs*). Then they would let me go. I get on well with my brother who has always helped me a lot.

I don't think that Cairo changed me a lot, I suppose it was difficult at first going to college and meeting all these men. Here, you know, we're not allowed to mix. So I felt a bit strange at first meeting and mixing with men and talking to them. It takes a year to get used to it, after that it's alright. It wasn't really hard for me because I get along with people easily. Anyway, I spent most of the day in the college from nine o'clock in the morning until six o'clock at night, then I went straight back to the hostel. I didn't go to cafés. I could have, nobody would have stopped me if I had wanted to go. But I wouldn't have done it. Why should I go on my own? If a girl went out on her own to a café in Cairo at that time, people would look at her and wonder why she was alone. Still now, in many Arab countries, people will stare at a woman if she is alone. If she's together with two or three other girls it's alright.

I spent seven years in Cairo, six years studying and one year training. I met my husband while we were studying, but we didn't marry until later. At first my parents wouldn't even hear of our marrying. And they knew him well—he's the son of a close friend of ours and his sisters are among my best friends. They knew he was a good man and he liked the family. What upset them was the idea of my marrying a foreigner. This isn't true in Bahrain. There it's quite normal to marry a foreigner. Also if a Qatari man marries a foreign woman no one takes any notice. They don't talk. But for a woman it's different. I don't know why really. After all, he's Egyptian, and so an Arab. We're all Muslims. There's nothing in our religion against it. It's just a social custom in this area, in the Gulf.

I don't know how I eventually convinced my father. My husband's parents came here twice, but my father said: 'She's still young.' I wasn't really young, but that's what he said! Then two young men here asked to marry me. I said no. My father asked why, he said: 'They're perfectly nice.' I said: 'I don't want to marry now. You said I was too young' (*laughing*). 'I still want to marry the Egyptian.' When my father saw how determined I was he gave way. All this took a year. Some members of the family criticised me, but not all of them.

If my father had not agreed in the end, I should probably have married somebody else. You see, here in our country, you can't say no to your father. I wouldn't go against his wishes. If he agrees then it's fine. If he says no, then it's finished. Suppose I had married against his wishes and gone to live in Cairo. How could I live without my family? I can't. Also I don't like to be away from Doha. I don't know why—it's just the feeling that this is home. When I'm on the way home in the plane, I'm happy. I like being here. I even like being here more than I like being in Cairo.

But when I came back here I wasn't all that happy for the first six months. You see, I had left all my friends behind—girl friends, of course. I didn't have friends here because most of the people I knew well were in Bahrain or Cairo or they were married. I was bored. All I had to do was to visit my sister's friends with her.

After six months I got used to it. I made friends with some of the other doctors in the hospital. I liked my job. I like helping patients, it's a nice feeling to be able to help. I had a very high status as a doctor, while my personal life was very restricted but this didn't really worry me. It's just the custom here. I never tried to change it. Why should I? I never felt I wanted to go out on my own, or with men, or anything like that. Here if you do anything like that people talk. It's a small society, everybody knows everybody else and you get a bad reputation if you do certain things.

In the hospital I deal only with women, it's a maternity hospital. I couldn't treat the men as patients, but I do come into contact with them as husbands and fathers. In fact, I was worried at first whether they would accept their wives being looked after by a Qatari woman, even that the women themselves might not trust me, or that they might talk against me outside the hospital. But they liked me and they all asked that I should treat them. Maybe it's because I'm dealing with women especially in obstetrics and gynaecology that they ask for me. They feel shy, you see—maybe that's why they like me, (*laughing*). Also I'm gentle with patients.

People here are shy about sex. They are not given sex education by their families. They are not told anything. People find out for themselves, after marriage. At least the girls find out after marriage. For the boys it may be different, (*laughing*). Even patients, if they have something private wrong with them, they won't talk about it easily. A woman will only tell you after you've probed a lot, and if you're alone with her. It's natural to be shy about things like that. We have to keep our virginity until we are married, which means that girls do not have sex before marriage. Our religion forbids sex before marriage, for men as well as for women. Some people are still shy of sex after marriage. This is the way they have been brought up—to consider sex a taboo subject. We are not used to discussing it.

When I was young and going to the secondary school, I never talked about sex to anyone—perhaps just occasionally to my girl friends, but even then only superficially. We have books here about the first night of the honeymoon. I don't think that they're allowed in the libraries, but it's easy to get them. They're not pornographic or anything like that; they just give the facts. But my

parents never provided me with one before I was married! Since I
had studied medicine, nobody bothered! It was easy for me. My
friends used to come and ask me questions—I was everybody's
general consultant.

I wasn't brought up very strictly, although my mother did allow
my brother to go out more than me. She let me go out to play with
other girls but not automatically, as she did him. When there was
a school picnic she would sometimes refuse to let me go if the place
was very far away. For my brother there was never any problem.
But she never made us do the housework, me and my sister. I
think this was wrong, really. She always wanted us to study. So
when I went to Cairo I found it difficult even to make tea. I had
no idea how to boil an egg. I asked her to teach me basic things
like that, but she wouldn't. She used to say, there will be time. I
don't know why she was so keen we should study. Perhaps
because I did well at school; I was always first. I was happy at
home. But I wouldn't ever take orders from my brother; we were
always quarrelling (*laughing*).

My father used to be stricter with me about going out, but I
never felt he preferred my brother to me. Some men here do prefer
their sons. Even in the hospital when the women deliver, the men
are most happy when they have sons. If a father has a girl he is still
pleased but less so. Sometimes the women prefer to have girls,
because the boys leave them but the girls remain closer to them.
The younger men now don't care so much whether they have a son
or daughter. But it was traditional in the desert to prefer boys,
since boys could help their fathers.

I have never discussed sex with my mother. I would feel shy,
even now, to broach the subject. I could speak to my sister, but
not to my mother. I don't know why. Perhaps, because I was
brought up this way, I've just grown used to it. Some other
mothers do tell their daughters about sex, just before the marriage.
But my mother is not that type; she always keeps silent. (*laughing*).
They will say this and that will happen, and not to be frightened,
that it's all quite normal. They try to calm their daughters down,
because this night will be the first time for them; they have simply

no idea what is going to happen. But girls nowadays are not as ignorant as they were. I think they might have some idea about sex. They don't see anything on television here. What they know they discover by talking to their friends. But most of them still don't seem to know much before marriage. For instance, I have two nieces, one is sixteen, the other is fourteen. They are so innocent, they really don't know a thing. And they don't ask me anything either.

Men—I don't know so much about them. But they can talk more freely about sex than girls. Society gives men more freedom in all the Arab countries. Of course, it's not right, but it's what happens! If a man does something wrong, everyone would blame the girl but not him. If I had a daughter I don't think I would give her as much freedom as my son. I would teach her everything, explain everything. I wouldn't allow either my daughter or my son to have sex before marriage, but maybe the son would go his own way. . . . I don't think giving the girl that much freedom would work in our society. People would talk. But also I don't think it would be right. I don't know. Anyway, by that time everything might be totally different.

I have seen a lot of changes in this hospital. At first the women wouldn't allow a man to help with the delivery. But now they don't mind. Now they think of him as just a doctor and that's it. You see, it's *haram*—it's forbidden by religion—for any man who is not her husband to see a woman. But religion also maintains that it's alright for a doctor to examine a woman because his motive is good rather than bad.

Another thing I've noticed is that the hospital is cleaner now than it was, the wards, the corridors. I think people care more about cleanliness now.

Also my friends—educated girls—know much more about looking after babies now. If they don't know something they will go to the pediatrician and ask. Even the uneducated women come and ask: 'What should I do? What should I give the baby?' In the past, people didn't know about vaccination. Now they are concerned that their children should be vaccinated and they go by

themselves to the vaccination centre at the Rumela hospital. I once
went there myself and saw that it was crowded with women and
their babies. We doctors speak to them, and they chat with their
neighbours so they get to know about it. Besides, it's easy and it's
free. It doesn't cost them anything.

We have our difficulties, of course. In the past, women in this
area sometimes used salt to make the tissues of the cervix shrink
when they were slack after a delivery. And we still come across a
few cases from time to time. It's very bad, sometimes the cervix
closes completely. Last year a woman came to me and told me
what she had done with the salt. I said: 'Why did you do that?
It's bad for you!' The problem is that they think it's good for
them; that the salt will make the tissue as firm as it was before.
They think that the salt will have the same result as exercises, only
without the effort! I explained her mistake to her and she promised
me she wouldn't do it again. Nowadays we see very little of this
practice.

Difficulties arise also when we have to operate; sometimes
women won't agree to this. At first it was a problem to get people's
consent for operations, especially if the husband couldn't be found.
But now the new consultant has made a rule that every patient
must give their consent in advance, even if the case is normal. At
first it was very difficult; sometimes they were afraid. They would
argue that if the delivery was normal, why should they consent to
an operation. We explain that it's just a matter of routine and we
don't have much trouble.

Sometimes, it's difficult to explain things to the patients, say
when they can't have a baby. You try very hard, but they just can't
understand. They keep coming back and tell us we have to do
something for them, we have to cure them; they just can't accept
that you can't do anything. It's difficult for a woman to come to
terms with the fact that she can't have more children.

It's normal now to use contraception. Most of the women here
do; they come and ask for it themselves. Young people now want
about four children. My sister wanted four; she says that's enough,
she couldn't take care of more children properly. If the women

Nura, television set-designer

The Doctor, his sociologist wife and daughter in their *diwan*

Working dhows moored in Doha harbour

Aerial view of Doha showing the Diwan Emiri, in
which Sheikh Khalifa has his office

work they want only two or three. I myself have one and I only want two! I have a boy but I wanted a girl.

The women sometimes won't believe that I am a doctor. They say: 'No, no. *You* can't be a doctor!' They're used to seeing old ladies. They say: 'You can deliver a baby? You can do oper, ations?' Then they get used to me. If they don't know my name they refer to me as the young doctor. Or the slim doctor!

My own friends prefer to come to me. When I came back and started to work, they were all natural with me; they would ask me all kinds of things, about contraception and such matters. Most of them had graduated from university themselves, except for my sister. My sister has four children. The oldest boy is twenty-one; she had him when she was fourteen. In the past girls used to marry at that age. She didn't want to go to school. My father tried to make her. I remember he even beat her. But she wouldn't go; she married her cousin. Now that her eldest child has gone to school, she has started to study again herself. She went through primary school and now she's in her final year of secondary school. She just studies at home, but she takes her examinations with schoolgirls. Most of her friends do the same thing. She doesn't want to go to the college here and she can't go abroad, of course, so she's thinking about studying languages, French for example. She already speaks English but not very well; she attends a course at the British Council. I think she might go to college in the end. Her husband is often busy and so she is usually alone. It's better for her to study than to wait for him. Before she was always complaining and telling him to come back early and so there were constant quarrels. Now she doesn't care!

I am going back to Cairo for two years to complete a Master's degree and a specialist course in obstetrics and gynaecology. My husband has agreed; he likes me to work. But it's quite difficult all the same. I have to leave my husband and my family. It is true that Cairo is not far away. If I have a few days holiday I can always come back to Qatar. My family don't mind. Since my husband agrees, they wouldn't interfere. Other people accept it; they think it is quite natural. Many girls here are doing extra-mural degrees anyway. They aren't satisfied being just teachers, so they study at home and go and take their exams. They work here first as teachers if their family won't allow them to be abroad or if they find it too difficult to go off by themselves. I know many who have graduated this year. So people are used now to women going off on their own to take exams or to study.

After my two years in Cairo are over, I intend to go to London for a further course which will make me a Fellow of the Royal College of Gynaecology. I have to do these courses. First of all because I am the first Qatari woman doctor. I can't just be a general practitioner; I want to do something better, (*bursts out laughing*). Because I am the first I have to be a model for the others. There are at least three or four girl medical students in Cairo. Also I just want to go on to get a higher degree for myself. I'd hate just to stay a junior doctor! I want to give my country something. The better qualified I am the more I can give my country. I have to do it. This is my country. Also my brother is in Cairo doing further courses. He is twenty-seven—one year younger than me. Perhaps we are competing a bit! Anyway, all the first wave of Qatari doctors are going on getting better qualifications. So why should I just stay here and be satisfied with a junior post? I hate being ordinary. Even if the men didn't go on with their studies, I would.

Latifa, the Headmistress

Latifa is one of the Qatari girls who might have stepped out of a Victorian novel. Her hair is parted in the middle and waist length. Her dresses have long sleeves and skirts.

In character she is very like Dorothea in George Eliot's *Middlemarch*: determined, intellectual, high minded and very much of an individual. Like Dorothea who sponsored model workmen's cottages, she is greatly interested in social problems and if given free rein would probably turn out to be an immensely energetic and intelligent educational reformer. She parts company with Victorian young ladies like Dorothea, who were dreadfully earnest, in that she has a great deal of humour, the bent of which is ironical and slightly mocking. She has a laconic turn of phrase. Qatari girls in London, she says, 'stroll around a bit'.

Latifa is around twenty-four and unmarried. This is where the Victorian parallel reappears. For Qatari girls, like Victorian girls, are expected to marry young. Many now wish to complete their studies, and reach twenty-two or twenty-three before they marry, but this is later than society would wish to see them safely settled. Latifa herself claims not to be over-anxious to marry and one can very well see why. Given her own high standards and quality of character, she will be lucky to find a young man of her own age up to her own level and could easily find herself marrying intellectually beneath her. This is one of the major problems that the modern educated generation of women in Qatar face today.

Latifa's mother is present some of the time. Once the door is safely locked —just in case the neighbour pops in—she removes her face-mask. The face is strong and striking; she sits forward on her seat, arms resting on her legs which are firmly planted apart. Life now is too serious, she says. Your life (addressing her daughter) is tedious. Children are always having to think of their lessons. I have four sons and three daughters. Mothers are responsible for their homes and their children. Do you see what I mean? The older generation never took off their mask except when they went to bed: they were too shy to show their faces to men, young or old. But don't write about the mask, because Westerners always distort the fact when they write about us. I don't read magazines or newspapers. But I have heard it said that Arabs are so backward that they cover the faces of their women. But, in fact, we have our own civilisation and we know what we are doing. We can breathe and see easily. When I go abroad and don't wear the mask I feel as if I were not wearing anything. I feel shy. (Aside to her daughter. No, don't say so to her. Tell her it makes no difference to us; we feel nothing.) I don't want my daughter to wear the mask, mind you. It has no importance now. Times are different. When I was young, everybody else wore it. Now girls go to school and university and it doesn't suit them.

I have wanted to go to university ever since I was in my third year in the secondary school—anyway ever since I was young. I just felt I wanted to go on with my education. It was as simple as that. Besides, everybody knows that the more educated people are, the more civilised their society becomes. Also I can serve my country by taking a higher degree. The truth is that I would like to learn as much as possible. I hoped to take a Master's degree and then a

PhD. I wanted to get every degree I could because the BA is no longer important now; anyone can get a BA.

I studied Arabic literature, but I really wanted to study psychology. But psychology is a practical subject which requires regular attendance at courses and my parents wouldn't let me go abroad to study full-time. They thought it was all right for a girl to study, but that she should remain within her own country. They had heard that there was an extra-mural course at the Beirut Arab University, so they suggested I try that. I studied by myself here during the year and I went to Beirut to take the final exam at the end of each year.

It was the grammar that gave me the most difficulty. You know, there were no teachers here of university level who could explain things to me. I used to miss the special opportunities that universities give: discussing with professors and other students and writing research papers. I was limited too, in finding references, by the books I had.

When it came to sitting the exam, I went with my mother to Beirut. For her, it was as though she were sitting the exam herself. She was always with my sister and myself, encouraging us to study and, on the day of the exam, she was as anxious as we were. She lived on her nerves until we had finished. Perhaps she would have let me go to study in Beirut. But what could my mother do? Tradition is very strong in our society. (Mother interrupts to explain that there were no hostels available for girls in Beirut at that time.) Where could girls stay? Also they didn't want to expose us to the dangers and difficulties we might encounter in travelling. So we were obliged to fall into step with what society wanted. Now girls go abroad to study quite frequently—there are at least thirty girls in Egypt and more elsewhere. And now there are special hostels for girls. But at that time, when I first began to study, it was difficult, and not only because of the lack of accommodation. You see, we were the first group of girls to graduate from the secondary school in Qatar. There was no one on our side, no one supporting us. We paved the way for those who came after us. Actually there was one Qatari who graduated with some

Egyptians and Palestinians before us. She went to study in Kuwait and her mother went with her and stayed with her for the whole year; she's now a school inspectress. But we didn't have anyone to go with us so we waited. Our mother couldn't just leave the younger children and go off to the Lebanon.

The Lebanon was the first foreign country I visited. I liked it very much—the people were so cheerful and the way of life so free and easy. What always struck me as I came off the plane was the beauty of nature. When I was young I had read stories about rivers and trees and such things. I dreamt about such scenery and I used to say that in the future God might change Qatar's climate and we would have more rain and we would have rivers, (*laughs*). Of course, that's impossible. I would love my country to be like the Lebanon. Also there I felt youthful: one can come and go so easily, go into bookshops, buy books, look at things. I never stayed for more than one or two months at a time. But what used to get me was that it was always summer when I left Qatar and it was still summer when I came back. I love the winter—winter in Qatar is beautiful.

When I graduated there were few professional openings for girls outside teaching. So I became a teacher. I worked for two years and then was appointed as head of the secretariat section of the inspector's office. Nominally, I was head of section but I didn't consider myself as such because all I did was to open and close files and answer the telephone—that is to say we did no productive work at all. I requested a change of job but had to wait for three years. Now I'm just finishing my first year as a headmistress. There are seven hundred and fifty-five girls in my school.

Why did I go into education? Because I would like to see changes in our educational system. I would like to make a thorough study of the syllabuses and curricula we have in Qatar and possibly improve them. At the moment they are very packed. They are not always up to date; what we learn at preparatory and secondary school is not necessarily the most recent knowledge available. We should be keeping abreast of modern discoveries and educational techniques.

In Qatar and in the Arab world generally, pupils usually study subjects separately. On our educational courses we learn to give them projects so that they can study related subjects and under-stand the connection between them. Also these projects should not be too theoretical, they should have a practical application. We should teach children to think and invent. This is what I would do if I had the chance.

I have a lot of ideas. I took a course in educational studies at the College in Qatar last year. But for the moment I don't have the power to make changes because the syllabuses are prepared centrally by the Ministry. I can contribute by paying more atten-tion to school activities, by guiding teachers so that they don't turn the entire lesson into a lecture but involve the students more. I can make the girls compete both in their studies and in keeping the school clean. When they write Arabic compositions they shouldn't be given a landscape to describe, but subjects related to their own environment: what's lacking here, for example; how the hospitals are run—that kind of thing. Then the girls would be more concerned about the society they live in.

I have a lot of criticisms—of the classrooms for instance. We have fifty girls in a class at the moment, while there should be no more than twenty-five. As for the desks, some are big, some are small; in most cases they're not suitable for the pupils. They ought to be changed. Then it's hot in the summer and cold in the winter. If we had air conditioning the girls would be more enthusiastic about coming to school. We lack sports facilities: there are no playing fields, just an open courtyard where they are exposed to the sun when we line them up. If the courtyard were roofed, we could use it for sports. We have no halls for parties.

We have to change the girls' attitudes to school. They don't always absorb their lessons as they should because they feel that study has been forced on them; they just read bits of information and forget them by the end of the year. I've tried going to the classes and explaining that this information is relevant to their lives.

But they don't see school this way: as a place where they can develop leadership qualities and come to terms with their rôle as women of the future.

Nevertheless most of the girls here want to carry on with their studies. The country is just beginning to develop and careers are opening up for women. Not all of them want to go on, of course: we have some girls who are training to be nurses and some who want to be secretaries. They haven't completed their education. Because professional opportunities for women are restricted for the time being, most of them go in for teaching. But they are keen. Many of them would like to be doctors. If they could work easily in ministries as in Bahrain, for example, they would do that. Then there are people who would like to study politics or economics; others who are interested in design and decoration. I'm surprised that girls in England don't aim higher: so many of them become nurses or graduates of intermediary institutes, even although they have every opportunity to go on. I wish we had universities here. In Kuwait, they were studying before we were. We feel the pace of progress here is very slow.

I feel there is a generation gap already between me and my friends who are in our mid-twenties and the younger girls of say fifteen or so. When we were at school, the teacher would tell us to shut up and we would shut up. We wouldn't move from our desks. Now the girls discuss every order with you: 'Why should we shut up? What have we done wrong?' There is a certain amount of boldness and rebelliousness; they challenge the rules. Maybe because they know more, because they are more aware of and open to external influences. I don't know.

We were good girls. When I was young and we were listening to the radio, we would switch it off when my father came home out of respect for him. Now my little sister dances in front of him and he doesn't say a word. Compared to my sister, I was quite shy at that age. Maybe she's bolder because there are now more activities at school—education has the greatest influence. Maybe because she was brought up with boys. She always expresses her opinion forcibly. My older sister and I were just a quiet couple living with my father and mother. We obeyed orders. We would never have behaved the way my sister carries on these days. Maybe she will become a bit more moderate now that she is teenager, but she'll always have her own opinions and a strong personality. She'll be a pop fan but not the way Western girls are. In the West they swoon over pop singers.

Television has also been a big influence. Television opens people up. Even the common women are influenced by the women's programmes. They've gradually begun to listen to advice and to understand how to treat their children as the announcer tells them. Where the Western serials are concerned, I think the girls just take in the essence of a story, but are not further influenced by it. They are still tied by tradition. If a girl sees a Western woman in a play walk about the streets in trousers, she can't do the same because someone would stop her. There are distinct borders between what people see on television and what they experience in reality. But television has had the effect of encouraging girls to sing and dance in school plays; ten years ago they were neither so good at singing and dancing nor were they encouraged to do so. Now they have become bold. I don't think that activity which is supervised is likely to clash with our customs.

Travel may also have had an effect. They learn how other people live. If they see a different kind of house or garden, they might come back and change their own. But when women go abroad, they don't go to restaurants, they just stroll about a bit. They might go to a park or to a market, but they wouldn't go to night-clubs or cinemas. But this depends on the family; each family has its own customs. The girls generally go, have a look around, and come back. They might be more influenced by foreign people and ways if language were not a barrier. They're not really able to mix. All they see are outward appearances.

It is true that our social life here in Qatar is very limited. Girls don't visit each other very much. I have spent my entire school years with some girls and yet only ever visited them two or three times. There are no clubs or societies. I wish these things existed. Most of the time I read; I love reading. Sometimes I write, just very simple articles, memoirs, diary, mostly about Doha and the problems of our society. I write when I am interested in a subject or if I think something is wrong and I feel strongly about it.

Women in this country really want to progress. It's not only the young women who are learning but older women with children are going back to school. I find the women in this country superior to the men, both at work and in their studies. Women do their utmost to get on. As for the men, I would like to see them involve themselves more in the problems of our society and do more to, help it advance. Once they have their job they don't bother (interruption by mother: 'Why should you talk about them like this? They are all good boys'). I would like everyone to participate in society, whether men or women—that's what I want.

I come to work between six-thirty and quarter-to-seven in the morning. The bell rings at ten-to-seven. We line the girls up in columns and then they go to their classes. After that I do mainly routine work. Most of the time I spend coping with problems. There are problems with the *farrashes* who clean the school, problems between teachers and students, sometimes the girls bring their parents into their quarrels. I have clerical work. I organise the reserve teachers. I have to draw up time-tables at the beginning of each year—my sister helps me with those because she's been a headmistress for three years. Then the Ministry is always keeping us busy preparing statistics, about employees, their experience etc. Providing statistics is a bit of a nuisance it is true, but we must help practically; we can't just restrict ourselves to ideas. If we're going to change, we have to change the syllabuses, the teaching methods, the type of teachers we employ. We'll need new teachers who are able to use more advanced methods. The whole Ministry will have to involve itself in these changes; one individual can't just act by herself.

I leave the school at half-past-twelve and go to college; I stay there until four o'clock or even until six. Then I go home and do some research or prepare lessons for the next day. So I get very tired. That's why I wanted to be free to study this year, because next year I shall be sitting for my diploma in Education. Next year I may go to Egypt and study for an MA. I intend to complete my studies.

People criticise me for not being married. But one shouldn't be affected by that kind of talk. There are lots of people like me who haven't married. I have never been in love. Never, since I was a child, have I ever been in love. Maybe because I have such stringent conditions for marriage. I don't know that I could say what they are. Of course, our religion stipulates that we must get married. In Islam there are no nuns.

I'm afraid that when I get married I shall be given more freedom and then God knows what sort of problems I'll get myself into. Now, praise be to God, my family gives me enough freedom. But I'm afraid that we don't know much about the person we marry, whether we have got to know him on the telephone or met him. God knows best what his real character is. We don't know men before we marry them. And it's quite possible to live with a husband for two or three years happily and love him dearly, and for the marriage still to fail. One doesn't know anything about these men, what they're like. Here a man can be as good as gold for ten years, and then he might suddenly divorce his wife; this can happen, especially these days. It depends partly on circumstances —for example, an educated man is more reliable.

There are a lot of girls of twenty-seven who are not married. I'll tell you why. Look, now the boy is educated and the girl is educated. The boys are afraid—and God only knows best—of what they are letting themselves in for, what a girl might be like, what they are taking on. They don't see any girls, they are not allowed to meet them. They have no more information on her than a photograph and maybe a telephone conversation. This is why they don't get married.

Anyway, marriage is not something that concerns me. What I want to do is study. I don't know what will happen in the future —Glory to God—maybe. That's for God to decide.

Miriam, the Secretary

I decided to become a secretary, which is unusual for a girl in Qatar, when I heard that Shell were looking for them. I took courage and applied for the job. Being divorced at seventeen I could do whatever I wanted. I wanted to be Qatari's first woman secretary. There were then no Qatari girls working for the company. I was the first. I thought my move would encourage other girls to follow. When I saw the advertisement, I was seventeen-and-a-half. I'm now nineteen.

I was still at school then. I'd just passed my intermediate exams and I was going to secondary school. I decided to work instead and to continue my studies at home, but circumstances were not favourable. My father was in hospital suffering from burns, so I couldn't go back to school for the last year. I knew what the work of a secretary meant—typing and other office work—because we used to see our school secretary at work. I always like to work. I like typing. I like being busy. I didn't think of working for the money. I had no financial problems. I just wanted to be a secretary.

Before I thought of becoming a secretary I had intended to finish school and then work as a nurse or as a telephonist for Cable and Wireless. I was glad to get the Shell job, because it's what I wanted. I felt relaxed when I went for the test and I went there on my own. There was nothing unusual about my first day at work and I wasn't surprised when I found myself surrounded by men because I knew what I was in for. Everything was normal, except that they all spoke English which I couldn't understand. I wondered when I'd be able to speak like them. One thing I learned from work was to be on time. This was a bit difficult for me at the beginning. But I got used to it. Now if I stay at home in the afternoon I get bored, because I got used to coming home at 4 p.m. I do figure work, typing, but no shorthand, because of my English. I'd like to be able to speak English. I understand everything. I watch films. I can pick up words but it is difficult for me to concentrate because of the noise my children make. Here at work, I can concentrate.

I have two children. One is three and the other one-and-a-half. When I go home at 4 p.m. I play with them until they go to bed. I give them a lot of attention because I miss them when I'm at work. After they've gone to bed I carry on with the rest of the housework. I have a daily help who stays until the afternoon, until I come back from work. She doesn't live with us. My mother also looks after the children. She loves them and takes care of them much more than I do.

I was fifteen when I married. I saw my former husband before we were married and I liked him. I divorced because of my mother-in-law and for other reasons. He didn't leave me. But he never gave me any money and he didn't let me visit my mother. Moreover, he drinks. So I went to the *Qadi* and asked for a divorce. I told him my husband didn't want me to go to school. The *Qadi* told my husband: 'I can't stop her from going to school because that would not be in the interest of the State. If we start with this, then others will follow and there will be no girls going to school. Then the girls will not be useful to the country.' My husband told the *Qadi* that he would take me back only if I gave up school. The *Qadi* said to me: 'We cannot force you to give up school, but if you do, we can make your husband give you a monthly allowance.' My husband didn't give me any money and refused to let me go to school, so we parted. I was granted a monthly allowance of 200 *riyals* to be paid by my husband. I never bothered to collect the allowance. I could support myself and my children, God be praised.

My husband married again. But we have no financial problems. Sometimes my mother buys me something, like a skirt. Otherwise I support myself and the children and also give my mother some money. I'm saving money for a car. I can get a driving licence because I am working. There is a law which says that only working women are entitled to get licences. This law comes into effect in 1977. It will take me about a year to save for a car.

The problem I had with my mother-in-law was that the man I married was an only son. My mother-in-law used to say to me: 'Don't buy anything or go out without my permission.' I could only see my parents when she gave me permission. This often happens in Qatar. Some mothers-in-law are good but when the mother has complete control over her son, then it's worse. If the son is educated, then he will try to establish an understanding between his mother and his wife. When the couple gets married, the wife is expected to live with her husband and his mother. But the rich have several houses. If the man works for the Government, he gets a house in which he can live with his family. The father or the son supports the family. When two married brothers live with their mother it often happens that the wife of one of the sons ends up by doing the housework while the other wife does whatever she likes. Even if the wife is willing to do the work, her husband may not like it and he may say to his brother: 'It's not fair that your wife should go out while my wife does all the work.' This creates problems. Then again, the mother may prefer one son or one of the wives to the other. This leads to more problems. Some of the wives take it out on their sister-in-law's children. Also if one cooked something they didn't like they would complain:—'Why did you cook this, why didn't you cook something else.' Before I got married I had worked out how I would deal with my mother-in-law one day: I planned to ignore her. But it didn't work out that way!

I bring up my children differently from the way I was brought up. When I was a little girl our parents used to beat us if we did something wrong, I tell them not to do it again and explain why they shouldn't. But if they continue doing it again and again then I beat them so that they will be afraid to do it again. At school we studied psychology. I also borrowed books from the hospital. The doctor provides expectant mothers with books about child care. I have no problems with my own mother. If I introduce something new to her she doesn't mind. My mother doesn't even mind if I correct her when she speaks. When we talk she tells me how we were as children, or I tell her if I've heard something new or about rising prices. Sometimes my mother tells me of the many things they used to be able to buy for a rupee. When we were children my father used to buy lots of dates and bread and other things for a rupee to last the family throughout the pearl-diving season.

My mother still wears the *batula*. She's used to it. But she doesn't force me or my sister to wear it. She lets us wear whatever we like. She wants us to wear modern styles. She even told us not to bother about giving our children old names: for example, instead of Aisha we could use Huda. She advises us to use fashionable names. When women of my mother's generation were little girls, they saw their mothers wearing *batulas* so they also wanted to wear them in order to appear as grown-ups. In the past when a girl wore a *batula* it meant she was married. It had a social significance. The girls liked wearing them because it made them feel important. But when we saw women older than us who didn't wear it, we also didn't want to wear it. We have different values now. My mother was twelve when she got married and she then wore a *batula*. Now this has no meaning for us. In the past they wore a *batula* as soon as they got married, whether they were nine or twelve. We didn't give up the *batula* because of Egyptian or Palestinian influence! We did not imitate Egyptians or Palestinians! The fact is we never wore it at all. When the upper class stopped wearing it, the rest followed.

The stories I tell my children are different from the ones my mother used to tell me. When I was a little girl, if I couldn't sleep my grandmother used to tell me frightening stories about genii. I tell my children nice stories until they fall asleep.

I'm quite happy. When I learn something I feel I'm improving myself and so I'm happier. I want to continue my studies. I always like to learn. I want to work and serve my country. When I marry again, my ideas about marriage will be different from what they were when I married last time. I wish I could find someone who would understand me. I would want him to under-stand and appreciate me. I would like him to accept what I do with an open mind and to trust me. I would want him to let me work and visit my friends. If a man wants to accept me as I am, then he is welcome. My parents agree with my ideas. It is difficult for them to accept new ideas all at once, but they gradually come to terms with them.

Leilah, Headmistress and Diplomat Manqué

I think family solidarity is our strong point—the strong point of the Arab world and the whole East. I believe that excessive and absolute freedom causes the break-up of the family.

At the same time, lack of personal freedom is also a problem in the East, particularly for women. Women are deprived of their freedom, this is quite plain for anyone to see. We simply don't have any freedom. In the first place, we aren't able to choose any profession that interests us. I, personally, would like to be able to choose from a wide range of professions other than just teaching. If I had had the choice, I would have worked in the diplomatic service.

I have no vocation for teaching and I'm not interested in school administration. I worked in the first place to still my conscience and secondly to occupy my time and do something useful for the country. It was better to teach than to stay at home doing nothing. We have so much spare time.

Of course, I had a struggle. My family were not all that happy about my going to school. The worst difficulties we had were when we were at primary level. By the time we reached secondary school, there were practically no problems, because the country had developed a lot. But at the beginning it was very hard.

When I first went to school I used to think of my older sister who was not allowed to go to school. She had been kept at home to look after the house. I used to think that if I had been the older one I would have been sitting at home. Later she learned to read and write and to study books and so on and she is now a competent housewife.

When I had finished my secondary education, there were more difficulties. Of course, my family opposed my going outside the country to complete my studies. From the time I was very young and still in the primary school my ambition had always been to come top in my studies. My greatest wish was to manage somehow to go right through the whole education process. When I had finished school and found they did not want to let me go abroad, I wrote secretly to the Minister of Education. No one knew about it. I wrote that I had heard that there was a system whereby one could study at home and that I was prepared to pay for everything, but that I didn't know how to go about enrolling myself. The Director of the Ministry, who was married to my first cousin, helped me. He obtained a place for me in the Arab University of Beirut and he provided me with the books. So I began to study as an extra-mural student. Then my older brother said: 'What on earth do you think you're doing studying? You've finished your education.' I said: 'I'm studying in Beirut.' He asked: 'Who will take you there?' I said: 'Everything will be alright at the end of the year.' And it was he who took me, he was forced to take me to sit my exam at the end of the year. I finished the year successfully, thanks to God, and then I went on.

My father was not an educated man and so my brothers had influence over him, but he didn't refuse—he didn't really know anything about it. My elder brother was the real power in the house. My father used to go out all the time but my brother stayed at home. He had the final say in all family matters. If he said no, then no it was. My father always listened to him because he was the eldest and this is the Arab way.

At school I was good at Arabic and I used to write poetry. I also wrote short stories which were published by a local magazine. My Arabic mistress advised me, from the day I came to school, to concentrate on my Arabic.

Throughout the time I was taking my extra-mural course, I had to grapple with administrative problems. It was all very difficult. Besides, I didn't really want to be a head-mistress when I finished. But a new school had just been opened and the Ministry chose me to run it.

Even if my brother had absolutely refused to let me go on studying in Beirut, I would still have done my utmost to go. I would have sat my exams in spite of him. I would have moved heaven and earth to get to Beirut. If my brother had refused, I would have gone to my father, I would have tried to move my whole family. If my brother had refused to accompany me to the exam, I would have tried to take my mother and my sisters and the rest of the family with me. I was absolutely determined to go and study. I am ambitious, even now, and not easily satisfied with half-measures. With me, it's all or nothing.

Elder brothers here don't help their sisters much. In fact, in seventy five per cent of all cases, it is the elder brothers who create the difficulties for girls. This is because the brother can come and go and so has been around and seen many things and is frightened in consequence that his sisters will do the same as he did. This is, of course, a mistaken view. Because although the girl may have the opportunity to go wrong, her self-control is normally very much greater than a boy's.

Girls here don't have even one per cent of the freedom boys enjoy either at home or abroad. There are strict rules governing a girl's action, whereas boys are left very much to their own devices and not cross-questioned if they do something on their own initiative. But the code for girls is different. Men are contemptuous of women in some way I don't entirely understand. The man is allowed everything, the woman is allowed nothing. The man is all-powerful, he can do as he pleases and no one, not even his wife, has the right to question him. In my view three-quarters of the problems a woman faces arise from the fact that men neither consider her nor respect her feelings. If women had more confidence and self-respect, none of these things would happen.

I am speaking less for myself than for a great many others. I have not had to face as much pressure as many others. In some families the pressures on women are quite extraordinary. You might even consider me lucky. Other girls might have had real problems about questioning or defying certain accepted social norms, but this has never been the case with me. I don't attach too much importance to social convention and refuse to be ruled by the tyranny of appearances. I have fought and won, many times. But I have colleagues and friends who have suffered so much from this kind of thing that they fell ill and had to have treatment from a psychiatrist.

We have a habit here of marrying our cousins, this is normal for us. The girl is brought up believing that she belongs to her cousin, that she is the girl of X. She will stop seeing other people, she can think of nothing and no one else, because all her thoughts are concentrated on this one man. So when she grows up it comes as a terrible shock to learn that the young man on whom she had pinned her hopes and with whom she envisaged spending the rest of her life has gone off to America or England to study and brought back a wife from there. She loses all her self-confidence and all her confidence in others. I know lots of girls to whom this has happened.

The solution to our problems lies in more education and general culture. The generation now coming forward is already beginning to change. They are even different from us. Travelling abroad and the presence of foreigners here have helped, too, in broadening people's minds.

Travelling really changed my own personality and my view of society. If I had not travelled abroad, I might be less agitated, less concerned, less aware of our painful situation. We always felt sore when we went abroad and compared other societies to our own. I used to go abroad every year after my examinations, to Beirut or to London.

We have quite a number of visitors even at home. But they are women, not men, and even when families come to visit, the women sit with the women and the men with the men. Although, of course, in another country, they'd sit down with us and we'd all chat together. Nevertheless, we avoid the men and we are as formal with them as it is possible to be, especially if the visitor is from Qatar. It would be quite impossible for us to see him without another person present. If, on the other hand, we met another Qatari family in London, we would all sit down together, the men and the women, because we would be far from home.

My mother has always been my sole source of aid and comfort. All mothers here are close to their daughters like that; they are always prepared to help their daughters. A girl will always run to her mother if she has any problem. The first year it was my brother who accompanied me to Beirut, but thereafter my mother went with me. She always helped and encouraged me.

When I sit down with my mother and we discuss the problems of women, we don't always have the same views. Sometimes she's on the side of the elder people, the mothers, and sometimes she sides with the girls—I mean she supports progress. She will always say: 'I don't intend to have any prejudices. Praise the Lord that you now have all this freedom. What were our lives like?'

There is always this envy. Those who aren't part of our generation would like to have had all the things we have: education to know how to read and write and to live the life we lead. My mother says, 'We would like to have been able to do that. Look at your lives compared to ours! We envy you your lives. We never dreamed, when we were young, that such a thing could happen!'.

Contrary to what outsiders might think, my mother and her contemporaries are very proud of their veils. They won't even hear the matter discussed, they are so convinced it is right to wear the veil. But I don't believe in it at all. The Lord preserve me from wearing it! I wouldn't even consider it. But, of course, I can't impose my opinion on people who are older than me and who like it and are convinced of its utility. I couldn't tell them to give it up—good manners prevent me as much as anything. On the other hand, we wear the Gulf female dress—the thin black *abbaya* we slip over our dress—and we like wearing it. Even when I go to London I sometimes wear my *abbaya*. Most of the time I walk about just in trousers and shirt. But then I take the *abbaya* and wear it for some hours. Here in Qatar, I like to wear my *abbaya* and wouldn't like to be without it. I'm proud of it because it is our national dress, in fact our Arab national dress. I feel better, more relaxed when I'm wearing it. Without it I feel uncomfortable in the street and I don't know the reason. The *abbaya* is very light; it's made of a kind of chiffon and I just put it over my shoulders. It's not stifling. It has a certain style and gives you a special stamp.

When I get up in the morning, I go off to school immediately. After school I go home and have a short sleep. If I ever have spare time in the evening—and I rarely do—I always spend it reading. In fact, all my spare time I spend either reading or writing. There isn't one single second from which I don't profit. I don't like to go out, even on Fridays. I'm always shut up in my room by myself, leafing through a book, or reading a magazine or writing. I very rarely go to parties—only occasionally as a duty. It is not in my nature to go out to enjoy myself all the time. Sometimes I visit my friends; we talk to each other on the telephone every day. My mother would prefer me to go out more often.

I read mainly literature. I don't like detective stories or political books and I read very little history. I like novels and poetry. If I find a poet who pleases me I'll go to the ends of the earth to get his book. I also watch television, but not all of the programmes—some are bad. I do watch 'Forum of the Week' which is a literary programme. I also like the late night showings of foreign and Arab films. These films we see on television have given us a complete picture of life in the West. It was mainly television that made us all so eager to get to know that society. After we had seen a film we would always get together the next day and discuss it among ourselves. We would sit together and talk about freedom and so on and its effect on the personality and character of the girl. So we really welcomed some of these films.

I've read about Women's Liberation in the West and heard about it. I've tried to follow it up. I've read a lot about it and I'm not sure that liberation is necessarily a good thing for a woman. But it depends what you mean by liberation: there is personal liberation and intellectual liberation. And liberation doesn't necessarily mean following through an idea to its logical conclusion. We are free to express ourselves. We are free to think. I can act within the bounds of freedom which I am permitted, but I do not have the freedom to do things which would harm or damage my family or my society. That's what I mean when I talk about freedom—I'm not talking about what happens in Western society. I don't for instance, think that a boy should go out alone with a girl, because the families would not be happy about it. Nor would society accept it; people would talk. You know what their opinions are in advance. It might be done in the West because people there have a different mentality. When I go to London I talk to the boys who address me in the street. I do this because the view of and intention behind such things are different in the West. Here I can't go out into the street and talk to a man. My intentions might well be honourable, but people would say—well, you know what people would say. Of course, we shall change, because these kind of problems are on everybody's mind.

I can speak to young men in the West, but about young Qatari men I know nothing at all. If circumstances allowed us to meet each other, then their judgement of us and our thoughts about them might be totally altered. The obstacles between us give us a bad impression of them, and make them negligent in their attitude towards us.

When television first began I was a teacher at Doha school. They were looking for Qatari women to broadcast, and their first offer came to me at the school. At the time I was often involved in plays and usually played the part of the heroine. But when they made me an offer I got angry and said: 'Why me? Why did you have to choose me? It is an insult to me and to my family.' It's not normal, in fact it was considered rather disgraceful for a woman to present programmes on television. I got very angry. I was afraid because people really gossip a lot here and I knew that they would say that so-and-so who gets up in public and is seen by everybody can't really be the daughter of a good family, or that she has no one to look after her. This offer was made six or seven years ago. In twenty years or so from now, it might be possible.

The idea that we had inculcated into us has always been that nobody should see us. If anybody saw a young woman, the question would always be asked: 'How is it that you saw her?' So we were all used to this situation. We had got used to the idea that no man could come into our house and see us. This is something engrained in us—that we shouldn't let men see us. It's shameful to let men see us. I don't know, it's in my blood. So I think I wasn't in a state to think clearly about what was being offered to me.

We haven't gone out with my brother in his car in a very, very long time so that other young men won't see him with his sisters and so get to know that he has sisters. People don't know who my brother is. A lot of people come and visit me here, for instance, ambassadors whose daughters are in the school, and two days ago we had somebody from the Armed Forces. When they come, they say: 'You look like someone in our department.' Once I admitted that he was my brother to someone who asked me, and I told my brother afterwards. He said: 'Why did you do that?' I don't know the reason exactly but my brother doesn't like it to be known that he has sisters. I think it may be the behaviour of some young men—just some of them, not all of them—who never see girls. When they see a girl they like, they start pestering her. We've been pestered ourselves sometimes when we've been out. As soon as they see a girl they try to find out about her because girls are forbidden to them and when anything is forbidden then you try and find out what's so secret about it. They try and find out who she is, whose daughter she is, whether she is married or not and their intention is to try and get to know her. I'm not saying that they're wrong to do this. But we have problems with our families if we see them or, for example, if they're trying to get to know the house. If they succeed in finding out where it is, they pursue us and ring us up and try to get to know us. It's because we're afraid of this kind of thing that we don't see them.

It's a vicious circle, but in what sense are we to blame? This has made the girls really very afraid of young men and always anxious to avoid them. To meet a boy and no more is enough to blacken the reputation of a girl. They don't realise that we, like all Eastern women, can be harmed in this way, by the smallest word spoken against us. Our entire future life and the honour of our family can be damaged. So we avoid them. We don't know what they're like; they don't know what we're like. Society is stronger than either of us.

Nura, the Television Set-Designer

Nura is a very sophisticated twentieth-century young professional woman. Mid-twenties. Just had her first child, a son, and returned to work after a month. Wears modest clothes, but very assured and strong minded. In the evening she likes to walk with her husband along the corniche; in the summer she travels abroad to Paris, London and Cairo. Her hobby is painting.

They're not as well-educated as I used to think, the English. Sometimes I think that they don't know as much as we have learned in our schools. Some people here are really well educated: they follow the news every day and they read a lot. Especially the girls. The girls, in particular, are well educated in literature, art, and above all, social studies. They know more than the men because they work hard by themselves. Maybe it's partly because we have no clubs here, no place to go in our spare time. All our spare time we devote to reading books and magazines and listening to the radio. You will find that it's always the girls who write to the radio programmes here, commenting on them or suggesting new ideas.

When we read in books about highly civilised and cultivated societies, we want to be like them. It's our dream that some day we will resemble them—that some day we shall achieve something. This dream is already being partly realised. The girls teaching in the schools here are providing their pupils with a very high level of education. They are winning through. In the beginning, of course, it was difficult to rely on them. It was all so new— education, everything. But the authorities had to depend on them. The whole thing was an experiment and nobody knew what the result would be.

In time the fact that the girls are often more highly educated than the boys will create problems, not just in Qatar but in all the Gulf. The young men and boys learn because they are prodded and pressurised. First of all they have to go to school, but then the Government encourages them by assuring them high positions and high salaries. For the boys everything is easy; everything is handed to them on a silver platter. It is one of the faults of our social system that when a young man graduates, even if he only has a low degree, he's immediately given a high managerial post. I don't approve of giving these kind of opportunities to people who have only just begun to work. First they should learn and acquire experience and then they can be promoted. But what is there to motivate them to improve if they are given high positions and high salaries at once?

Take myself, for example. When I came here to work I had specialised as a television set-designer. This involves some knowledge of engineering and architecture as well as art. The course I studied was quite difficult. It wasn't very usual for a girl to take this subject and even the boys had difficulties. I ended up not with an excellent degree, but with a very good one. It's difficult to get a very good mark in engineering.

If they had placed me in a high position when I came back here, this would have reduced my drive. I told them I didn't want a top post. I said: 'I'll prove myself to you over the years'. Of course, I want to run my own department. And now, after two years, I think I could. Yet some of my friends have come back here and have refused to work if it meant working under somebody else.

I can tell you for a fact that when I came back, I knew nothing. I had trained in Egyptian television for three years after my studies. I knew all the theoretical side of television when I came here. But to deal with the workmen, to control their work, to achieve discipline, to plan for the future—all this takes time. I don't mind admitting that I was afraid. Besides, I was the only girl and it's difficult for girls in our country to direct men. I was frightened that they would refuse to accept me as an engineer. Maybe if I had been aggressive, if I had stood on my rights, I would have had my way—but I would have lost their friendship. My way was to start at the bottom, to show them that I was no better than they were and that I needed their help. At the same time I made a point of demonstrating my skills to them.

It was difficult for them to understand how a woman—and especially a very small woman like me!—could come into the studio and tell them what to do. But, in time, I found that they were asking my advice more and more frequently. Now they come and consult me on any problem that arises. They don't go to anyone else. This is particularly true of the Qataris, but it's also the case with the foreigners. In my section there are between forty and fifty people; most of the workers are Indian or Pakistani, but I also have more than a dozen Qataris. They are carpenters and things like that. The less educated they are the harder it is to manage them. My men friends might respect me because I've been to college with them. They have worked hard and I have worked hard and so they feel we're equal. They don't try to oppose me. But it doesn't occur to an uneducated man that I might have studied and worked hard. One of them said to me once: 'You earn a lot of money.' But I don't believe he was really thinking about the money. What was in his mind was the question: how was it that as a woman I could be holding this position? I found it difficult to explain to him. So I just said: 'Maybe if you work hard, you will have the same job as mine.' I encouraged him to get on and now he is working with me. As he had never finished his schooling, I encouraged him to study and learn the same job as I am doing. He has taken my advice and is setting about going off to study my subject.

I'm encouraging them. At least I'm trying. It doesn't speed up our work here to do this, but I'm thinking about their future. Unless someone helps them, they'll end up as carpenters and I don't think this is the best they can do. As a Qatari myself, I feel that they are my brothers and that I am more responsible for them than the foreigners who work here. They are happy to find someone who feels for them and also understands their problems. Just this morning one of them said to me: 'If those in responsibility here looked after me I would work all night without overtime.'

They do for me. Really. When I ask them to work unpaid overtime for me, they do it. But I don't like to ask them. I have started to look after their earnings. I check that the hours they have worked are set down and taken into account. I want the young men to get into the habit of working regular hours. To get people to come on time is still a problem, particularly in this department where timing matters so much. With me—because they feel I'm trying to help them—they don't like to be late. Sometimes they even come early. I try to explain to my friends that they should do the same, but it's not easy to get people to co-operate. Also the workmen tend to think: 'He's not going to do anything for me—he's a foreigner.'

One of the main problems of starting a new enterprise, like here, is lack of planning. People don't seem to believe in plans at all, at all. . . . I try to plan, but I'm one of the few who do. I feel responsible for the way things go. My family is well off and so is my husband so I don't need to work for the money, but I want to help build up my country.

People here don't always understand women working. Some say that it is against religion for women to work. This is not true at all because in the early days of Islam the women fought together with the men. Of course, it's right to wear long clothes—to cover yourself up. This is our particular tradition. But religion does give women the opportunity to work side by side with men.

Maybe a woman isn't as strong as a man, but this is no reason to prevent her from developing as a person. Yet this is the way it is everywhere in the Gulf—we all have the same blood and mentality, we all came originally from the Arabian desert. Men in the desert all think that they are strong; each one considers himself a king. Yet in bedouin life, the women do all the work while the man sits and drinks coffee. She herds the sheep, she brings in the milk, she looks after the children. If anything is planted, it is she who plants it. She even puts up the tents, which is hard work. They don't mind her doing physical labour but they don't like her to think; they feel it diminishes them. If women think too, what is left for them?

I'm not against men. I like men to be strong and I like the man to be everything in my own house. At the same time my husband understands and respects me. He's Egyptian, but that doesn't make him any different from the men here in the Gulf. Sometimes he is even more traditional than the Qataris. Some of the young

Qataris allow their women to do anything just to prove that they are modern. I don't like this. I don't like women to have so much freedom that they forget our traditions and customs. I'm not thinking of driving a car. That's not a disgrace. But one of our customs is that women shouldn't sit together with men alone, I mean indiscreetly. I do sit with men myself. But I like to show respect for my husband whether or not he is present. I don't like to see women talking and laughing with men immodestly. I would sit down with a man at a cocktail party but the conversation would be open and general. I like to dress properly because our religion stipulates that there are certain things we shouldn't wear. I wouldn't wear an open dress, for example. Some Qatari girls do because they think this is the way modern people behave.

Some people here don't understand freedom. Some kinds of freedom are wrong. There are Qataris who allow their wives even more freedom than an Englishman would give to his wife. But I hold to our traditions. I like everything to go smoothly. I don't want to make the older generation unhappy; I don't want them to disapprove of me. It's very difficult to explain. What I want is for us to change—but wisely. Change in this area is a very sensitive matter. Trouble arises when people try to be modern too fast. Change should take place within the framework of our habits and traditions.

If we don't safeguard our own identity, there will soon be no difference between an English, American or Arab woman. This is what we are trying to avoid. I am an Arab. I feel Arab and I won't change. Perhaps wearing covered-up dresses is one of our most important traditions. I wear these three-quarter length dresses and dresses that stop just a few inches below the knee, but not dresses that are only knee-length and certainly not mini skirts!

Also I think an Arab woman must be true to her religion: one important aspect of our religion is that from the beginning it preached respect for women. I don't like a woman to drink. It's very unladylike. We don't like drink, not just because of religion, but because science too proves that it's harmful.

I don't like the woman not respecting her family. I think a

woman should obey her father. If he had prevented me from marrying, I would have respected his wishes. Of course I would have tried to change his mind, but I would never do anything that my family would really oppose. The best thing we have are our family ties. I would not disobey my father. Maybe today he says 'no' to something, but I can always persuade him. In time I can change his mind. If not, then of course I will be very sad. There are some parents who force their children to do things and this is one of the problems in our society. But I would still do what my father wanted. If my father said 'no' to my marriage, I wouldn't marry. Maybe this would break my ties with my father, it would change my feelings towards him. To some extent it all depends on oneself, how one goes about things, one's timing in particular. I would talk to my mother and my brother and we would all put pressure on him together.

Because my husband is Egyptian it wasn't easy for him to be accepted here; it wasn't easy at all. Even my husband—you know what he told me? He said: 'If your father had prevented our marriage I wouldn't have blamed him. I would have done the same thing in his shoes. I would excuse him because tradition here is against women marrying foreigners and it's not pleasant to be out of step with one's society. I wouldn't blame him, but even so I would keep coming back until I wore him down and he gave way.'

As it was, our father had always taught us that we were responsible for choosing our own husbands. There is just one thing I wouldn't accept—if my father chose a husband for me whom I didn't want. Then I would fight. I would even leave. But if I chose a husband whom he didn't like, I wouldn't leave.

One of the important things about our culture is that we can't live without our family, outside of our society. I want my children to grow up with their aunts and uncles, and for my mother to look after me while I am having a child. You don't know how happy she is because I'm expecting a baby. She is very happy. I can't give up this happiness. Because if I left with a man, what guarantee would I have that our marriage would be happy?

You're safer with your family. We have grown up in an atmo-sphere of family love. There are some things I respect in Europe: if you find one of the family sick, maybe you feel very sorry for him, but you are able to cope with the problem. But we start crying and immediately fear that we might lose him. We are very sensitive in our feelings for each other and not only for our family but also for our friends. This is the basis of how people live, think and behave in our society.

I can't live without people at all: without neighbours, without friends. But in England we stayed in a building with over one hundred flats and we didn't know any of the people in them. Here you can go to any area and everybody knows each other. Maybe the streets have no names but you can ask for the house of Mrs So-and-So and anybody will be able to tell you. The character of our society is bedu: it is based on groups. Nobody can live alone outside of the group.

Johina, the Social Worker

We've got a story almost like Cinderella. They called her Suweifi, I think. She was living with her step-mother who ill-treated her. Then a fairy appeared to her, dressed her and took her to a party where the Emir was present. Then she forgot the shoe. There's almost no difference, except in the setting. For instance, in our story she went to the sea and caught a fish which was really a fairy—because our environment is coastal, you know. When she caught the fish it was crying and it said to her 'Set me free and I'll make you rich.' When the Emir came, the feet of Cinderella's step-sisters didn't fit into the shoe, only hers did, so he married her. People didn't wear shoes then, of course, only sandals. Maybe the story came from India.

I also remember being told a story that was almost the same as Oedipus. By Allah, it was the same story: he married his mother and killed his father. I think his father didn't want him, so he took the son out to the desert to kill him, because his father had dreamt that the boy would one day kill him and marry his mother. But the shepherds who found the boy didn't kill him—they brought him up. So he went back again and—I think he killed a dragon, so the queen married him. Then he killed his father. I asked myself, when I grew up: 'How could our families come to know this story?' But I've never asked anybody so far.

When we were young our home was by the sea. What I remember most is that we used to catch those little fish. We would take a tin—like a jam-tin for instance—and put a little date in it. Then we used to tie a piece of cloth around it but leaving an opening and lower it into the sea. The fish would go in and stay in because they were very small.

When we grew a bit bigger our families gave us dolls. They would take a piece of wood and shape it into a small doll—the same kind of dolls that you find nowadays. We used to make a mother and children and the dolls would visit each other.

Boys were not given dolls, of course. So they used anything they could find to play with. From what my mother says, they used to take bones—animal and fish bones—and fix them to look like people. They would even dress them up with *batulas* or just anything they could find. But boys weren't supposed to play with dolls. That's something shameful for them—or almost.

We were always swimming. Because, as I was saying, our house was by the sea, so I always remember the sea. We lived with my grandparents. I had a sister and a brother—we had another sister but she died when she was three. My father, also died when I was young. Then my grandfather died and my little sister—all within about a year-and-a-half. Life was hard.

We had property, praise be to Allah, to keep us. We lived by ourselves, my family. But my cousins all lived in one big house, six families together. Now they are all building houses for themselves and being dispersed. My aunts would take it in turn to cook, or two would cook together. They all ate lunch and dinner together, even if there were as many as fifty people. The *majlis* was big.

This family I'm talking about, they had houses for rent and the sons worked. So the grandparents kept the rent money and bought most things that were needed in the house. The father of each family would only have to buy small things, like clothes for his children. But as for the rice, all the food, the grandfather and grandmother were supposed to provide it.

Our family is small, but we don't like to be alone. Of course, one likes to be alone when one is depressed, but at other times one ought to meet people and live with them. But I wouldn't go back to the past and live in a big family. No, by Allah. Life has changed. There is no one today who gets married and stays with his family, especially as the Government provides them with housing. A man may stay with his parents for a year or two, but in the end he will leave with his own wife and children. It's become a habit. And, of course, the wife likes to be independent. At least she feels that she's mistress in her own house and that she can bring up her children as she likes.

In the past, boys and girls played together until the age of eleven or twelve. Then a girl would put on an *abbaya* and stay in the house. Now girls remain without *abbayas* until the preparatory school age. They don't wear the *ghishwa* or veil as before. In the past they were forced to cover their faces with this light silk veil. Now, it's worn only a little. Then girls even used to have to hide from their cousins if they came into the house. They would play with the neighbour's sons, live and be friends together with them, then after the age of eleven they would all suddenly become afraid of one another. These customs still exist, but it's better than before. People can greet each other sometimes. But we still stick to some old customs. Sometimes guests come but they don't greet the women. Our neighbours whom we have known for a long time— when we see them we're supposed to hide and not speak to them. Even these days. It's natural to us. But in other ways it's not natural. Someone I know like my father, whom I have lived with and eaten with, I should like to be able to greet them. I should like to greet our neighbours, but one is afraid to do so for fear of being considered a woman who does not hold to tradition. The strange thing is that they allow us to speak to any man who is not Qatari. For example, if a salesman comes in—an Iranian or a Pathan or something—we can go out and speak to him. But if a Qatari comes wearing a *thaub* and headdress, we're supposed to shut the door and go inside. That's what they tell us. We ask: Why? Are those from whom we don't have to hide men or are they not men? We have male servants and we don't hide from them. We don't hide from anyone, even a Qatari, provided he isn't wearing a *thaub* and headdress.

Of course, we hope for a change—because women are unjustly treated here. Women—what can I say?—it's forbidden for a woman to go out. Someone must take her and bring her back. We can't just get into a car and go. That's shameful or something.

At one time it was shameful for a woman to travel. Then our families allowed us to travel. Last year, for example, my family sent me to Jordan for three months to study. At first, they didn't even allow us to go to school, except when they were forced to. But then when they saw so-and-so's daughter go out to school, and somebody else's, they said: 'You ought to study like them, at home.' It was we ourselves who forced the pace sometimes. But soon even our families accepted the idea of our studying. When they saw more and more girls doing it, they wanted the same thing for their daughters.

I had only my mother and we accepted each other's ideas—praise be to Allah. Of course, people older than my mother don't accept that we should have more freedom. They're inclined to be old-fashioned. In my mother's case, she can accept a little change. Of course, we are more open-minded than her generation and the next generation will be more open-minded than we are. My mother will accept some things, but not others. She takes into account the opinion of her social group.

The older women feel inferior in so far as the younger generation of women have been educated while they have not—that's for sure. And an indication of this is that nearly all the women have joined literacy courses. My mother hasn't, though: she just stays at home, with my small brothers. She says 'Let's see if this experiment

The Emir of Qatar, Sheikh Khalifa bin Hamad
al-Thani (right) in conversation with Sheikh Zaid,
Ruler of Abu Dhabi and President of the United Arab
Emirates

The Minister

succeeds and then I will go'. But my mother is learning by herself. Now she takes a copybook and sits writing in it. She even remembers the old songs. In the old days, at Eid, we had what they call *mrada*. They used to wear gold and sing.

My mother has fond memories of the past. They had more freedom then. When the men were away diving they used to be able to come and go more freely. In the diving season, no one stayed at home. They all went out into the desert. They could walk for long distances without feeling tired. When the men were here in the winter, of course they didn't go out.

All of us here—my friends and myself—we studied at the teachers' training institute for women. At first we were teachers. Then the Ministry offered some of us jobs as social workers. In view of our situation *vis à vis* our families, we made it a condition of acceptance that we would not work with men in the Ministry. So we were given a section to ourselves. This in spite of the fact that I study commerce at university and all my three colleagues study law.

Our first job was to check on people who were receiving social assistance. Some people were getting money in the name of people who had died—three hundred *riyals* a month. Our job was to investigate: to see if the woman was alive, or maybe divorced or re-married. But then people complained. I don't know why. At first we used to go out by ourselves—maybe this was why. Anyway, we don't do that any longer. Now our job is to wait here for widows and divorcées who may be in need to come to us. We have to check whether they are really divorced and have not re-married.

Our work here is different from the social work we did in Jordan, where we visited mother-care centres and charitable societies. We studied social work there. But, *inshallah*, we shall see what happens. I like the job. It's more comfortable than teaching. Then, at first it was really nice. We came into contact with people's problems. We had ideas. But now, what can I say? We are still hoping to be given a chance to serve the community. But for the time being we are in a situation of stalemate. We can't come and go as freely here as in Jordan, nor create charitable societies. The younger generation of women might be prepared to do it, but the older people could not accept it. We still need some time before our society can accept charitable societies or that women go to aid centres, that their husbands allow it. Qatar has only had ten years of development.

I hope that women will be able to participate in the community beyond just being employees, that they will soon be able to set up groups to think about the problems of the community, for example. Even if these groups were quite small and informal, it would be better for the women to think than just to sit around chatting.

We are all extra-mural students at the Beirut Arab University. I've heard that we're going to be allowed to go and study there. I am in my third year. Of course, when we started we didn't know that we were to become social workers. I like mathematics but as it was not available I chose commerce, because the course includes some mathematics. I study management and economics. I don't know what I shall do with my degree—perhaps go on to a doctorate. But I hope to be able to work sometime. I like commerce.

Aisha, the Radio Announcer

I was born in Doha. My father used to go to sea, not as a pearl diver but as a trader in a small way. Now everything in Doha has changed greatly and for the better.

The first women to work were not really accepted. There was opposition. But I am speaking of the women who went to work in jobs together with men. Of course women had already begun working as teachers and nurses but the teachers only worked in girls' schools and did not mix with men. But now things have changed totally. This change has taken place in a period of about six years. When I started my work, my family was against me but finally they came round, thank goodness, to accept it. But I have been lucky, and have had encouragement. Members of the family are usually not too worried themselves, but they are always afraid of what somebody else will say, relatives, neighbours. The difficulty was really only at the beginning with my father.

My father trusted me: he was simply afraid that people might criticise him and might say to him 'What are you doing, making your daughter work?' This would, in their eyes, mean that he was in straitened circumstances, if he had to put his daughter to work. But I pointed out to him that this was untrue and I said to him 'What on earth should a person like me do? Should I stay sitting at home? What am I going to do with my life? Be a teacher? I don't want to be a teacher.' I brought him round to my way of thinking. He was simply afraid of criticism from others, and the fact that I was setting a precedent.

When Sheikh Khalifa appointed the first woman radio announcer, an Egyptian, there was a lot of criticism; people asked what it would sound like, especially the sheikhs. But he said to them 'Let her speak morning, noon and night' and this is the answer. There were some extremists who opposed these moves. but the directors of the radio station, the people running the news section, took no notice of these criticisms.

Since I was very small, I have always liked the idea of working for the radio. I liked soaking up different subjects. It was always my ambition to be an announcer. As soon as we had a radio station here I thought of joining it. When I applied I was successful in the voice and other tests. They needed Qatari girls.

I have no desire to act. From time to time, people ask me to take a part or use my voice in a play but I always make excuses and don't do it.

I always listen to the other Arab radio services, and to the Arabic programmes of the World Service of the BBC which we can receive clearly. I listened to the BBC when I was small and as soon as Qatar had its own radio station I listened to that. And as soon as I heard it I thought about working in it. I am now a broadcaster and a producer. I read the news and I prepare pro⸗

grammes and select the material, such as songs. I produce a programme called 'Listeners' Choice' and another called 'Good
Morning'. Both of them are daily.

I have been working at this job for six years. The Radio Station
opened in 1968 on an experimental basis but opened properly in
1969 and I joined the Station a year later.

I trained here at the Radio Centre for five months. At first I presented only recorded, not live. During my training I relied on my
colleagues but when it was over I relied, of course, on myself. I
was then sent on a training course in America where I saw radio
and television stations. I went to ten different States and to the
radio and television stations in every town I visited. The course
lasted fortyfive days.

In our radio station here, the most important qualification for a
broadcaster is a good voice, and a good command of the language.
I fulfilled both conditions. I used to feel a bit strange to start with
because I was the only girl among my colleagues but they showed
me every respect and treated me as though they were my brothers
and I found no difficulty or embarrassment in the work.

Although I have always liked broadcasting, I never wanted to
work in television. It involves too much fuss and bother. It's not a
question of my face being seen. My picture has often been published in magazines.

I received a lot of encouragement from people. From my colleagues at the radio, from my family and my relations and all
other people, mostly girls whom I knew. In the beginning when
they heard my voice, they used to encourage me more by saying:
'Your voice sounds very nice.' At that time, there were very few
female voices to be heard on the radio.

I get a lot of letters and postcards and telephone calls commenting on the programmes.

As the first Qatari girl's voice to be heard on the radio, I
received nothing but expressions of admiration.

The letters I received were mostly from girls, but some of them
were from boys. But most of the girls telephoned. This may have
been because their family might have seen their mail. Many of

them would have liked to have done the same thing as me. But they were probably afraid of the same problems which I had at the start. I mean, everybody was frightened simply of what people might say. So, most of the girls who went to work, went into teaching. But now times have changed. There are women assistants in colleges. There are women broadcasters on television. All sorts of things. The position is different even from what it was last year. There is a woman doctor and there are Qatari girl nurses. They are working, all of them, in the hospital and this is something which didn't happen before.

There are now quite a few more women in the television centre. There's even a woman engineer. Now, girls are able to go into all fields of activity. Into journalism, into information work. They can become university graduates. There are large numbers of girls from Qatar now studying abroad—in Kuwait, in Cairo, and other places. I am very happy about it.

PART FOUR

Pillars of Society

I. PROFESSIONALS

The Minister

The notables of Doha (barring the businessmen) are like the squirearchy
of eighteenth-century England—amiable huntin', shootin', fishin' types, by
and large. The Minister is different, more like a cultured French aristocrat of
the same period, immensely charming, exquisitely correct and polished,
perfectly discreet—but with it all a Qatari at heart, more complex than most
and also much less direct (too skilled a politician to be that), but still
humane and approachable. In fact, like virtually all Qataris he is a self-made
man who started with very little and built up his fortune by his own efforts.
But there is nothing in the least ostentatious about either the man or his life
style. His villa is large and comfortable and filled with Iranian carpets—but
by no means luxurious. There are always fresh roses on the tables. He
entertains often in a relaxed rather than grand manner. 'Tell me an Arab
proverb' asks a guest teasingly. Without giving himself time to think the
Minister says at once: *al insann tawkum wa rraghba*—man is all passion.

I had been interested in philosophy for many years. Then, one day,
I met a gentleman in Bahrain, an Indian. We were talking together at a party. I was speaking about the problem of justice in
life and how everyone should have their rights. The next day we
met again. He said to me: 'Last night you were speaking of
justice. You know there is no real justice in this life. It is too

219

difficult a goal to reach. Why is it, for example, that someone who is educated and knowledgeable may not succeed in life, say in his business affairs, while another who is ignorant may do well? You see, there is no justice.'

After this discussion, I also came to the conclusion that there is, indeed, no justice in life. I decided it was useless for me to go on as I had before, trying to discover the reason why everything is as it is. So I stopped. That was about ten years ago. It was not the Indian alone who convinced me. I myself had long thought that if you ask yourself ceaselessly why one man should succeed and another not, why one woman is beautiful and the other ugly, you will find no answer and reach no end. I didn't stop struggling to change things, but I stopped trying to discover reasons. I said to myself, 'There never will be an answer.'

I never studied philosophical questions formally, at school or university. I just read books by myself. I began to read books on philosophy when I was about forty years old. I wanted to study everything, really. Before I began to read philosophy books systematically, I used to wonder in my own mind why this should happen like so, and that like so; and, above all, why there was no justice. Then I began with books. I bought them in Cairo and other places. I read Arabic translations of the Greeks: Plato, Socrates, Aristotle. There have been few great Arab philosophers: philosophy is not an Arab subject. Islam is the greatest influence on Arab thought and I read many books on our Islamic religion too. But religion is different from philosophy. Religion never questions why things are as they are: you just have to accept. And Islam is like that.

I still read now, a great deal. I have one bed for myself, the other bed is loaded with books. But I no longer read philosophy. After I spoke with that Indian in Bahrain I gave all my philosophy books away. I didn't even want to have the books around me. But even now there are times when I can't stop myself thinking, when something happens, something I consider to be unjust, 'why should it be?' I come back to that. I stop again and tell myself, 'It's no good thinking about it.'

I have also been interested in politics and social questions for as long as I can remember: from the age of sixteen, at least. I didn't read in those days, but I used to think things over. I worried about poverty. Most people here were poor at the time. But why? This was my question. Also I saw that people were poor the world over and I asked myself: 'Why not develop a social policy to help people?' I used to discuss the matter with anybody who would listen. Their answer was always the same. They said: 'You can't do whatever you want. It is God who decides, particularly according to our Muslim religion.' I have come to terms with this now, to some extent. . . .

In those days, when most people were not able to educate them-selves, I was sent to a school in Bahrain. My father was a general merchant. I was about twelve years old. When I was here in Qatar I learnt the Koran and Arabic grammar, but in Bahrain I learnt everything: history, geography and mathematics.

After Bahrain, I went to Saudi Arabia because the economic situation in the Gulf was really very bad. Most of the poeple here emigrated like me mainly to Saudi Arabia, but also to Bahrain and elsewhere. The pearl trade came to an end very rapidly. The poverty that resulted lasted for at least fifteen years, until the late forties. During that period people here had just one meal a day. When I was living in Saudi Arabia people would come from here to buy dates, they had so little to live on. I used to ask myself: 'Why does God allow this?'

In Saudi Arabia, I worked with the customs, the finance department and finally the police. I read a lot and I attended the courses in English and Arabic. I had learnt English in Bahrain and wanted to improve it. I also wanted to know more about Arabic grammar so as to be able to speak the language better. I now speak Arabic well, very well, but I still want to do better. In any language, however far you go, you can never say: 'I know everything.' This is what I really want: to learn everything—as much as I can anyway. This is why I have always been struggling with myself, internally. At the same time, I'm a very sociable person, I like to be with people.

When I first heard about oil, before the war, I didn't think much about it. I did expect that there would be some changes, but I didn't foresee that they would be as momentous as they have been. I imagined that a school would be built and that people would live differently because they would all be earning more money. In the days before oil we only imported food and some material. Nobody at that time would have dreamt of bringing in furniture. So there was a great difference between the era of pearl diving and the oil era, even at the very beginning after the war when our oil revenue was still limited.

The first imports that came into Qatar, when people began to have a little extra money, were radios and cameras—that kind of thing. Then, little by little, we imported furniture—cheap furniture. We changed the way we lived in our houses. At that time I was working with foreigners, mainly with the English and the Dutch. I tried to learn something from these people; I wanted to understand how they lived and to improve my English. I learned how to prepare food we didn't have ourselves at the time: steak and sweets. I liked the way they arranged the furniture in their houses; I used to watch how they did it when I visited them. I thought that they had become civilised before us and so had more experience than we. I watched everything they did to learn what might be useful for me. I bought new furniture for my own house and placed it like the Europeans did. I didn't find them arrogant. Of course, they were employers and they treated the Qataris as employees. In time they respected us more, not necessarily because of our money, but because we ourselves were more educated.

I came back from Saudi Arabia to work as director of customs in the oil area. I was very young at the time, just twenty-five. I liked my job as head of customs because I was able to help people. I came back to Doha around 1954 and worked in the palace for two years. My responsibility was to look after letters and complaints and convey them to the Emir. Sometimes people would ask for a piece of land or some kind of help. In those days the Emir held his *majlis* three or four times a day. Anybody could come.

People used to call the Sheikh simply by his first name. Qataris were like one family.

From time to time I went to Egypt to learn French at the Berlitz Institute. I really care very much for that language. I like learning languages: I had studied Persian and speak some Urdu. So I wanted to be able to speak French too. But circumstances prevented it: I was called back here as Director of Immigration. This was very far from what I had in mind for myself, but I was appointed to the job. So I had to do it. I was always interested in politics really. If I were young now, I should study, of course. But I wouldn't change profession: I should go into politics (*laughs*). I took over the Ministry of Social Affairs in 1970. It was smaller then than it is now.

Recently I have set up co-operatives where people can buy more cheaply than in the ordinary market. We don't give a straight Government subsidy; members of the public hold stock. The government adds whatever extra capital is needed. But these co-operatives are meant only for certain areas, particularly where people with lower incomes live. Since the experiment has only reached the end of its first year, we don't yet know what the result will be. We have five or six co-operatives. The idea behind them was to provide people with facilities in their own area and to give them cheaper goods. If you live outside the centre of Doha, you need a car to shop there—that costs time and money. Now you have whatever you need on the spot and at the end of the year you are given a share of the profit.

I am also opening an Institute to teach women how to make things by hand. I provide them with machines, instructors, everything. The women who will attend the classes are dependent on social welfare and receive a monthly allowance from us. I want to increase their income but also to teach them something: how to be a useful member of the community. I am thinking of bringing over experts from Iran to show them how to make carpets. The women like the idea and have agreed to come. I want people to work, not just to sit at home and collect money every month. I also think they should participate more in the affairs of the community.

My main problem in running this ministry is housing. It takes time to build, but people always want houses immediately. Families here still want to live together, in the same area. People are always coming and saying we are fifteen, sixteen or seventeen families, please give us houses next door to each other. We arrange it for them. Besides it suits us too. If neighbours were not related, there might be many more problems between their children.

Every Qatari has the right to a free house from the State. The delay at the moment in getting a house is around one year, sometimes even longer. We are short of manpower. Prices go up and the housing materials we need never arrive on time.

The biggest houses built by the Ministry have four bedrooms, a sitting-room and a dining-room. That's suitable for one family. We don't build houses where they can all live together as in the past. We don't want that and they don't either. The old days were different. Now everybody wants their own house. People want more independence. I accept this myself with my own children. But it's less a question of money than of education.

The most important change created by oil wealth in this country has been education. The more educated people are, the fewer the problems they create They become more disciplined, more co-operative towards each other. Recently we were discussing family planning at the United Nations. I said that I thought it was useless to lay down laws forcing people to have a limited number of children only. This is not the right way to go about it. What we have to do is to educate people: to show them the way and then leave it to them. When they begin to understand how the economy of the country works, when they realise that they can only bring up a few children well, they will do the best both for themselves and for society. But it's useless to impose laws because people won't accept them—that's the nature of human beings.

Nowadays I can afford certain hobbies: I like to collect carpets, especially Persian ones, prayer beads and old swords. Swords are a symbol of power; this is what I like about them. In the old days people used to pray with beads—they recited God's name, say one hundred times, as they held them. I collect them because they're beautiful and because they make me think of religion and prayer. I always use this green one—I like green things (*laughs*). The Persian carpets I collect because they are the best in the world. Their colour never changes and their price always appreciates. I like some paintings—of huge palaces and greenery, such things. I like music, Arab and Western.

I am still the same person I always was (*laughs*). I only change my furnishing and my eating habits, but there has been no change in my personality. I have become more liberal, partly as the result of travelling. But money has not affected me. It's only a means to improve your life. Some people say that if you have money you can have whatever you want: but I don't believe that.

The Doctor

The doctor is a highly strung young man in his mid-thirties with severe squarish gold-rimmed glasses which are contradicted by the slightly rakish air imparted by a gap between his two front teeth. He wears well-cut European clothes and an expensive-looking jewel-studded watch. In London he throws out invitations to the Hilton rather easily. But this does not make him a play-boy. In fact, he is one of the most professionally dedicated people in the country, a young surgeon who, as an older Amercian colleague admiringly put it, can resist wielding the knife and whose diagnosis is first-class. His early life was not easy and this has marked him. As a child he grew up in Bahrain because his father had emigrated during the hard years——he was a journalist and political activist, a leader of the opposition to the British in Bahrain. He was sent to St Helena for sixteen years all because someone threw dirt at Selwyn Lloyd's car in the tense days after Suez.

The doctor's home life is both traditional and liberal. He lives in one house with his brother, his brother's family and their mother. At the same time, his wife, who studied psychology in Kuwait, is now studying sociology in Cairo; she takes their small daughter with her and is expecting a second child. She is a quite exceptionally good-looking woman of thirty with a face like a medieval madonna, only more alive. He says he hopes she will do a Ph.D. She reddens and makes a grimace in his direction as she dishes out the meal: pastries, chicken, boiled beef, macaroni and salad. Qataris, apparently, don't care for his kind of fare when they go out. All attempts to convert them to chicken and steak have so far failed. The doctor sighs: they must still have lamb.

Because of our family circumstances, my mother, although she is not educated, was the one who made men of us. My father we respected and he had a great influence on us because he was educated at a time when very few other people were. He was a journalist but he was self-educated; he taught himself by reading books and travelling. I think he was one of the first people in Bahrain to speak English then.

I was sixteen when my father was arrested in 1956 for political reasons and taken away to St Helena. I left Bahrain, where we then lived, that same week. We were afraid that we, too, would be affected by the political climate. It is difficult for me to find words to describe my father. To me, as well as to others, he was great. And there is no doubt that his ideas and the way he lived affected our personality as well as the whole course of our own lives. He was a strong personality. His way of treating us was completely different from the way that other people, our neighbours, treated their children: he never interfered with us at all, never. When we were at school he never made us work, but just said that he would be happy if we were among the first in the class. He interfered in one thing only in my life: he told me he wanted me to be a doctor. I obeyed out of respect for him. I myself was interested mainly in literature, I write poems, and, actually, I failed in my first year of medical studies. I didn't go to take the exam. I used to go to other classes, the literature and law classes. Then, one day I got a letter from my father in St Helena, and he said he wanted me to succeed in my studies. After that I never failed an exam again. But in other matters he let me go my own way. He even knew that as a student I belonged to a political movement which had different aims from the one he belonged to. He just kept an eye on me. He was strong enough to free himself from his own father.

My mother was very young when she married my father. She was the most loyal woman to her husband I have ever known. She did everything for us. If I never get tired, this is a characteristic I have inherited from her; and if she does get tired she refuses to admit it. She is also a very, very strong personality. When they took my father away, we were not left destitute, but we hadn't much to live on. When he was sent to St Helena my mother decided to keep the same dress on her back until he returned after fourteen years—and that's what she did. She worked to collect money for us, to keep up our standard of living at the same level as before: she sewed and she traded. Even now, if I am out working until four o'clock in the morning, she never sleeps until she knows that I have come back. My wife will sleep, but my mother—never. Whenever I move, she thinks I need something and she jumps out of bed. I try to stop this, but she can't act any differently.

My father used to treat my mother differently from the way other men treated their wives. Of course the Eastern mentality was in him and in my mother also. But the way my father treated my mother, with respect —he really respected her, there is no doubt about it—affected us too. Men in Qatar used to expect everything to be done for them, without giving anything in return, I don't believe in this, of course. I can't force the rest of the community to follow my ideas, but in my own family I treat everybody as free agents and allow them to act as they think right. This is my philosophy in life; this is the way I myself was brought up.

I don't really know why my father wanted me to be a doctor, I never asked him. Maybe the main reason was that he wanted to keep me away from politics—in fact I am sure about this. Maybe, he also thought that as a doctor I could help people. Certainly, he was determined that I should steer clear of politics. At that time, in the 50s and early 60s, everybody in the Arabian Peninsula was involved in politics, either on the left or on the right, but anyway they were active. I think this marked a stage in what I might call the Arabian revolution. At this particular time there were a sufficient number of educated people around to start saying 'No' —to the British or to anybody else. People had a new confidence in themselves. Now there is less reason to be involved in politics because people in the Gulf live better than almost anywhere else. In the past, this was not the case: even the sheikhs were poor.

At that time we knew we had oil, but we also knew we were suffering. We needed scholarships, but nobody gave us them. When you know that you have everything in your house, but that you can't have it, you revolt. This is what happened. All students were affected by this situation. In my case, having been a member of political parties and movements increased my knowledge. Now I can think; I can plan. This is very useful to my country at the moment because we need such skills. Today I have no prejudices against foreigners, except if they don't do their job well. But in general I would help a foreigner as willingly as a Qatari. I think this is the official attitude, too: expatriates have served this country for a long time, so they should be given every opportunity since they helped us with their energy and work when we had nothing. It's very rare for anyone in Qatar to be told to leave the country, even though very big mistakes are sometimes made.

The policy of Qatar is to encourage students, especially medical students, to carry on gaining higher qualifications for as long as they like, without anyone having the right to question what they are doing. I think that this is a good thing when you are starting to develop the country like we are, because then, when you come back, you are on equal footing with expatriates who may have a lot more experience than you. I myself had some difficulties when I came back, but I was able to win through because I was well qualified: I was fighting on solid ground. The first thirty or forty doctors in Qatar, I think, should only come back when they are very highly qualified. Besides, the longer they stay abroad and the more educated they are, the more qualified and surer in their judgement they will be. At the moment there are several Qatari medical students in the UK and the US, but the majority— around 65—are in Cairo. If they want to come back to Qatar for one year, straight away after graduating, they would be welcomed, but we can arrange for them to go on to any university abroad or any teaching hospital. If a doctor stays for one year in a British hospital, he gains more experience than in two years in one of our own hospitals.

I took my first medical degree in Cairo in 1966; and I completed my final fellowship in Edinburgh. That was in May 1973. During the whole period of my studies I was supported financially by the Qatar government. It was Sheikh Jassim, the Minister of Education, who helped me, as well as others of my generation, most; when I was in trouble with the authorities for two years he paid me from his own pocket. He was really a great man, in every sense: in helping people, in being kind to people. When people met him the first time, they might have thought he didn't know much, but in fact he knew everything. He himself had very little education although he could read and write, but he was one of the first people here to travel a lot outside Qatar. When he took over the Department, a number of people here opposed education, some on religious grounds. He really fought very hard and it was thanks to him that our education system started in the 50s rather than in the 60s. He was especially supportive of the girls, in the face of a lot of opposition. Every girl in this country should know of the debt she owes to Jassim Bin Hamad.

He travelled a lot because as a Minister he had to attend many conferences where he would meet other Ministers and foreign experts. These conferences are very useful. I go to two kinds of conferences, medical and administrative, and I think that I learn a lot in both areas. For instance, I am now on the board of the World Health Organisation. It is a great thing for me, at my age, to sit with these experienced people on a committee which sets the guidelines for the health services of the whole world. I can't say I was apprehensive. I always work things out within myself and I only go ahead when I am sure of what I am doing. At any conference, I can take the microphone and speak. I don't hesitate since I know that my arguments are solid. The whole world elected Qatar to be a member of the Board. There was not one single dissenting voice. The whole General Assembly gave us the vote.

I completed my fellowship very quickly, in just two-and-a-half years—many people take five years. I was in a great hurry to get it over with as I wanted to come back and work in my country and help to improve the medical services. Mind you, when I came back here, all was not plain sailing. The Government has a Qatarisation programme but it is inevitable that people who hold positions of power aren't happy about giving them up; this happens every, where. But any Qatari who has personality and qualifications can pull through. This wasn't the only problem I had to face. To be honest I was a little taken aback at the state of medical services in my country. I had been a long time abroad and found that the level of medical care here was lower than I had expected. I became director of the Health Ministry after some time and had to face a good many problems. Nobody knew what their exact position was nor whom they should approach. Sometimes I was sent notices complaining that the assignment of sugar and tea was less than in previous months—can you imagine, this kind of thing, coming to a Director! Anyone going on leave had to apply to the Director, if they wanted to scratch their head they had to go to the Director. . . .

One of the things that was wrong was that because Qataris are kind and generous and often give presents, even important and busy doctors would occupy themselves with minor matters, such as removing stitches, so as to be given all the credit for looking after the patient. Moreover, there was a gap between consultants and junior doctors, organisationally speaking. I wrote a memo, randum on the subject, questioning our system. I proposed instead something akin to the English system, that the hospital should be separated into divisions and these subdivided into sections. Each section would be headed by a consultant; below him there would be a specialist of registrar level and under him a junior medical officer. I concluded that the job description of the medical officer should exclude from the job most of those who were actually per, forming it at the time. I knew, from my own experience as a medical officer, that in general they are young, energetic, eager to acquire additional qualifications, ready to be on call twenty, four hours a day. But when I arrived back most of the medical officers were much older than me, they had fifteen or twenty years experi, ence, they had family responsibilities. They would look at their watch before the end of the working day, like any other employee. But a man is finished as a doctor if he regards his job as a routine affair with set hours. Of course it wasn't possible to get rid of these people, they had settled in this country and made their lives here. But when the new medical centre was created it was agreed to avoid using these kind of people, and instead to find people who would be immediately available in case of emergency. Previously, for example, the doctor on call might live out near the airport. Yet suppose somebody had a car accident or was bleeding seriously. This doctor would have to drive all the way from the airport to the hospital, and even if he drove fast it would take him not less than twenty minutes. Twenty minutes is too long when a patient's life is at stake. I wanted young and energetic people who would be immediately available on the spot and I succeeded in finding them. Now at least half of the medical officers are such people.

At the same time we are planning health centres outside Doha to take some of the load off the hospitals in much the same way as GPs do in England. We plan to have seven health centres and when they materialise I could transfer the medical officers to these centres after a period in the hospital, because if, four or five years after their graduation, they are not working for any further diplomas or degrees, then it is clear that they will never do so. These kind of people will be moved to the health centres and be replaced in the hospitals by younger and keener people, eager to learn, and to improve their qualifications.

I also divided the hospital medical staff into the three categories I mentioned before: consultant, registrar, medical officer. As far as the surgical department goes, I have completed the reorganisation. I think the new system here will make a lot of difference. You see, the medical officer is usually the person who sees the patient when he first comes into the hospital. Now, in our country, people are very demanding. They want to see the top man, the consultant or specialist. When there is only one consultant available, without any go-between, and this consultant is reluctant to come in the afternoon, which they usually are, then the medical officer himself will be affected and become equally reluctant, so it is important to have a specialist category available who will be able to treat the patient with the most modern methods. The job description of

these new specialists is that they should have seven years experience after graduation, so most of them will be between thirty and
thirty-six years of age, and still energetic enough to work hard and
usefully. The system has been in operation in the surgical department for the past year and it is working well.

I am now a member of the Action Committee: it's difficult to
describe its functions. This committee is formed by the Cabinet,
one of the ministers is chairman and I am reporter and secretary.
The work of this committee is not just to plan, it is also responsible for following through its own decisions. My position on this
committee has given me great leverage and has enabled me to get
things done more easily than would otherwise have been the case.

At the hospital itself, I am working now as head of the surgical
department. I have seven consultants, seven specialists and fourteen
medical officers under me. But there is one department which is my
very own: there, I am the consultant, specialist and medical officer
all rolled into one! This is the endoscopy department and it is new.
I studied the subject in Japan. Endoscopy is a fibre-optic technique
whereby you can examine the inside of the patient by inserting a
tube through the mouth or the anus. It's a new branch of diagnosis
which could have an interesting future as there is a possibility that
we might be able to perform small operations in this way. This
technique is useful, for instance for looking at the stomach. An
examination will show you only 80 per cent of what's happening,
an X-ray possibly 90 per cent, but endoscopy will give you the full
picture.

Another subject which has interested me personally a lot for the
past nine years is burns. The burns unit here is my unit, actually. I
look after it. What I have done is to apply old techniques that were
used here before the days of modern medicine. You know that here
we, as Muslims, practise circumcision. For two or three days after
the circumcision, the boys are sent to the sea. The wounds heal
quickly—just two or three days—which indicates that the salt in
the water helps the healing process. I use this method now. I
immerse the patient in salt water and just now I am measuring the
optimum quantity of salt to be added to the water. I have got

very good results with this. I have even succeeded in reducing the number of grafts and operations we do.

These ancient techniques can be usefully applied today, but it takes time to work on them. I even created a research budget for this purpose, of 200,000 *riyals*. Anybody in the Ministry who wants to do research can have access to this money, but up to now nobody has applied for it.

I am convinced now that apart from my job as head of the surgical section I can be of most use as a planner. I write all the memoranda and reports for plans myself, in good Arabic, because I am a poet and write Arabic well. I think my reports are con-vincing. It is a matter of pride to me that I am now able to assess what is needed here in the medical field more competently than any external specialist or consultant.

I like my work, but I might in time join the staff of the W.H.O. and become an expert in health services, then my country will call me back as an expert. Our countries have great faith in experts. I once saw a Kuwaiti comedy on the subject. Six or seven problems common to most of the countries in the Gulf as a whole are dis-cussed and, in the end, when the question is asked 'What's the solution?', a group sings 'The solution is in the hands of the experts'.

The Editor

'Shall I tell you a secret?' demands the editor within five minutes of your entering his room, a shambles of books and papers like any newspaper office anywhere. He crosses to the huge safe in the corner and withdraws a manuscript. 'I have written this. It's a history of the whole area. But the time is not ripe, the time is not ripe. . . ' He returns the manuscript to where it came from.

Hs is one of the few eccentrics in Doha: rich businessman, showman and journalist—in that order. The stories that circulate about him are greatly relished and probably true. He is in his mid-fifties, smallish and balding, and in his office he wears a beige *thaub* without the head-dress, making him look like Friar Tuck. He begins a discussion quietly but in no time at all works himself into a rage, shouts so that the dust on the bookshelves rises in agitated clouds, then settles as he calms down, and rises again as he returns to the charge. Some foreign diplomat has just, it appears, complained to the Ministry of Information that the paper has attacked his country. This outrages him, quite justifiably: 'If I complained to *his* Government about one of their papers attacking Qatar, they wouldn't do anything about it—that's what I told the stupid man,' he yells furiously. 'Now take the American ambassador. We're always attacking his country. Yet he's friendly—comes here and drinks tea. He wouldn't go and complain to the Ministry. So, sometimes I tone down my attacks a little.'

He is, above all, proud of his daughter, who will soon become the first female journalist in Qatar. At the moment she lives with his first wife from whom he has separated but has never divorced. 'She's retired,' he remarks amiably.

I was the first journalist in Qatar and my magazine was the first to be published in Qatar. There was never anybody before me. And listen to this, I was not only the first with the magazine, I was also the first to open a book shop, the first to import newspapers from abroad, the first to set up a printing press, and the first Qatari Petroleum Director. In my life there is nothing but first, first! I love anything, just as long as I'm the first to do it.

A long time ago when I was Director of Customs and Petroleum and Passports at Umm Said, I was preparing myself for the day when I would work in journalism. I used to write memoirs of my life and things like that, but I had to interrupt my writing to work. There was an airport at Umm Said at that time—and not yet one at Doha. I began to import newspapers, mainly Egyptian and Lebanese, on a very small scale—not more than ten at a time. Then in 1954 I opened a small bookshop here. I continued to import newspapers, but also other things. Even in my early life when I was abroad, it was the same thing—I loved anything to do with journalism and writing. I loved the idea. I thought of it as some kind of adventure.

In 1955, I left my work at Umm Said and opened the Telmeth and the al Oroba bookshops in Doha. In 1956 I worked as a contractor and did well for myself. I bought a printing press and I opened an office, but what we produced was sent abroad. I also wrote memoirs and I'm still writing memoirs and until the day I retire I shall be writing about my life. When I was young I led a different kind of life because I lived in Saudi Arabia for seventeen years. But I am a Qatari and my father is a Qatari and so is my mother. All my forefathers have been Qatari right back to the eighteenth century.

In 1964 the first magazine ever to be published in Doha appeared: this was the *al Oroba* magazine. It's still going. After a few years we published the *al Arab* daily newspaper. *Al Arab* was first issued as a weekly, then it became a daily when the government began to support us financially. Of course, I consider *al Oroba* as a patriotic venture—I wanted to do something for my country. I have no way of showing my patriotism other than through journalism. I love journalism and I have a purpose.

There are people who think in terms of money and people who don't. I belong to the second category. I'm one of those who simply want the paper to succeed. Then there are my sons. I want to create a publishing house which will be an asset to them as well as me; to found a publishing dynasty.

I consider myself as having been a pioneer in publishing *al Oroba*. I didn't bring an editor from outside the country. I got the help of four or five of our Palestinian brothers who were working in the Education Department. They used to come to us for three or four hours at night and they helped us until *al Oroba* was published.

I wanted to make my children journalists. My son Abdullah is the first Qatari journalist to graduate from Cairo University. He graduated from the Faculty of Media which combines journalism with other media. My daughter is the first Qatari girl to graduate this year from the same Faculty. My son finished two years ago and now he's editor-in-chief of the daily paper. I have another son who is a journalist and one who graduated in law. So I am the first Qatari father to make his sons journalists and to create a publishing house for them.

My opinion is that journalism can only serve the country if it is patriotic. My patriotic desire is to spread awareness, interpret events, provide information. If I bring a chief editor from outside, he will come here to earn money, not to serve Qatar. If somebody offered him a thousand *riyals* more, he would leave me and go. That's all there is to it. We've tried so we know. But my sons who have graduated as journalists are also Qataris, while I have the necessary journalistic enterprise.

A Qatari will serve his country. I will tell you why. I left this country when I was seventeen and it caused me much mental anguish to do so. But at that time there was no electricity, no oil, no means of livelihood. A lot of people left. Our fathers were prosperous but only relative to their own time, not by today's standards. The situation was the same throughout the Gulf. Dozens of people went like myself as emigrants to Saudi Arabia. I worked for five years in Aramco, and for five years as petroleum manager at Ras Tanoura. For the rest of the time I was in contracting and in business, and I had a hard struggle. I've got pictures of myself with a beard, pictures which show me as thin, pictures where I'm wearing workman's clothes when I was working as a driver for geologists in Saudi Arabia.

I wanted to be a journalist from a very early age. I am now sixty-one years old. Nowadays when a young man graduates he is given a job, a villa and land by the Government. There's no struggle. The Government helps, his father helps and when the young man is ready to work he finds a huge salary waiting for him. But then we lived in hard times and we suffered in the desert, we had to struggle to survive. That's what struggle means—the dust and the sun and the heat when there's no air conditioning and no fans and I don't know what. This struggle has given birth to education and a better life and stability.

I wanted to study abroad, of course, and at that time it was a bit difficult to find anywhere to go.

I left here when I was around seventeen years old and went to Bahrain where I studied in an American mission school. They called it Hakkam school because the teacher's name was Hakkam.

I was determined to go. I fled from Qatar in a sailing boat taking gypsum to Bahrain and I took refuge in the house of one of my uncles; he was the head of the family. My father looked for me after a time but he couldn't find me.

My father was Director of Customs here for around thirty-five years. Originally, customs did not exist. The first man to found the Customs office was my father. He's now 120 years old and he's still alive. He worked on a contractual basis. The system was that he had to pay the Rulers a certain fixed sum per year. So he had a free hand, (*laughing*). He was also an important pearl dealer—not just one of the small ones. He had ships and slaves and servants, not like other people.

Before I went to Bahrain my father brought a teacher to Qatar for us. We studied the Koran and I also studied Arabic, reading and writing. Even in the customs office itself—at that time school, house and office were all the same place. My father was very concerned that we should be educated. He was one of the first people to register the dates of birth of all his sons. If you ask a lot of people, they don't know when they were born. But he wrote down all our names, mine and my sister's. He had nice handwriting—he himself was educated. People then were taught either in the Koranic schools or, if they had money, they brought clerks from abroad. My father brought clerks from Kuwait and one from Iraq.

He didn't want me to go to Bahrain; he didn't want me to leave here. All fathers at that time were against their sons leaving them because they thought that if their sons were educated in the Lebanon, they would no longer be Muslims but become infidels. People were fanatical then. I remember when I was twelve years old, my mother wanted to go on the Haj and I went with her. Of course, a woman couldn't go without a chaperone. My aunt went with us, also her husband and other relatives. My father didn't want me to go, but my mother did. I made up my mind to go and indeed I went. I rode a camel from here to Medina—it took forty-two days! There was nothing to fear in the desert. There was never any danger. We went as part of a caravan and we slept in the desert. There were fifty of us and there were many other people travelling on the road, so we had nothing to fear as long as we didn't diverge from the beaten track. At the beginning the Al Saud Government in Saudi Arabia was severe and that considerably lessened the danger from looting by bedu tribes. Maybe it was more dangerous in the interior, off the road.

After I had been in Bahrain for a couple of years, I went to Saudi Arabia. I was not the only one to leave Qatar; there were dozens of others like me. This country was bare and entirely with-out resources then. There was no life here. You just lived with your father and mother. There was nothing but the family.

Later I came back to Qatar to live. The money with which I started my printing business in 1955-6 I earned through various contracting jobs. Of course, I was planning to create this printing business so I began by buying some small machines. Gradually I inched my way forward, until today I own almost the biggest printing press in the whole region, all offset, all colours.

It was the first printing press here. Previously, if people wanted things printed, they would send them out to Kuwait or Bahrain or Beirut. At first I used the press for commercial purposes, printing letterheads, envelopes etc. The operatives came from Jordan or Beirut. But I had it in mind to produce a newspaper. It was called *al Oroba* newspaper, published weekly. Then after some time I changed the name and licence and called it a magazine. I took a second licence for *al Arab* newspaper.

This was an experiment as far as this country was concerned. We progressed slowly. But, quite honestly, the first issue was not bad. But it was hard work and we lost money on it for the first four years. A year after *al Oroba* was published as a magazine, we began to feel we had got over the worst and our job became easier. At first, readers here hadn't a clue what a magazine meant. But gradually they began to understand the importance of reading a local paper. When we started to publish *al Arab*, we printed 200 to 300 copies only. Now we publish 9,000 copies a day. It was difficult. There was no news. And there were few readers. But, nowadays, if the newspaper hasn't reached the shops by eight o'clock in the morning, we are besieged by telephone calls and with people weeping, wailing, or cursing on the line. So people have become interested in newspapers.

My sons and I are all one hundred per cent patriotic in what we write. The policy of our paper is to support first Qatar, then the Gulf, then the Arab world. And I think it wouldn't do any harm for me to tell you that we want unity. What is important to us is the unity of the Arab world as a whole. Our nationalism is known. We are pro-Arab. We stick to this line. But, of course, as Qataris, our country is more important to us than any other country.

After all these years I am still a working journalist and at the same time I run a printing business. We print commercially, books and other materials. The Government is one of our clients. But we specialise in importing and selling paper; we are agents for paper companies. We import all kinds of stationery, also office equipment and furniture.

Of course, I also get involved in other business ventures that arise and I am both shareholder and partner in other companies. I take on some contracting, but only as a small-scale operator these days—I used to do more in the past. I already have a registered company which I am reactivating, because contracting has become more profitable. I'm waiting for an engineer before I can go on. I want to construct some buildings. I know that other contractors will take at least 60 per cent profit on them—I know all about their profits—so why not derive the benefit from my own land? These buildings will cost in the region of 40 million *riyals*. But if I build them myself, they'll cost less, won't they? I can get an 80 per cent loan, from abroad—I have many contacts outside this country. In three to four years I will recover my capital. This is because rents here are very high. And the Government can't take over the entire construction business. How can it? We are only a small country and without private enterprise no one would build. Land is very costly now. My land cost me ten million *riyals*; the building itself will cost between ten and fifteen million, at least. Right? If I didn't get my money back very soon I'd sell the building and never have anything to do with construction again. If I and others did this the Government would lose, the country would lose. In the meantime, the Government wants everyone to build. In about five or ten years maybe they'll put the brakes on because no more buildings will be needed. But from now and for the next ten years there are still plenty of opportunities.

That's where the big money is—in construction. But con-tractors face a number of difficulties. Sometimes they can't get hold of cement; and sometimes they can't get electricity and water installed. The town is expanding rapidly and it's impossible for the services to catch up.

On the other hand, contractors all want to put up two, three or four buildings simultaneously and so they spread their efforts too widely. They're greedy, so they take on more work than they can cope with.

My contracting work I deal with directly, but most of my other business goes through agencies. Between eighty and ninety per cent of my business is with agencies. Without agencies I wouldn't work. I have some exclusive agencies; if the products are sold to other people I take a commission.

I was the first person in this country to deal in paper products and for a long time I had no competitors. But nowadays there are a lot of stationers and a lot of people importing. Of course, there is competition today, but I don't think it counts for too much because of the long delays that port congestion creates. Besides, whatever the product, the name of the company still counts for a lot. Profits here are reasonable: between 60 per cent and 70 per cent. Although clothes shops can take up to 500 per cent. My wife owns a clothes shop.

In truth, I'm a businessman. My life is business, it's in my blood, it rules my soul. I must go to the international exhibitions. I'm keen on travelling, taking on new agencies. That's why I've been successful. But I still like journalism in spite of the fact that I'm a businessman.

My sons have taken over 60 per cent on the journalistic side. I just deal with the politics in the paper. I don't read anything that is not political, but all that is I check and edit carefully. We are a small country and we depend on having friendly relations with other countries. We don't want to stir up controversies or touch on sensitive points. Even if circumstances allowed us to be free to write what we want, we wouldn't do so. International friendship is too important to us, friendship with Arab countries, Asian countries. If we want to criticise a country, we do so without actually naming it. We apply the brakes. The principle and aim of journalism is service: service to a company, to a name and also to a country. Not many businessmen serve their country as I do. One day it will be said that I was the first man to start journalism here.

My sons—I have sons from two wives—aren't all identical. They are different from one another, but I bring them up properly—that is to say, not to waste money. Before my sons came back from university I was alone here and could suit myself, spend my money as I wanted, eat as I wanted. When they came back I wanted to make them realise the importance of order in life, so what I did was this: I fixed salaries for everybody in the family, sons, my wife and even the smaller children.

Once I had paid them their salaries I said to them: 'I am not responsible now even for your food. You can go down to the *souk* and buy what you need. Take your salaries and from now on you must depend on yourselves. I won't give you anything from the house.' I gave them a house to themselves. The boys who haven't yet married are living with their mother, who also has a salary. My daughter at university has a salary and even little Khalife has one. He gets two hundred *riyals* a month—that's a salary too. If he asks me for money I just tell him to live on his salary. He laughs and says it doesn't matter.

But I am sixty years old now and I've got to rest a bit. When it comes to money, people are always ambitious to acquire more. They never think of death—that's a human failing. I have a house in the Lebanon and a house in London. I chose to buy a house in Chelsea because, after carrying out a wide survey, I discovered that Chelsea is a respectable, quiet and aristocratic area. Some other parts of London are not like that, not nice at all; you find unbelievable things there. But Chelsea is quiet, and it's a long way

away from those areas where you find every different kind of
nationality all mixed, as in Earl's Court, for example.

Last summer I spent three months in London. I had a complete medical check up and had false teeth fitted and spectacles
made. I went there at the State's expense—the State pays for our
medical treatment. My family was with me—my wife and my
sons. I don't stay up late at night myself. By ten o'clock I'm
asleep, whether in Qatar or in London, because I wake up early.
That's the way I live. I have lots of English friends in London,
also lots of people from our country went to London last summer.
So much of the time we visited each other. Exactly like in Qatar.

One day I shall have to retire. I am famous as an amateur stamp
collector. I am the number one and best—the greatest stamp collector in all Qatar. I have stamps the Post Office long to have in
their possession but can't lay their hands on. And in addition to
stamps, I like collecting old currency. You may ask why? One
day I'm going to retire, like I said. What shall I do? Sleep? I need
something to keep me occupied. So I'll do gardening and stamp
collecting and acquiring old currency. It will keep me entertained.
What would you expect me to do—sit waiting for death? I
couldn't bear it. I want to do something which keeps my heart
happy. I'll work within limits. I'll stick to my albums. I'll enjoy
the old things and my memories.

The Head of the Department of Religion

Islam to me and to any other Muslim, means preserving Islamic
teachings, the directions of the Koran and the path that was
adopted by our forefathers. It is to guide us to follow the directions
put forth to us by our prophet Mohammed, God Bless Him and
Give Him Peace.

However, every person also has his own goal. As for myself I
was brought up since my childhood as a searcher of knowledge.
My trade is knowledge; my ambition is to learn. I am very keen to

follow the instructions of Islam. I am anxious that as long as I live I should be useful to other Muslims by offering guidance. Islam calls for co-operation in this life. Islam has made our path very clear. It instructs us to fear God, to shun evil.

To be a good Muslim a person must apply the five pillars of Islam. To witness that there is no other God but God and Mohammed is his messenger; to worship (prayers); to pay alms for poor (*zakat*); to fast in the month of Ramadan and to carry out the pilgrimage to Mecca if possible. The pillars of faith mean to believe in Allah, and his Messengers, and His Scriptures and the Last Day, as well as fate (good or bad). Goodness is to enjoin right conduct and forbid indecency for God sees you even if you do not see him. A Muslim should not only believe these things at heart, but must also apply these beliefs practically. He who follows the good path enjoys the Almighty's blessing. If he follows the path of evil he would be remote from God, he would incur God's displeasure and therefore his fate would be hell.

God Almighty described paradise in many verses of the Koran: 'And Gardens where enduring pleasure will be theirs.' 'There are the fair ones with wide lovely eyes, like unto hidden pearls.' Muslims are immortal in paradise. They do not fall ill. They do not feel miserable. They do not suffer fever. They do not feel sad. They do not sleep. They spend all their time in pleasure, affection and harmony. The greatest blessing of God to those who enter the Paradise is that they can look at the Almighty. They assemble there once a week and look at God. Such a sight is worth more than all the happiness they enjoy in heavens.

It is said than an old woman came to the prophet, God Bless him and Give Him peace, and said, 'O messenger of God, please ask the Lord to admit me to Paradise'. The Prophet answered her jokingly that no old woman enters Paradise. She left crying. The Prophet called her and said smilingly 'Haven't you read the Koran?' She said, 'No.' He told her that she would be young again for the Lord said, 'We have created them anew. And made them virgins, lovers, friends.' He (the Prophet) added, 'You will be a thousand times more beautiful than when you were young.'

You might ask whether we imagine Paradise as green and pleasant because on earth we live in a desert where there is no water or shades of trees. On the contrary, trees, valley, rivers and flowers are samples of Paradise which God has shown us in the world. But they are not the same as those in Paradise. Nor is the wine of Paradise like that of the world. In Paradise there are 'rivers of wine delicious to the drinker' which do not harm man's liver or make him feel intoxicated. In Paradise there are rivers of milk and honey. There is no heat.

There are no monks and no priests in Islam. The most learned, religious person in Islam still carries on a normal life. He trades, works, goes to the *souk*. There are grades of religious men. This depends on each person's knowledge of religion. Any man can lead the prayers in a mosque.

An Imam is a religious person who explains religion and the way to worship God and who has followers adopting his creed. This is the general meaning, applying to such as Al Shafil, Ahmed and Malik, who collected the Prophet's directives and sayings. They also laid down Islamic legal rules. They devoted their lives to studying religion but none of them considered himself a priest or isolated himself from others. The Prophet did not isolate himself but used to sit with others and considered himself equal to them.

Praise be to Allah, Lord of the Worlds, the first time I went on pilgrimage I was twenty-three in the years 1361 of the Higra. I am now in my late fifties and I have been to Mecca several times. When I first went on pilgrimage I stood in awe of the glory of that occasion. I felt as if I possessed the whole world. I forgot everything else when I looked at the 'Kaabah' and when I started going around it. I found myself bursting into tears although I felt a great happiness when I stood at Arafat. I was so thrilled to achieve something that I had considered a great dream. Since then I have made the pilgrimage about thirty-four times, thanks to God. When there were fewer pilgrims they seemed more submissive and more God-fearing. More of the pilgrims then were poor and a believer who is not rich is always more submissive to

Sheikh Hamad bin Khalifa al-Thani, the Heir-Apparent
(in white *thaub*) talking to his younger brothers, Sheikh
Abdullah and Sheikh Mohammed, with (on the left) his
uncle Ali bin Hamad al-Attiyah

Vegetable market in Doha

Pouring coffee for guests in a *diwan*

God. Those who become rich get more absorbed with their wealth and their ambitions become more worldly. When a man has more love and faith in the Lord he is devoted to Him, but if he has more love for the world, for higher positions, leadership in Government departments and cars and luxuries, air conditioners, his desire in the Hereafter becomes less.

Jesus's message is recognised by us. No one would become a true Muslim unless he believed in the message of Jesus. If a person says There is no God but God and that Muhammed is the messenger of God and does not recognise and believe in Jesus as a messenger of God, such a person would not be considered as a Muslim. But Islam worships Allah as being unique while Christianity makes Allah one of three; the Father, the Son and the Holy Spirit; Islam does not accept that the Almighty should have a partner. Jesus himself called for the worship of one God. But misinterpretation of the Bible led to Trinitarianism.

In Christianity a man is allowed to marry one wife while in Islam he is allowed to marry four. How, you may ask, could this be since women have equal rights to men? Islam respects the woman more than any other religion. Islam aims to give the woman her rights and enables her to accomplish her ambitions. When the Almighty created men and women he made men in charge of women. You can see that fighting, tough business and heavy work is for men and not for women. Originally man has been created physically stronger than woman. That is why women are tender and soft and they need to be taken care of. God created man for hard and tough things but woman is created mainly for the continuation of the human race. She is put in charge of the most important mission of bringing up the children.

Islam does allow women to work. During the time of the Prophet and his Caliphs, women used to join the army, taking with them medicines to heal the sick and the wounded; they carried water and arms. We have no objection to such work, but we do not approve of her working as a dancer or so. Islam does not approve of letting a woman go out at large and so lose her respect among others. Islam wants her to be something of nature and not to be made cheap.

Some Muslims marry more than one wife without recognising the orders of Islam to be equally just to all. This is irreligious. The youth have been affected by Western traditions and prefer to have one wife. There are also other factors. Now people are more and more engaged in studies and are busier at work than before. That is why a young man does not want to be occupied with more than one wife. Of course, education and our relations with the world have an effect on the views of the younger people on marriage. Both educated and non-educated Qatari women object to their husband having more than one wife. The non-educated are more fanatically against the idea. An educated woman who has studied Islam can understand the religious justifications for having more than one wife. But the non-educated is the one you cannot argue with. The poet said; 'It is a catastrophe to talk to one who does not admit his ignorance or one who does not understand.' Therefore, the educated women are more able to be convinced.

Islam is a flexible religion. If you look at what we have been allowed to do and what we have been forbidden to do you find that we have been forbidden to commit those things that are not approved by any good person. We have been allowed to do the things that are acceptable by all good people. Islam does keep up with changes in civilisation, provided that they do not affect our moral values.

The Multi-Millionaire Businessman

Sultan is in his late thirties, tall and powerfully built with immensely broad shoulders and curly black hair—an energetic character with great charm which with typical Arabian caution he holds in reserve until his judgement is made. He is an enormously rich businessman to whom gain is not the name of the game. His pleasure in business is derived from the intellectual challenge; like a chess-player, he always thinks several moves ahead in business and in other things. For example, having worked out that children finishing their education in the Gulf only end school at twenty, he has decided to send his sons so school in England, so that they will finish earlier and speak fluent English into the bargain. One is going to Eton, the other to Harrow: a kind of controlled educational experiment. He is curious to see which school will produce the better result. Hopefully, they will then go on to Harvard. Another interesting educational experiment: cross-fertilising the best of British and American education.

He lives in a pleasant but by no means spectacular house from which he will soon be moving into a new luxury villa. Some idea of the rocketing land prices in the Gulf can be gained from the fact that he was recently offered twelve million *riyals* (which he refused) for a piece of land he bought two years ago at just one and a half million *riyals*. The plan for the villa was drawn up by British architects in Singapore, on the basis of his own suggestions. There is a separate entrance for guests so that they can come and go without disturbing anyone. A dining-room table moves up and down by a switch, so that one can choose to eat either Arab or Western fashion. There is a small Arab dining-room beside the main one where one can eat sitting on the floor. In the garden are a sauna and covered swimming pool. He has done away with the showiest suggestions—and the bookcase in the sitting-room. Why should he allow other people to see what he reads, he observes with a humorous glint in his eye? A man who is not easily checkmated.

We are agents for Peugeot and Citroen and for Mack trucks from America. But now we are concentrating mainly on big industry, as agents representing large companies for big projects. We help them to make contact with the Government; if they undertake a project, we help them expedite the work through the supply of labour, transport, Government formalities etc. For example, nearly two years ago we succeeded in obtaining a steel project contract for Kobe Steel of Japan which, jointly with the Government, will produce 400,000 tons of steel every year. The project is under construction at Umm Said and will start production at the end of 1977. The Government wants foreign companies to come and help Qatar to develop, but it also wants local companies to share in the overall benefit. If a foreign company is going to build or to make something locally in Qatar, it is absolutely essential for them to have an agent. This has been Government policy for more than thirty years.

Another example of our business is an energy project in Qatar to liquefy the gas we are now producing. It's being undertaken by a Japanese company called Mitsubishi; we are agents of Mitsubishi and Shioda.

My family started up a business here in 1958 when I was fifteen, before the oil money really began to flow—a transport company to take pilgrims from Qatar to Mecca. The journey lasted twenty-five to thirty days each way. We had big, used trucks bought from the American army and rebuilt by us. We had breakdowns most of the time. That's why we took a month on the journey. Normally, it wouldn't take more than fifteen or sixteen days. We used to travel twenty trucks together.

Usually we carried about 1,000 passengers. We had to take a lot of big water tanks with us, but the water was always hot because we had no ice to keep it cold. We did have a way of cooling water, though. We used to fill thousands of small canvas bags: in the night the water in the bags would cool—because it was often cold in the desert at night—and we would drink this water during the day. Our price included everything: water, food, accommodation in Mecca. We used to charge about fifty US dollars per person. In those days if you had a thousand dollars you could buy half the world. A camel cost only three dollars. People would usually go only once in their life to Mecca. Nearly 20 per cent of our passengers were women. We carried them separately in cars.

Eventually we stopped taking pilgrims to Mecca, but meanwhile we began the first transport service by road to Lebanon. There was no road to Lebanon and Syria then, only desert. We crossed the desert and brought back fruit from Lebanon to Saudi Arabia and Qatar. We used to take guides to show us the way. We used the same lorries as for the Haj: after the Haj we would go to Lebanon. There was a big demand for the fruit. Everybody bought it, not just the sheikhs.

Then in 1957 I went to the Damascus International Exhibition where I saw European cars. We got the agency in Qatar for Peugeot, Fiat and Citroen. If we had had enough money at the time we could have taken most of the agencies. But we didn't have the capital to buy so many cars, paying cash in advance before we started to sell them. At that time, in 1958–9, some Qataris began to have money, and the cars were very cheap.

In that same year, 1959, I went to England to study business administration for four years. That's how I learned English. I went to Brighton first, to the Technical College to learn English. It was hard at first. I used to go to school in the morning, I had a special teacher in the afternoon and in the evening I took correspondence classes on how to write business letters in English. To pay for my studies we had to borrow money from the bank—that was on top of the money we already had to borrow for the business. The Government offered to pay for me, so did Sheikh Jassim who was Education Minister at the time. I refused the money. I felt shy about accepting because I didn't intend to work for the Government when I came back. I wanted to run my own business.

I was very happy in England. I lived with a family all the time; I paid them three guineas a week for bed, breakfast, lunch and dinner. I had some Iranian and Iraqi friends and we gathered together every Friday and made our own food. We used to buy a small lamb and make a special meal.

We have a lot of English agencies. But unfortunately we have not yet taken on a big project with these agencies. We have projects of one million or two million pounds, but not any really big ones. The reason? Well, English prices are no longer competitive with the Japanese: they are often nearly 30 per cent higher than Japanese prices. And often the English don't follow the matter through seriously enough. They don't study the situation sufficiently carefully before they put their prices up. I have been dealing with the Japanese for five years and it is unbelievable the way they calculate prices and costs. Sometimes the Japanese come to us and ask: 'We are going to fix our prices like this—what do you think?' We give them an idea, yes or no. This will work, this won't, this is expensive, this is cheap, and so on. We discuss the matter with them. Well, the English never do this. Everything is top secret as far as they are concerned. But being an agent, you are in a position to help; otherwise why bother to have an agent? The English never consult. And because they look at Qatar as if it belonged to them, they don't think they need much help. This is a big mistake.

I learnt a lot myself in England: how to manage companies financially, how to treat customers, how to deal with your mail every day. I read a lot of books about business administration then and I still do.

When I came back in 1963, I was working in my own company so I could make my own mistakes without anyone noticing. I could afford to make mistakes and I wasn't ashamed to ask for advice. When I started, actually, we didn't have much business. Even half-an-hour a day was enough to finish the work I had to do. Then I gradually became more and more busy. People nowadays don't just come in unannounced, but then, when they did, we couldn't do anything: we just sat and had coffee and talked. But I used to have two offices and no desks in my offices. So if people came who wanted just to sit and drink tea, I would put them in one office and say: 'Excuse me for one minute' and go and do business in the other office before going back to them. If I needed a desk I'd go to the Pakistani accountant's office and sit at his desk. If someone came I'd leave the accountant to his work and go to my office to talk with them.

When I first came back I was in partnership with my four brothers. We were heavily in debt. I thought that it would be best if we all split up and worked on our own as we were not getting on well together. My different background made it difficult. For instance, when I came back I wanted to sell cars for cash. I wanted to advertise. I wanted to buy more cars and borrow from the banks to pay for them. Some banks said: 'We don't believe Arab promises. You may not pay.' So I said, 'OK, try me and see.' Soon we were paying the bank back.

A lot of people wanted to buy cars then, but we didn't have the money to buy them, nor the spare parts, nor the mechanics, etc. So my first move was to go to Paris to buy cars and spare parts. I bought fifty cars at once, with money borrowed from the bank. Then I advertised: 'If you buy a Peugeot car and have trouble getting spare parts, you will be given twenty dollars daily while your car is out of action.' As it only cost five dollars a day to rent a replacement car, people thought this was nonsense. But we had the spare parts. . . . We carried out our promise. In three cases we had to admit we had no spare parts. We kept the customers' cars in the garage and paid them twenty dollars every day. Soon they were spreading the news all over the country. People started coming to buy cars, paying six or eight months in advance.

By 1969 we thought that the car business was not big enough, there was not enough future in it, so we started on large projects. The first one we were involved in was at Umm Said, a water desalinisation project. Then I created a mechanical-electric contracting company to build this project. We now have a company called Manco (Mechanical and Electrical Engineering).

This is how we succeeded in getting this contract. They wanted a subcontractor. So I said, 'OK, we can be subcontractors'. I went to Lebanon and asked some Lebanese to give me a quotation to erect the project. They provided it, I came back, added my commission to the bill and gave it to the company in question saying, 'This is my price for the project.' It was cheaper than the price of another company, so they agreed. Then I took the tender and commissioned the Lebanese to start building. After that the Lebanese didn't leave but stayed on and are still working with me, in my company.

We are now engaged in very big projects, another water desalinisation plant and a cement factory. We fitted gas turbines and built the power station at Ras Abu Fontas, supplied by Mitsubishi. One of my advantages at the beginning was that I had good contacts. I travel a lot and I always take with me letters from banks and embassies, and recommendations from other people. I go to Lebanon where I know people; I ask them to find out things for me. I don't send other people, I go myself. For instance we have one of the largest transport companies here. I went to Korea last month and made an agreement with the largest Korean transport company to take on the management of my own company. Now the Koreans are very successfully running my company here.

An important ingredient of our success is that we have a top class company doing our accounting. In Arab countries generally, we are still not up to date in our accounting methods. There is a tendency to look for cheap people, while in my company we look for the most expensive—it gives you more business.

My studies helped me a lot from the very beginning. If I had not studied in England, mixed with English people and taken the correspondence classes, I would not have achieved as much as I have. To ensure success one needs good management and sound financial direction. Our company is now doubling its turnover every year.

I enjoy it all very much. I don't mind working seventeen hours, sometimes eighteen, until two o'clock in the morning. It's the work I enjoy, I don't care about the money. I mean, I have a lot of money. If I wanted to live in any country in the world I could do so and support my wife and children, but I enjoy business. I think people should work even if they have money; they shouldn't sit idle. I soon get fed up with activities which are not connected with my business. I can't read a book for more than one hour a day. I read newspapers; I read the *Financial Times* and *Newsweek*. But books, not much. In my spare time, mostly I am invited or invite people to my home. They're not always business invitations. A few years ago we used to gather with our Qatari friends almost every night, but now we don't meet even once a week. It is sad, but times change.

In our office it's difficult to meet people because of interruptions by visitors, so I like to discuss important business in the evening or over dinner. If Qataris come to the office they will meet some of my employees, but they like to meet me as a friend. It's an insult to them to be told that I'm busy. The personal friendship angle is still very important in Arabia, even in business. I think friendship comes first. Western businessmen have come all the way from Europe to visit you, so you must respect this and give them a friendly reception. As far as Arabs are concerned, if you are not friendly with them, they want nothing to do with you; they won't ever come and see you.

As for the past, we have lost something of course, but I don't think it's good to cry over what you've lost. I am very happy with the present, with the Government of the country and with my business. My special ambition is to try and create more industries in this country. Last year we began a joint venture with a British company in steel structures. We import the finished steel from Japan or America and we manufacture from it platforms for the sea, sheds, foundations for big factories etc. We cut and weld and design ourselves. We are interested to develop our manufacturing side further. But we have problems with manpower and the delivery of all the materials. When we set up our steel manufactur-ing project we were nearly six months without any steel because of shipping delays from the UK and Japan. But I don't foresee our rate of expansion slowing down much in the near future. The country is getting bigger and bigger, there is more money and more people are coming in. We have a lot of resources: we have oil, we have gas. We will continue to develop our industries and bring in more people to work here.

We are thinking now of starting more consumer industries, such as vegetable oils. I am one of the directors of the Qatar Plastics Company which plans to produce all kinds of plastics, household appliances and paper. The Emir is setting up a national company, the National Light Industry Company, which will produce a wide range of consumer items like oils, soap, paper, carpets. This will bring prices down and relieve port congestion.

We have about four Qataris working for us in a company staff of 1,500. Most Qataris prefer to work for the Government or run their own business. We would like to employ more Qataris and we pay more than the Government, but people think working as a civil servant is easier. Besides, it's easy to set up your own business, although you may not have much of a profit unless you have new ideas or agencies.

I liked the old days when we ran trucks to Mecca, very much. Now we are more sophisticated, but at that time we were healthier. We were happy, we didn't think about business. Now we don't walk at all, we take no exercise. Before, we used to walk all the time. The problem is that here there are no sports grounds, no clubs and swimming pools to join. I have a swimming pool in my home, and I have swum in it only twice in two years. I travel so much. Actually I am now building a big swimming pool in my new house, under cover, inside the house, which one can use throughout the year. It's air conditioned in summer and heated in winter.

Having money has made life easier than before, having a comfortable house, comfort in travelling: I spend a lot of money. I have two drivers, one cook, three boys and two nannies. We are six in the family, four children, my wife and myself. My wife complains about my hard work; she doesn't like me to work like that. I can't help it. I leave my house every morning at five-thirty or six o'clock. I became accustomed to this when I was young, so I still keep to it. Sometimes I relax, when I travel. My wife travels with me and in the school holidays the children come too. We used to go to Lebanon a lot. I have two houses in Lebanon, one in Beirut and one in the mountains. And we have a good air service from here to Beirut. I used to take the family nearly every two months, but the closure of Beirut has made it very difficult for us. The only place for us to go now, as a family, is London. In other countries there is the language problem. For me it doesn't make much difference, but for my family it does. Last year we spent Christmas and New Year in Las Palmas in the Canary Islands. We didn't enjoy it. It was very cold and windy, and nobody spoke English, not even the hotel operators and taxi drivers.

I suppose one day I'll not work so much. I will travel more. It would still be business, but not as hard as now. For instance, now I go to London for two days and come back. If there were other people running my company here, I could go and stay one month. I go to Japan and come back within seven or ten days. I would like to sit still more and relax.

2. THE OIL MEN

Servant of the State

I came into the oil industry by design. I graduated in 1962 from high school and when I went to college I wanted to do petroleum engineering. Later on I changed my mind and I did my studies in geology. But I think I was the first person who wanted to be a petroleum engineer; I was the first Qatari to start, at least. When I was still at school here in Doha, we used to be taken on trips to the oil fields, and to the small refineries at Umm Said, and I got interested in oil. I saw the oil installations, the rigs where they were drilling. It was fascinating to see something coming out of the ground that is worth such a lot of money.

As a petroleum engineering student I had to take some courses in geology, and then I became fascinated by the geology. Geology is closer to nature and its working than is petroleum engineering. I thought that I could be as useful to the country, as we needed geologists as well as petroleum engineers. I graduated from the United States in 1968.

The first oil well was drilled here, I think, in 1941. It was covered up because of the war and after the war they resumed drilling. The first shipment of crude oil took place in 1949. I don't really know how much money came from that but I believe it followed the oldest concession agreement in Qatar which provided for a royalty of three rupees a ton, in addition to a nominal rental of the concession areas.

I remember when Doha was nothing but a couple of strips of houses along a ditch. I first felt the influence of oil when QPC (Qatar Petroleum Company) offered a bus to our school, and that was probably in 1952. Everybody was in favour of the oil, there wasn't any feeling against it. Everybody talked about how the oil would affect the country, but nobody dreamt it would develop in the way it did develop, not at that time. The first real effect of oil money was felt in the late 50s when the Government started spending money on building roads, Government buildings, on the medical services and expanding education. The second stage was when the Shell Oil Company started production in the mid 60s. All the road building, medical services, all the social benefits expanded. After the 1973 oil price increase, the scale of develop‑ ment and the amount of expenditure was again noticeably increased.

Before I left for the States to study, the only places I had been to were Bahrain, Abu Dhabi and Dubai. I went to the States in 1962. I felt terribly homesick. For the first few days I felt ready to cry. I was about eighteen or nineteen at the time. Life there was so completely different from Qatar. There were so many things that distressed me. The food, for example, presented a real difficulty: I didn't know how to order in a restaurant. And then when I did manage to cope with that, the food I got was different from the food I was used to. And life seemed very complex compared with the easy life we were used to out here. Family ties have always been strong here. You don't have to depend on yourself for much, because you are always protected by your parents. Then, all of a sudden, you are propelled into a very strange country where you don't know anybody at all. Then, I didn't understand the language. It took me three to four months to understand what people were saying. When I could talk to people I was able, at last, to make friendships and things got easier from then on. I lived in the country for six years and after a time I got used to it.

I think that some people, when they leave and go abroad, forget what their own countries are like. A lot of Arab students in par‑ ticular when they had finished their studies and were ready to go back, expected their countries to have changed very much in their absence and to have come much closer to the kind of life they had become used to in the United States. But I never had this idea. I had no illusions as to what I would find in my country. I knew I would have to re‑adjust. I mean, I didn't expect the people in this country to adjust themselves to me. For someone like me who knew only one society and a fairly small group of people, the experience of living abroad was very helpful: it taught me so many things, to depend on myself for one thing. This is a great change in any person's life, to be totally dependent on any group—parents, family—and then for a period of six years to rely only on oneself.

I was also impressed by American efficiency. Qatar has never been a business-oriented society. We were a semi-nomadic community living for the most part at subsistence level. But now we are developing and moving closer to Western civilisation or, at least, to certain aspects of it, such as industrialisation. So we have to adapt in some ways, notably as far as running our industry and business is concerned.

The most logical place for you to start is the place where you are working. I don't know how much I have achieved, but I know that everybody else in my generation is also thinking about this kind of thing. The older generation had a way of life which was really beautiful, I think, but it's not suited to industrial development.

When I came back in 1968, I was employed by the Department of Petroleum Affairs as a geologist, but I wasn't doing geology as such, or what I really wanted. I wanted to work for one of the oil companies, either QPC or Shell, for at least two years, but since I was only the second Qatari to be employed in a senior position in the department my superiors decided that I should stay there. The function of this department is to supervise the oil companies. I thought that if I worked with one of the oil companies and then joined the department, I could be more useful to it because I would at least know more about the practices of the oil companies, and I am still very sorry that I didn't have the chance. In this department, as in other departments, they wanted as many Qataris as they could lay their hands on—there were only seven Qatari graduates in the whole of the Department of Petroleum Affairs.

My main aim at that time was to learn as much as I could about the operations of the two oil companies here, which were Shell and QPC. QPC, at that time, was run by IPC (Iraq Petroleum Company). I was particularly interested in how they dealt with technical matters, with petroleum engineering and geology. I wanted to find out about the geology of my own country. It was scientific curiosity, in part. It was also my job to discover whether the oil companies were doing what they ought to be doing, namely producing oil in the most economic way, for the least number of cents per barrel. We were particularly concerned to understand how they spent their money, especially as the operational costs were deducted from taxes and royalties. In case of waste, this country stood to lose.

The other purpose of the Department was to see whether the oil companies were really doing their best to discover new petroleum reserves. Instead of sitting on one giant field, like the Dukhan field, they should be exploring for new fields, even if these turned out to be smaller and less economic. This was their duty within the terms of our contract with them. But of course, the oil companies—like any other economic enterprise—were most interested in the fields which would give them the highest return for investment.

In the 1930s the oil companies used to pay the Qatar State three rupees per ton royalty. When I first joined the Department in 1968, I think the tax was 55 per cent of the net income, and royalties stood at $12\frac{1}{2}$ per cent. So the oil companies were making a lot of money. I don't think that many people were well-informed about the situation and, besides, it was current throughout the whole area. Because it wasn't special to Qatar I don't think very many people thought about it, with the exception of the top authorities and the officials in the Department of Petroleum Affairs. Then the Organisation of Petroleum Exporting Countries (OPEC) appeared and began to study the oil situation in general—and pricing was a very important element. Tax and royalties were being re-studied, and the moves to limit the incomes of the oil companies relative to that of the host country began to be made. At least, ideas tending in this direction were current at the time. Gradually, taxes and royalties were increased and in 1974, I believe, royalties were increased to 20 per cent and tax to 80 or 85 per cent. This still left the oil companies with a good profit. I felt quite strongly about this situation at the time, because I knew what the full implications were. That is to say, I knew the oil companies were making a lot of money that they were not really entitled to.

Another change since I joined the Department was the acquisi-

tion by the Government of a 25 per cent share holding in both
Shell and QPC. This rose to 60 per cent and now we have taken
over QPC and Shell. The existence of OPEC is mainly responsible for this development. When the oil-producing countries got
together they were able to achieve more than they had in the past
when each of them was dealing with the oil companies alone. The
oil companies had a lot of power in the past, you know. The
existence of OPEC also served to make public opinion in general
more aware of certain facts, namely that the oil companies really
make much more or, at least, they used to make much more, than
the host Governments. I have met many Western people who have
come to realise that this was true in the past. I can't say I know
much about the general public in the West but I talk to many
people in the oil business and I think they now understand the
situation. Local people here read a lot about politics and everything, and I think they are very well-informed on the oil situation,
or at least they have been since the late 60s. People knew there was
something wrong. I've discussed the subject with many people.
Most Qataris—and this is true of myself—are in contact with more
than just one particular sector of society. I mean, we talk every day
to different kinds of people, to people in high positions, to colleagues and to relatives. This is a place where everybody talks to
everybody. There are no class distinctions.

There will be some changes when we take over. The oil business
in Qatar is not yet run completely by Qatari nationals. We don't
intend that every position should be Qatarised. But we want the
Western staff who are still working in the oil companies and the
Petroleum Authority to be directed, policy-wise, by Qatari
nationals, and to be working directly for us. I think that that will
make a great difference. The oil companies had one thing in mind
and that was to make as much money out of the concession as
possible. Although commercial considerations will remain
important to us, at the same time we shall have to think about the
people employed in the industry, about their welfare status, we will
have to take better care of the environment. There are many things
to be considered. When the oil companies put out a tender, they

were concerned only to negotiate the cheapest possible price. Even if a local company, owned by a local person, were able to perform the same service at almost the same price, and almost as efficiently, they would plump for the cheapest offer which would usually be made by a foreign company. I think we have to re-examine the situation so that not all contracts are given to foreigners, that not so much money goes abroad. If part of the money stays here, I think it can contribute towards developing the country. This way our oil income will be more evenly distributed around the country. When you give a contract to a local contractor he will probably employ more people than would a foreign firm. The Japanese firm which is doing some work at Umm Said, brings everything, and all its manpower, from Japan.

The foreign companies never trained enough locals. When you walk into an office like this, how many Qataris do you see? How many Indians do you see, how many Westerners? We only took over last October so we haven't had much time so far, but we want to do a lot. We have seconded staff: these are people who are working for the old share-holding company, QPC. We have a service contract with QPC and one of the conditions of this contract is that they will supply the staff. They supply staff for varying periods of time: one year, two years. We want to find suitable people—not necessarily Qataris—to replace such seconded staff at the end of their term with the service companies. We should of course try to get a Qatari, and if we didn't succeed we would get another Arab. We don't want to depend on foreign oil companies for ever. We have a service agreement with the companies for the next five years. Some of the people now working for QPC can stay on if they are willing to work for the Qatar Petroleum Producing Authority, our national organisation.

Our objective is to employ as many Qataris as possible. We shall try to introduce training programmes for Qataris who are now in QPA and for those who might join in the future. We think we still have a good chance of finding enough Qataris to work for us; not all Qataris have enough capital to open a business. It's true that the Qataris won't accept the lower paid jobs, as labourers and lower ranking technicians. We shall be concentrating on the middle range technicians and University graduates.

Our main long-term objective, besides Qatarisation and mini-mising the costs of production, is to study all possible means of increasing our oil and gas reserves. At the present production level and depletion rate, our oil reserves will last until the year 2000. We know we have more oil reserves but they haven't been developed yet because of technical difficulties. The Iddel Shargi field which is the oilfield closest to Doha has a second dome south of the one at present being worked, and we know that there is quite a large oil accumulation under it. This area has been drilled and tested. Of course, we can't see these domal structures which reveal the presence of oilfields, but they can be detected seismically. The offshore oil formations are usually at a depth of 5,000 to 6,000 feet and you probably wouldn't notice the dome even if you could see beneath the sea. We know we have more oil in certain places, but it can't be exploited with today's technology. but we hope that, since technology is always advancing, one of these days we will be able to produce from these fields.

I used to worry about the oil running out. But not since we discovered we have a lot of gas. We have discovered gas at Dukhan and another very big gas field in the north, offshore. And we know we have gas under each of our present three main oil-fields. That's a lot of gas. It should last us for a hundred years. We shall have enough to run our own industrial projects and be able to export as well.

So I don't think we'll have to go back to a bedu way of life—though I think it was a better way of life really. It was more serene. I think people used to enjoy life more. I don't think we have a choice now. But if we had, I would go back to the old ways. I caught only a glimpse of the old days really. This was during the early part of my life, which is also the most impressionable part of anybody's life. I would go back to that. I don't know why. Perhaps it was the people, the way they used to treat each other, the easy way of life. You didn't have to run after money. Nobody had any money and that made everybody almost equal. Then there was nature itself; we used to live near the sea and the sea was beautiful. You could go swimming and fishing and now you can't do the same things, at least not in Doha. If you want to enjoy the sea you've got to go somewhere else now, either north or south. You can't have the best of both worlds. Now you have to have money, you have to think about catching up with everybody else. It's like a big wave and it carries everybody with it. I remember poverty, but it's not so bad as long as you can have something to eat and still enjoy life, and that's the most important thing. Look at Western civilisation: there are no human relationships between people any more. It's really a sad thing, you know. I'm afraid eventually we'll catch up with the West. From what I remember of the past, if I really had the choice, I'd go back—but I don't want to be alone. Sometimes I discuss this with my friends. They are divided but you still find some who think of the past as having been better. Not that the present is really bad, but maybe the past was better in relation to where we're heading.

From Office Boy to Deputy General Manager

I started as an office boy and I'm proud of it, because it's rare for people to rise from office boy to posts such as the one I hold now, which is Deputy General Manager of the Company.

I remember the day I joined the company. I came to Personnel to apply for the job and was asked to go to the Materials Department. It was difficult for me to remember 'Materials Department', the words I mean. I thought, 'I don't even know how to write English', so I had to take a pencil from someone's desk and write down 'Materials Department' in Arabic. I was taken to the superintendent who, in those days, was a man called Jackson. He is still Materials Superintendent, by the way. I suppose that does satisfy me a bit, (*he laughs*).

I was then sixteen years old. I had had a Koranic school education and it wasn't that good. After I started to work here, I began to read Arabic regularly. I even learned English by myself: I read at home. Because I was very keen to learn English, I was given a part-time teacher by the company after working hours. I borrowed books from the Government schools, and started reading and asking the clerks in the office, what is this, what is that. Some people were very kind, but others got fed up with me. I appreciated those who helped me. Some of them are still working for the company and I'll never forget what I owe them.

From 1954 until 1957 I worked distributing the mail. Then I was made tally clerk. In those days there was no port in Doha. The port was Umm Said and all the ships were off-loaded there, so I used to go and sleep in the ships for two or three weeks to check the incoming cargo. I had to go from ship to ship and then sleep in the barges at night because there was no other place to sleep, no hotel. They just gave me two blankets.

At that time I spoke very little English and I didn't have much contact with English and Dutch people. I don't really like to criticise them, but the Europeans who came here used to be very proud and arrogant. In time, Europeans grew more considerate towards Qataris. I don't think this was a direct result of the oil. There are a lot of Europeans in Doha who are involved in business which has nothing to do with oil. And they became politer than others who came from abroad because people who want to do business have to be courteous and friendly. This didn't start with the British. The British were, in fact, a bit behind. It took them about five to six years to change—I mean to look for business and to be polite to the locals.

While I was tally clerk, they closed this port. I was brought to Ras Abu Aboud to work there in the warehouse. I had a nice English boss there, John Cots was his name. I remember he even used to eat dates. In the morning the operatives brought dates, for their break. He came outside and ate dates with them. He was a really nice guy. It was unusual for a man like that to mix with the locals. Mind you, by being nice and mixing, he got more work out of us than anybody else did.

He said to me one day 'Look, I really think it's time for you to be promoted'. I said 'To what?' He said 'To Intermediate Staff.' This was a big step forward for me, though I wouldn't think so now!

Being Intermediate Staff meant being a full clerk. It also meant I had a little more money. The day I was promoted I got married. They gave me the letter confirming the increase and that evening I married my wife. In those days you couldn't meet a girl and take her out when you wanted to see her. I saw my wife a few times at the house of some relatives. I could observe her but there was no chance for us to talk; in those days it wasn't allowed by the girl's parents. Before marriage I talked to her only once. In my case the marriage wasn't a risk: we are happy together. But, if I were single now, I wouldn't risk marrying a girl whom I had never spoken to.

Later, when I had become Senior Staff, they asked me to go to Bahrain as the company representative there. In Bahrain I replaced an Englishman who went on holiday for three months. I took advantage of the job to make some changes. For example, we had an office there in Manama and also a house to accommodate guests. As the guest house was not always fully occupied I closed the office and we created an office in the guest-house. Naturally the company man there didn't like it very much. But from an econo-mic point of view, it was quite a saving. When I came back to Doha in 1965 they created a post for me as Materials and Admini-strative Supervisor.

After two periods in Nigeria I was sent to the UK. These few weeks there helped me a lot. I'll give you an example. We have a workers' committee here, in the company—in the UK you have unions. Some of the workers in the English refinery were union members and I was surprised how they acted. I used to think before I went that people here in Doha were difficult. But one day when I was in the warehouse working, a man came from the workshop with a compressor to be repaired. The system there, in the refinery, was that if anything needing repairing it would be delivered to the Materials Department by the section concerned, but after repair, it would be delivered back by Materials to the shop. One day there was no car in the shop but there was a vehicle going to the workshop anyhow. I said to one of the people there—he was an Englishman—'Why don't you take this with you and deliver it?' He said 'No, it's not my job.' I said 'Why?'. He said—'If I do it once, they will always expect me to do it!'

It seemed to me a waste of time, since he had come from the workshop to collect something and he was going back there anyhow. Then he told me, 'Look, you are a trainee here, watch it and mind your own business, please.' I did mind my own business after that. I said to myself, 'Why bother, if this is the way they think.'

Still, that period in England changed my ideas. When people here say 'no' to something, I say to myself that this is not the only place in the world where they say 'no'. But it was surprising all the same to find this in Britain where people are supposed to be more educated than us. It made me more tolerant but it didn't make me weak.

In 1972 I was made Head of Materials and Transport, replacing an Englishman who is now in Abu Dhabi. I moved up very fast. But I worked very hard for it. Without boasting, I think I was a good worker and I still am.

Some people do say that the old days were better than today, but I don't see what was good about then. We didn't have all the things we have now, like nice, well-furnished houses, boats, cars. We live a luxurious life now. I don't remember everything because I was a kid, but the old days were not happy days. We slept in the summer without air conditioning. Okay, if you haven't seen an air conditioner, you do without it, but now I can't do without one.

In 1972 I was also given the job of Government and Trade Relations Officer, in addition to my job as Head of Materials. An Englishman had hitherto occupied the job and he left. Eventually, they concluded that the job should be given to a Qatari rather than to an expatriate. Besides, they knew I could handle it. The Trade Relations job was to oil the wheels of our official relations with the Government. If I ask a Government official anything, he knows me and I know him; I just ring the man concerned and say so-and-so.

It is a matter of confidence, you see. This doesn't mean we don't trust Europeans; we do trust them but we get better results from our own people.

I have become a good administrator. But I think if I had my life to live over again, I would become a technical man. I would become a petroleum engineer or something. Our main income here is from oil and so the State needs such people. Some Qataris will be graduating next year and the year after, but I wish we had some Qatari petroleum engineers now. The problem is we didn't do enough about training in the past. It's only within the past year and a half that we have tackled the subject seriously.

Certainly, one of the reasons we can't find enough Qataris to train is because of the money. Many of them are wealthy and when we offer them two thousand two hundred *riyals* a month when they are on training schemes, they say it's not worth their while to work for this. I don't see any solution for this problem at the moment. They have the money and you can't take it away from them. And because there are not so many poor people in Qatar you have to beg people to come and work for you here, to train anyway. I'm really looking forward to seeing the young Qataris come back from the States. Because the Qatari population is small, we don't get enough students to come and learn, they prefer to go from school to university rather than to come and work here. Also many would rather go abroad to study, rather than be trained locally. Then, many of them simply want to go into business; they work with their fathers or relatives. Some of them are educated but they don't want to work with the Government or with us, they prefer to work on their own, independently.

I have money now but I don't think it has changed me. It's nice to have money and it's in human nature that the more you get the more you want. You never stop. This applies to me also because I have money, but I'm still working the private sector to make more money. I make my family happy with it, I make myself happy, I travel. I bought a house in Cairo recently and I am planning to buy one in London shortly. There is a telex on my desk concerning a house in Lebanon which I also plan to buy. It costs six hundred and fifty thousand Lebanese pounds, (about £100,000) which seems quite expensive. We spend our leave in London because we like to go to Europe and the best place there is London. London is like home for us Arabs. Sometimes I travel with a jeweller friend, he buys and so do I. I like jewellery, and when we travel we always have to bring gifts for our relatives and family. That's the custom here. We feel the same way about giving gifts as we do about hospitality. If someone in Qatar invites you to eat, he will slaughter a sheep. You don't really need a sheep—it's too much. But a sheep must be there on the table, not just for Arabs but also for Europeans.

As far as my career is concerned, I'm quite happy as I am. I want to enjoy myself and at the same time serve my country in this job. I don't do this job now for the sake of money, but to help the country. It entails very heavy responsibility, especially as the Government is now taking the company over.

As for the future, when the oil finishes, we shall still have gas enough to last for a century. I wouldn't say that I worry a lot about the oil running out, although I do think about it, yes. It's true that a lot of our new industries are oil-based, but not all of them. I suppose we think that in the long run gas will replace oil. So we don't have to worry.

PART FIVE

The Young Men

'Change here sometimes seems slow. But then when you think of it you realise we've come a long way in a very short time.'

Abdul Aziz, Chartered Accountant

Believe it or not, I was supposed to be a teacher. It's lucky I didn't though. I can't stand too much noise from kids; they need somebody who can accept them. I don't think I could stand it. Nobody forced me to become a teacher, it was my own idea. Quite honestly, it wasn't even planned.

Choosing accountancy—that also wasn't planned. I was good at arithmetic, you see. I liked the subject, so somebody encouraged me to go into accountancy and I did. Do you know something; I'll be the first Qatari to qualify as an accountant? It's nice to be number one.

We don't do much planning, you know, even in our own lives. Ask a Qatari, 'What are you going to do tonight?' He says, 'I don't know'. 'Next weekend?' 'I don't know, I might do this or I might do that.' Then suddenly they do decide and ten minutes later they're off. Sometimes it's nice to act spontaneously like this, but sometimes it creates complications. If you don't plan, you don't get anything done.

Another thing about people here, they are quite reserved; this is a result of their upbringing. They are not encouraged, as children, to form their personalities. This is a mistake that is made in most families. If you join a Qatari *majlis*, when all the kids are present, you will find they are usually ignored and not included in the conversation. 'You shut up, there', is all that people say to them. I think we all suffered from this, including myself. As a reaction I try to act differently with my own kids. I let them say any rubbish they want.

I'm not a bedu. I was born and bred by the sea, you see. We are fishermen more than bedouin here. We led a different sort of life, we had a different kind of approach from the bedouin. As life is in the desert, there's no room to be shy. You have to be aggressive to survive. We must have had a much easier life here, on the shores of the Gulf, than these people in the desert.

I went to England to study in 1970. The life there wasn't strange to me because I knew Europeans here. I worked for a while in QPC, starting just as an apprentice. So when I went to England, I already knew what to expect. Also, in my generation, we understand foreign places better because we read books, see movies, watch TV. In fact, that's how I learnt my English—by reading.

I was taken straight to the West Midlands when I arrived in England but, my God, I didn't like that place! For a start it was too smokey. You had the M4 which was only about a quarter of a mile from where I was sitting, then there were the factories, the mixture of people, Indians, Arabs, Germans, you name it. This was because of the work. The Midlands is one of the best places to find work. I studied accountancy at West Bromwich College of Technology. I was told that it was one of the best colleges for professional accountacy in England. And it was, actually. I managed to get through the first, second and third year in a period of eighteen months, which wasn't bad. Then I became greedy. I did Part IV and V—and failed both! I didn't want to go back, when I failed, but then I said to myself, 'You'll have to try'. So I went back and spent six more months completing one part, then back to Doha for a year because the best way of tackling these professional exams is to work and study at the same time. I got my Part IV and am now waiting for the results of Part V.

I'm presently working for QPPA. I'm fully operational, as they say, already. You need accountants here as you need other professional people. Don't forget, we import almost everything. Also, it's one of the best paid jobs there is. I like the job. You can't get away from the routine in it, that's a fact. But there are always plenty of challenges.

You can be penniless in England but if you are an Arab you are regarded as a multi-millionaire. I enjoyed it for a while. But then you get tired of it; sometimes I would avoid letting people know I was an Arab. They have mixed feelings about Arabs, the English. Their image of the Arab seems to be that he has a big belly, a big moustache, a big beard, a big dagger. Nowadays the dagger might have been changed into a Cadillac or something, but they don't have very realistic ideas about us.

To me Qatar is the place of my family and my friends. I mean, you have seen Qatar. OK, it's beginning now to be better than before, but there isn't much going on in Qatar. If you want to go out for a day, having spent five or six days working, what do you do? I mean, I'm not suggesting we should have night clubs and cabarets and flood the place with liquor, but at least there should be somewhere where a family can go. As yet nothing has been done in this respect. When I'm abroad I miss the people, that's all.

We're not a big family. There's my parents of course, I have two brothers, I'm the one in the middle, no sisters. I'm married and we have two small daughters. We live with my parents in the same house. I could have lived in my own house ages ago. It's just that they need the company at their time of life. My father is well over eighty now. My mother's about fifty-five or fifty-six. I think it's inhuman at the end just to say, 'cheerio and thank you very much' and walk away. As soon as you leave the house, you don't have time to go and see them, just perhaps once or twice a week and that's by making a special effort. I agree it's not easy for the daughter-in-law. My wife has to spend more time in the home than I do, I'm out at work. A family where you all live together, like that, quite honestly isn't always without problems.

But we still feel a sense of moral responsibility towards our parents. I can't think now of saying, 'cheerio, byebye.' I might, later on. What happened in my case was that my elder brother moved out on his own quite a few years ago, as soon as I was able to run the house. I think I'll do the same when my younger brother graduates and comes back. When there is somebody to look after my parents then I can go. Later we could share them, I will have the father, he will have the mother. We'll do something —the main thing is not to leave them alone, lonely. It's a crime, honestly. Look at the stories you read in the UK of old ladies who die in their home and are found a month later, rotten, without anybody bothering to look after them. To what level can people fall? That's ridiculous, quite honestly. It's one of the things I don't like about Europe. I remember in 1970, I stayed with a family in the UK who had two kids of about eight and fourteen. Their behaviour I didn't like. The kid would tell the father to 'shut up'. I said to him, 'Stephen, you shouldn't say that to your dad', and he replied, 'Why not?'

My father is in hospital at the moment with kidney trouble, and only yesterday another man in the same ward was saying to him, 'Kids now don't care about their parents',—you know the sort of thing. I told them about this family I had stayed with and said they should thank God that things here haven't changed yet!

They were talking about wealth, and how wealth draws people apart, and I tend to agree with them. It may sound strange, really, but at one time round here, twenty or twenty-five years ago, a foreigner coming to this country would not have to cook himself a meal. I don't mean Europeans, because from the beginning the Europeans would keep to themselves. A foreigner wouldn't have to do any cooking, he would be brought food every day, no problem. At the Eids, we used to have festivals in the street, especially up in the North. In the North this happened until quite recently, ten years ago. People would dance, you would have it in the main street, you know. Men and women would be together if it was outside. You know something, we used not to have this sort of complication that we have now, with women. You don't see any women in the street now in Qatar, but before, women used to go and bring wood, go out with the sheep into the desert for grazing, they would do every sort of thing that you could think of. City life has changed it.

Also you could say we haven't yet swallowed the idea of taking women along with us in what we are doing, in our social life. A lot of Qataris can't do this. As far as the girls are concerned, they can't do anything about it. I don't mind taking my wife to selective parties, where selected people have been invited. If there is a party in a hotel and I'm invited, I come alone, because nobody is going to bring his wife. The problem is, it's difficult to be the odd man out. But there are solutions, you see, such as family clubs. I wouldn't take my wife to a place where there are bachelors, and hard drinking. Even if I was in the UK I wouldn't like my family to go to that sort of place. There's a difference where I go and where my wife goes. I think that goes deep inside.

You know, women in this part of the world have always been treated differently. A woman is, how shall I put it, one's pride. Nobody shall touch a woman. This must date back ages ago. It's social upbringing, part of the things that you take for granted. You don't always try to see the reasons, the why's and wherefore's. My wife has been pushing the idea here and there that we go to parties. I mean—don't get me wrong—we go to places where there are Qataris and Europeans, but always in a family circle. Last Christmas, we were invited to the house of one of my accountants. My wife and I decided to go. I asked him next day who would be there and were they bringing their families. He said, no, they weren't. I told my wife, so she said, 'I am not coming' and I didn't want her to go. She said, 'Why aren't X, Y and Z prepared to bring their wives, is it a bad place or some-thing? I'm not going to go.'

It depends how old one is. Qataris now in their mid or late thirties may have married at fifteen or sixteen, that was ages ago, and they are not going to bring their wives who wear a *batula* to any party. I'm twenty-seven or twenty-eight, and my wife doesn't wear a *batula*, but we don't jump in to every party. Say there are six

Qataris and four of them don't bring their wives. The other two Qataris who have brought their wives will feel bad about it. We are afraid of bringing shame on our family.

I was trying to avoid saying this, but it's the core of it all. In the old days—I don't think it could happen now—if a girl was found to have had relations with a boy, she'd be scalped for it. The boy wouldn't. It's the social system. It's not the religion, though. According to our religion, if something illegal occurs between a boy and a girl, both should be punished. But the social system allows the man to get away with it. Think of the UK two hundred years ago, or even less.

We don't even talk about these matters in the normal course of events. It's shameful; it shows a backward mentality. But I don't think this mentality is really valid any more. It's a contradiction to observe our old code and yet send our girls out to universities abroad. We can't have the two things going on at the same time.

This is why a lot of Qataris lead two social lives. One with the family, one without. Men sometimes spend part of the evening— not the whole evening—out on their own at parties. But we do feel torn. I feel guilty about leaving my wife and I phone her at various times in the evening when I am out. She accepts that this is the phase we are in at present. It's going to change, definitely.

We manage this double social life. But I would love it to be a bit different, not too different. Families, neighbours—they are all much closer to each other than in Europe. I'd really hate to see that just disappear. It's bound to happen if we get too Western-ised. But it's a trend. The more complicated life becomes, the more likely we are to end up like any Western society. Our community has already become more mixed, and people more remote from each other.

Show any economist the changes that have occurred here—the flow of money, the prices. He will say it is unbelievable. But what counts finally is the future of the whole area here and this depends on what the present generation does. Many government depart-ments are run by thirty-five-year-olds; these are the people who decide the fate of this place. What we build now is the foundation for the future, and this foundation is not yet all that solid; we need a lot of planning and foresight in the future or the next generation will suffer. If something isn't done now, then in twenty or thirty years when the oil stops, the industry will die. The yield from the natural gas we shall still have is not as much as oil.

We shall always find something when the oil finishes. We can fish—the Gulf is full of fish. I don't worry so much about the oil finishing. What concerns me is that we should have something to show for the money we have had. Every nation needs an income: you have to sell cotton if you no longer have oil, because you can't sell sand, after all. That's why I feel happy when I see places like Umm Said, where all the industrial plant is situated. But I hope they will keep it as far as they can from Doha. We can do without new problems like pollution.

I'll go on with accountancy in the meantime and keep my eyes open for what other opportunities are available. If you just have a salary, that's not going to take you places. You can't have the kind of life a young man wants. You want to be sure you can go on holiday every year. You want the luxuries of life: a good car, a good house, good furniture.

The house I already have, I built two years ago and it's now worth two or three million *riyals*. I have a 500,000 *riyal* low interest loan and 30–40 per cent of it is paid off already. I was thinking about selling it. When I compared prices here with prices in London the idea of buying a house there came to me. I thought that with £65,000 one can buy a mansion with acres of land too. But I don't think I'd do it. I want to live here. If I could afford it, it wouldn't be a bad idea to buy a small place somewhere in the UK, somewhere just to spend holidays.

I shall go into business in some way. I'm interested in land deals. It's a quick way of making money. But nowadays you need a lot of capital to start you off. You need three or four people working together.

There's one thing I'm not going to do and that is work in my office for eight hours and then go and work in my business for a further eight hours. It's not worth it. After all, what do you want money for? I want enough money to be secure. But I'm not going to kill myself for the sake of money.

Nobody's going to say 'no' to the good things of life, to good food and drink and to comfort. But there's a difference between enjoying life and greed; you have to draw a line somewhere. I don't want to become too Westernised and I don't want to go back to the past. I want everything in moderation, if that's possible. I don't know if it is possible. We'll have to wait and find out.

The Hungry Schoolboy

Falih is a jolly, fat schoolboy, aged nineteen. He comes from a very rich family and is himself potentially very rich since he owns a large piece of land in Doha; his brother was offered thirty million *riyals* for an equivalent piece. His brother, five years older, is a real traditionalist who would be quite happy to live in the old family home—a mud-brick house out in the desert where they all lived when they were children—and to spend his life hunting (instead of which he is going into his father's construction business because, as he says, there are too many non-Qataris running businesses). Falih, on the other hand, doesn't care much for hunting and is always wriggling out of expeditions to far off places. The fowl that interest him are mainly to be found in Kentucky Chicken restaurants. He disregards what his parents say, an altogether new phenomenon in Qatar. When threatened by his father, he merely shrugs his shoulders and says, alright then, put me in prison if you like.

Last year I went to England to Huntingdon Lodge to lose weight. I eat too much. I lost about 30 kilos in four months. Here I eat too much food and don't get any exercise. At Huntingdon Lodge, in the morning, I used to drink a little coffee, I also ate grapefruit and some bread, black it was. I don't know what it's made of. For lunch I had a salad, tuna or cheese. For dinner a steak. Here I don't try to lose weight. For breakfast I have tea, cheese, olives and a lot of bread. This is at home. Then I go out and after about two hours I have a meal in a restaurant. For lunch I eat a lot of rice and

The Deputy Director of Ports, Abdullah Goreiri

Bedu oil worker

Doha Clock Tower

Part of the Doha Museum, formerly the Emiri Palace

a lot of meat. Between lunch and dinner I go to a restaurant again —usually Kentucky chicken. I need a lot of food all the time. I just feel hungry. And I like food.

In England I go from one restaurant to another: from an Arab restaurant to a Chinese restaurant to an English restaurant, all in the same day. Sometimes when I'm with my brother in one restaurant, I say, 'Come on. Let's go somewhere else.' There are a lot of restaurants around Picadilly. Sometimes we go to four restaurants in about one hour, (*he laughs*). My brother's not fat, he's thin and he eats even more than me. Sometimes he drinks three gallons of pepsi in one day. At Huntingdon Lodge, they say he's crazy. But my brother takes a lot of exercise. In England he does gymnastics, in Qatar he plays football. I don't like exercise, except for skiing. I don't have the time for exercise—I'm always together with my friends. We say to one another: 'Come on. Let's go to the desert and shoot'. Sometimes I take my sleeping bag with me when I go hunting. But after I've walked for a kilometre I feel tired.

In England I sometimes walked for five miles a day in my track suit. Mrs Black at Huntingdon House was very angry with me. She used to say that I'd catch cold. Huntingdon Lodge is like a hotel: you pay about twenty pounds a day or something and they lodge you and feed you. They expect you to take gym, but I don't like that. At night when everyone else is sleeping, at about one o'clock in the morning, I creep down to the kitchen and have a snack. In the morning they tell me I'm wicked. At first they made me do the exercises, but now the doctor says I don't have to because it's not good for my back. So I spend all day shooting.

At Huntingdon Lodge I make a lot of friends. You meet people in the gym classes in the morning and the afternoon, and in the sauna. Sometimes I go to the sauna: I have massage, electric treatment. They pull and prod you—I hate that. This year I was at Huntingdon Lodge just for twenty days. But I didn't lose any weight, because now it's like my home. I tell Mrs Black that she's my mother and I go and eat when I want. Nobody says no. I like photography. There was a wedding at Huntingdon Lodge and I took pictures. I also had some pictures taken of the bride and me. I told my mother: 'Look I'm married,' (*he laughs uproariously*). She believed me and she showed my father. But he knows me.

My friends at Huntingdon Lodge were just like my friends here except for one difference: in England if you go to a party you just buy drinks for yourself. This friend I have doesn't like that either. He would buy for me and I would buy for him. He's Welsh and he comes from a poor family. I went to visit him once. There are good people in Wales, better than in London. In London there are too many foreigners: you meet Indians and Arabs, but not many English.

One thing that's different about London is that you can talk to the girls there. It's easy, not like here. I tell my English friends: 'If you come to Doha you won't be able to ask a girl out to have a drink with you. If you speak to a girl she'll hit you!' Sometimes in London they get angry if you ask them out and they're married. At first I found it difficult to talk to girls, but my friends helped me. At the beginning I used to shout: 'Go away and leave me alone.' I did that to about three girls, but I soon lost my shyness. In fact, one was very angry because I asked her out the first day. My friend told me, 'You can't ask that straight away the *first* day— wait a week.' But now I'm all right.

Here in Qatar it's not like London—there's not so much to do. I go out shooting in the desert with my friends, even at night. We tease each other. Somebody says: 'Look, there's a ghost coming!' and everybody gets frightened. It's funny.

Here in Doha I feel freer. In London I'm sometimes afraid. People steal your money so I never walk alone—usually I'm with about ten of my friends.

I still go to school, but not every day. If I'm tired, I sleep. My father gets very angry. Sometimes he threatens me, but I just tell him I'll run away, so he can't do anything. Sometimes I don't have anyone to go out with to the desert, because they are all at school. In this village I'm the only one who doesn't go to school regularly. Sometimes I go near the road to watch the girls, but I can't speak to them. You get into a lot of trouble if you talk to them. Maybe the girl would speak to you, but if her father knew you were speaking to his daughter, he would kill you. Well, maybe not if you just talk to her but if you tried to make love to her, he would. In the afternoon I talk with my friends and in the evening I watch television. Or I talk to my friends again in the Juice Bars. If I get bored, I drive my car, or I go to shoot. My father is sometimes away. Sometimes at night, I go out in the car and drive till dawn. My mother doesn't like that. She's tried to stop me several times, but I still go.

I don't really know what job I will do—but I want to work for myself. I don't want to work for the Government, I don't want to be a minister or an ambassador or anything like that. My friends in England want me to go there as an ambassador, but I tell them no, it's too much trouble, too many problems. I want to go into business. I think I might start my own company, perhaps a clothes business or maybe cars. I want to earn a lot of money and be free.

The Chauffeur

When we go hunting we take the bird with us, with a hood over its head and a string attached to its foot. When we see the bustard we remove the hood, the falcon straightaway sees the larger bird and goes for its throat. The *shahin* is faster than a *saker*. With the *shahin* we can only hunt in the afternoon, from three to half-past five because the bird feels hungry in the afternoon and is not very lively in the morning. But towards sunset the *shahin* goes off like an arrow from a bow.

On this hunting trip we had two or three guys from Qatar TV making films. We travelled over the mountains by car, it was very dangerous. There were ninety-two cars on the trip. We had two Rolls Royce generators for electricity. We had portable bungalows made in Qatar, in Kuwait and in America. All the bedus lived in tents, the sheikhs and their sons in the bungalows. For the hunting itself we had twelve cars. We stayed altogether fifty-five days. The camp was eighty miles from Damascus, up in the Syrian mountains. The roads were very bad, twisting mountain roads. We had everything we needed, just like in our own homes, except for our families. It was very cold, sometimes there was snow and ice, but we had electric heaters in the tents. In the morning, when we set out, we'd begin by filling the tanks with petrol; the food was put in my car. The bedu who live there come and tell us if they've seen a bustard and where to find it. The sheikh rewards them, whether it's true or not, because they are very poor people you know. There are not many bedu there because there's little grass for them to feed their animals. The land is mountainous and often cold. They live in big tents and wear big coats; they are poor and dirty. I have a lot of food in my car; apples, bananas. Sometimes I stop near the tents and give them some, saying, 'This is from the sheikh'. Or I might give them cigarettes.

When I left school I was very poor. I helped my father on our boat, a big *dhow*. We went out fishing. I enjoyed it, but sometimes the sea was really rough. One *dhow* might catch nothing, and another might catch a lot. It's just a chance, you know. We used to get up after praying in the morning at half-past-four. There was no jetty, we went into the water up to our necks. I remember as a child being carried on my father's back as he swam, to take me out to the boat. At that time it was very cold, early in the morning. Later it was all right, the sun shone. We fished far away from here, five or six hours' voyage. We'd fish for only three or four hours and then go back to Doha. There were four people from Oman, fishermen, working with us. My father and I would take half of the catch, and the four Omanis would have the other half. I was twelve years old at the time. I used to go out in the boat in summer, not in winter. My father was afraid for me: I might be seasick sometimes and sometimes you can't find your way back to Doha because it's really dark and rough and you are at sea a couple of days. Then the family at home get worried. They are down on the beach every day watching and waiting for the boat to come in. Sometimes the engine doesn't work and you come back by sail.

When I was seventeen my dad was sick and in hospital. The boat was laid up. We were sixteen children in the family, and I was the eldest. My brothers and sisters were small and someone had to provide them with food, so I worked for an oil company. I used to start work at six in the evening and come home at six in the morning. I really am sorry about having so little schooling, but I don't mind because I helped my family.

There were no oil Qatari drillers at the time. I had to look at all the gauges, some for water, and a gauge for a sandy material which is mixed with oil to keep the gas down. First you have a big drill. After drilling with the big drill, an 18-inch diameter casing in 30-foot lengths is inserted into the well—we call it the eye. Then you take out the drill and put the casing in as far as you have drilled. You put this sandy material down the sides and you drill again, using a smaller drill, 6-inch diameter. With a diamond drill you drill until you are near the oil, about 12,000 or 15,000 feet. You have to go carefully when you are near the oil, you don't use steel cable, but pieces of wood. You put them carefully inside the well. You go easy, easy, to arrive at the gas. After that you remove the diamond drill, put in a test pipe and take samples for the labora-tory. Then we put in what we call the 'christmas tree' down the pipe, and allow the gas to escape for a couple of days. Next we put on a big valve, take away the rig, and whenever we want to use the oil we just have to attach a connection, and that's it. The whole drilling operation takes two-and-a-half to three-and-a-half months.

For the English and Dutch who work for it, the oil company is like school. We Qataris work hard. We sleep like the dead, it's a very hard job. The Dutch come down to the job and they think we know nothing about the job, that we don't even know how to use a spanner. Yet we have to teach them for two to three months. Afterwards they say, 'No need to tell me, I know everything.' After three or four months or after one year, these people become drillers. Yet we work here for three to four years and all they do is tell us, 'Hold this. Do that'. I was made assistant driller after three or four years. I could have done the job of a driller myself if I had been trained. I can open a big pump by myself. I know how to recognise the problems: say the pump won't push the material, it takes two or three labourers to fix it. We are Qataris, all Qataris. We work for two to three hours and make the pump work. We do a fantastic job for the company but what do they care? Everybody knows me. It's in my file, that I speak good English and would do well in this job and so on. But they didn't promote me.

One day a Lebanese guy was brought to the rig. We were drilling. On the back side of the rig no one was allowed to hit with a hammer, make any noise, because the guys start from twelve midnight and work for twelve hours, so they need rest. The Lebanese was repairing everything on the rig: you know, doors, toilets, everything. That day we were sleeping. We feel every noise, the drill, the rig itself when it moves. This Lebanese was fixing a pipe or something: bang, bang. One of us went to the man and said, 'Please, our colleagues are sleeping, they are very tired. Do the job while they are having lunch.' But the Lebanese guy only said we Qataris were stupid. So we became edgy and everybody on the rig was told to stop work. We were all sent to Doha. The tool-pusher asked us to go back to the job. We said no. There were forty-five of us, all Qataris. We had no work for three weeks.

We wouldn't go back before the Lebanese was transferred some-where else. But then he said he was very sorry for what he had done. He said, 'I have kids. I didn't know what I was doing,' and so on. Qatari people have big hearts so we said, 'Alright, never mind'. We told him not to ask us to do anything for him, to hold a hammer or anything.

But from that day I became restless because the company wasn't playing fair. I sent a letter to them telling them I was sorry but I didn't like the job. I said to the labour officer: 'The Qataris work-ing on the rig are working for their country, for Qatar, not for Lebanese'. I could see the company were helping other national-ities, not Qataris. The Lebanese are given a school for their children. The Dutch are given a nice school, too, a nice bungalow, a ticket every six months to go back to Holland. We work day and night, twelve hours every day, the same shift for a week at a time. So why don't we get the same as the Dutch? They make them senior staff and yet they don't know anything about the rig at all. They don't know how to work the big spanner round the pipe. We know how to work it. They have a club, a nice house, a holiday abroad—so why not us?

I became really upset, seeing the company do so much for the Dutch. We all have kids here. So why isn't there a school where the Qatari kids can learn English? Why not? All we got was our salary. 1000 *riyals* a week was a good salary. We didn't worry about the future. Only I ate out my heart every day. Nobody helped me. Nobody felt what I felt. When I talked with them, everybody said, 'Yes'. But no one did anything.

So I became a driver for one of the Government ministries. I also worked in a sheikh's house: I sat talking and took poor people who came to the sheikh, who would send them to the cashier to collect some money.

The rigs are dangerous. When I used to leave for work on the rig there was always the possibility I would never come back. Now that I work in Doha, I see my family every day. I am happy, and my family is happy. We are building a new villa.

When I was young, we didn't have much money. In those days —around 1960—the Government wasn't able to pay the people. But after that the Government began to look after us. Everyone had salaries from the Government. We got free breakfast at school, free clothes, books, shoes, a salary—everything. Since then everything has improved. Now I get a monthly allowance for my family; all Qataris do. I've got 15,000 *riyals* for furniture for my new villa. We shall soon be getting 150 *riyals* per square metre for a piece of land belonging to my father on the corniche which the Govern ment is taking over. Sometimes I get nice presents from the Ministers or important people I drive around. Perhaps 1,000 or 1,500 *riyals*. That's enough for one day.

I also bought and sold land, in 1976, that is. A lot of people make money this way now. They come to me and say, 'I have land of such and such a size and ask for a price of, say, a million.' I find someone to buy it and they give me a percentage, a quarter of one percent, so I make 2,500 in a few hours. But I don't like it. I don't trust it. It's not really good, it's too like gambling. Some people have become rich that way but I am not interested. My salaries are enough; I get one from the sheikh, one from the Government. My wife also gets a salary from the school. *Ilhamd-illah*, it's good enough. If I had more, I'd become crazy. It's good enough for us. We can go to Europe, go to Cairo.

We have a good life. Perhaps there is not enough variety in our lives. We have a car, but we know all the roads, we know every place here, we know all the people. We need to meet new people, outsiders. I am happy when I have the chance to talk to English people. It gives me something new to think about. It changes my ideas. When I'm with my Arab friends, we're always telling each other the same stories, talking about the same things, like Friday fishing, either this week or three months ago. We need more things to distract us. Every day we just do the same, we go to the oil company club, play cards, billiards, or watch television. The lack of stimulation makes us restless. Every Friday, we take the car out to Ruas and go fishing, we sleep one night there and get a lot of fresh air. We fry fish out in the open and eat them, that's very good, that's what we need. Because, if we don't do that, what do we do on Friday? We stay in and watch TV. Some of the programmes are bad, so we get irritated and take the car out and drive it round the corniche. Then the next day we go back to our job. Our government knows that we can't change everything at once. We must advance slowly but surely. We don't want a boom here and the government doesn't want one, otherwise we might lose all our money. We have to be careful.

I don't worry about the oil running out, because the oil is no longer so important to us. We have plenty of gas—that is very important. The Shell company is looking for gas all round Qatar. When I used to work for Shell myself, we found a lot of gas everywhere—but we just closed the pipes—this was when we were looking for oil. I think that in the future our money will come from products other than oil. We have a very big ammonia factory and we are already exporting gas; both bring us a lot of money. We have two cement factories and two more are being built, also a flour mill. We export prawns everywhere, we have a steel plant. So I think that in the future there will be no cause to worry.

I want to see my country like any European country. I want the people to be direct and speak the truth. For instance, I am having a villa built. I go to the contractor and ask when it will be finished, he says maybe in six months. But they never tell you the exact time it will take—I call this cheating. There is no one to control them, to see that the contractor really does finish the job. But in the future, I hope that this will happen.

On the other hand, like in the UK, people should be able to do as they like. That's difficult now, but in the future, I think it will happen. In Bahrain it is already happening, because the country has a long tradition of contact with foreigners.

The situation is not easy here as far as girls are concerned. They would love to go out more, to talk freely with everybody. People who've been out of Qatar, who've seen how life is in Europe, how girls behave there, think differently. I've seen this happen. I myself walk outside the house with my wife and daughters. My father doesn't object, but if he did I would take no notice of him. I say to my wife, enjoy yourself, if you like walking, why don't you go out with your friends. I met my wife before we married and when my daughter is of the age to marry, she will do what she likes. My daughter will be free to talk to her friends and go out as she pleases. Anyone who has been to Europe, takes their family out to visit their friend's family. We all talk together. It's starting now. Not among the old people, of course. I take my wife out to the hotel for dinner, sometimes. I don't think people talk. She likes it. Because she's a teacher, you know. People here earn good money, but sometimes they don't know how to enjoy themselves. Where can we go?

I've been to London seven times. My wife says, 'Take me with you', and I always do. In London we walk a lot, go shopping, go to restaurants, to the cinema. It makes it difficult for her to come back to Qatar, but then we plan to go back to London next year. No young Qatari would marry more than one wife now. Because he likes his wife, because he had a baby with her. If there is a problem with parents-in-law, then he can just take his wife to a separate house.

We would like to change everything here. We would like to change the minds of the old men. It must come one day. I hope it will come as soon as possible.

I want Qataris to get good jobs and I hope that the young Qataris who are abroad studying can come back and take the jobs from the foreigners here, from the Palestinians, the Lebanese and the Egyptians, and I hope that these people will go back to their own homes. These people have done very well out of the Qatari government. They came here with just the trousers and shirt they were wearing and after a couple of months they have a nice villa and a good job. I don't understand what happens in these couple of months.

I intend to learn English. I know Arabic: I read it, I write it. I read stories like those of Youssef al-Sibai, stories about life in Cairo. But it's not enough for me. I need English too. If you know English you can do all kinds of things. While I was working with the oil company I could have become a driller if I had known English. But no one helped me. I kept asking all the time, 'Send me to the school. Just give me a chance for six months'. But nobody listened. But if I had been English or Dutch I would have had what I wanted straight away.

Next year I'll speak English well. I'll also speak a little French. French is the language of diplomacy. Diplomats don't write invitations in English, they use French. Then I can take a new job. *Inshallah*. I'd like to work in a Qatari embassy: issuing visas for the Qatari Embassy in London, say. I could help my country. Not all embassy work is diplomatic: you can get involved in business.

If I had studied when I was young, I could be an ambassador by now, a big man. I remember a lot of the guys who were my friends when I was young, now they have good jobs, or they're still studying in the States. My chance has gone alreaady.

But I'm still young, I can learn. The Government will pay for me, but I don't mind paying from my own pocket.

Mohammed, the School-Leaver

I used to like school very much. But I wasn't able to get enough marks in the last year of the secondary school to be accepted by the College or to be allowed to go and study abroad. Now I have just started to work.

My father really taught me everything in this life; he taught me how to take a book and read it all, not at once, but to finish it before going on to another. He also taught me never to start a job I think I might not be able to do. I always act on his advice because it's useful. My father was just eleven years old when his own mother and father died, leaving him alone. He learned English and worked as a telephone operator for an oil company. He earned two *riyals* a week. He used to spend one *riyal* on food and he saved the other *riyal*. He bought a lot of books and now we have a big library at home. He reads English, history and science books.

My mother is studying at school in the fourth class. She knows how to read and write and has always read books, but she wants to learn about mathematics and history. Her studying makes her happy—she's always studying at home. She's not old; she's only thirty-six. She's my friend more than my mother. She has good ideas about women: she wants women to go out and do whatever they like. I agree with her sometimes. But at other times I don't agree. Of course, I want women to go out and do what they like, too. But I must act as the people here do, otherwise I will be alone, like one white hair on a black head. My mother wants young girls to be able to love. But I think it's very difficult. Young boys here might tell the girls they loved her while they didn't really, so I think the experience might be a failure for the woman. Because when a woman's in love she's in love with all her heart.

My parents are not like most others; they gave me freedom from the age of sixteen. Many of the boys I was at school with have good ideas, ideas about freedom and the way society should be. They listen to pop music like the Carpenters, Abba and the Brotherhood of Man, they go abroad for their holidays but at home they still go to the *majlis*. They hate this—or at least many of them do—because they want to express their ideas. But their fathers want to see their personalities mirrored in their sons, so the sons end up being like their fathers. Because he is under pressure to be just like his father, the son often quarrels with him without knowing why. The boy will say he wants a car; the father refuses to give it to him. So they argue. But I think the car is not the real cause of the quarrel. Of course, the boy wants the car. But mainly he doesn't want to be told what to do by his father. Later, he will realise his ideas through his own son.

A lot of the boys at school travel to Beirut, to Cairo, to London. Qataris are advancing by leaps and bounds—you can see it happen. They meet different people with different ideas. This enables them to observe their own society more critically. I saw life in London myself and I thought it was a good life. Everyone does as they like; no one tells you what is right and what is wrong. Here, you only have to add something to your car, and they will all tell you: 'No, no, you mustn't do that, it's bad,' your mother, your father, your friends. They will all tell you no one is doing it here, it's bad to do it. For instance, I can't take off my Arabic *thaub* and headdress and wear Western clothes. The reason is not that I'm afraid of public opinion. But people would no longer see *me*—they would just see my clothes. They would forget my personality. Things are changing, but it's going to take time.

The Painter

I come from a family of artists. My maternal uncle was an embroidery designer. I was fascinated by the designs he made. I used to wonder how that noisy machine could produce those bright and beautifully designed dresses that were worn on wedding feasts and other occasions. My uncle still designs embroidery and is regarded as the best designer in the Gulf. Now my uncle is in Bahrain. He first learnt his profession in Qatar under the top master designer. When the master moved to Bahrain he followed him there. Gradually he developed his own style. Because the chiffon material he uses is very fine, he starts on the embroidery without a preliminary sketch, relying mainly on his eye. The machine follows his hand.

My mother used to design birds on cushions. I used to see her at work. The process was very simple: she made two lines and then drew a circle on them. The result was either a bird or a rose or something else. I thought it was a simple thing. This was before I went to primary school.

I started to draw on walls, imitating my mother's designs. It seemed easy to me to imitate her. Whatever I drew turned out to be a bird or a fish. My hand was getting used to drawing such things. When I went to school I saw a lot of colours. It was an eye opener.

Art was my favourite subject at school. I preferred to draw with colours, and to use plasticine. I was just following my inclinations. I tried to create an impression with my paintings. My dream was to become another Leonardo da Vinci, because Leonardo da Vinci was a perfect man. He was not like other artists who excelled in one field. Leonardo was versatile and excelled in everything he tried. The artist is a creator. The creator and the inventor speak the same language. Leonardo da Vinci excelled in poetry, medicine, the art of flying, mechanics and mathematics. His intellectual and artistic capacities were super-human.

In the Arab world, art is not given as much attention as in Europe. Our teachers simply trained us to draw and use colour. When I do a portrait I try to improve on the original. But when I was studying I didn't get any encouragement worth mentioning. It's our will that sustained our interest in art. My teachers showed a limited interest in my work. I was good at drawing and could copy objects very well. The teachers should have shown a similar interest in the other pupils' work, but they didn't. They just gave them paper and colours and told them to paint. I think they should have helped them to develop and refine their artistic sensitivity.

When I see a pupil drawing something beautiful, I'm interested in finding out what he's trying to convey. Then I ask him to draw his mother and father. He draws his father with a serious expression and his mother with a kind expression. This shows genuine representation. He uses the colours that he likes. We don't appreciate this kind of work sufficiently. All we do is collect the drawing pads and throw them in the waste paper basket at the end of the year. We don't give enough encouragement to pupils.

I paint in different styles now. When I started painting I tried to reproduce an exact copy of the original. For example, if I saw a beautiful scene I would paint an exact copy of it like a photograph. I have perfected this technique and now I feel I've had enough of it. In 1972 there was a competition between all the schools to choose the best paintings for the Arab Youth Festival in Algiers. I won the competition and five of my paintings were chosen. I was asked to go to Algiers with my paintings. In Algiers I met people and discovered new styles and asked all sorts of questions about them. The new styles I saw broadened my knowledge. I discovered that art meant not merely drawing a face, but expressing a feeling. If I wanted to paint this man before me I wouldn't just do a portrait of him as a kind and generous person. I'd try to bring out the essence of Mohammed Said by means of colour. Children's paintings confirm what I'm saying. Children's paintings are the ultimate form of expression. But we destroy their paintings for them when we tell them, 'You've got the face wrong.' I've trained myself to express what I feel. I've trained my eye to the use of colour, to find out which colours go together and which colours clash. I look at the canvas and imagine which colours will be most suitable. I don't stick to a particular school of painting. I did this painting before that one. The style of this one is new. I may not like this style. I may try to find another style. I'll go on experimenting until I settle on a style I like.

When I was a small boy I liked drawing. When people found faults in my work and pointed them out to me, I tried to eliminate them. I tried to do what pleased them. But with this method you gradually lose your personality and do what other people like.

Later I tried to find my own personal style. If my paintings were taken to Europe I would want them to be distinguished by their Arab character. That is why I began to look into the Arab way of life and to experiment with Arab calligraphy and to use distinctly Arab colours. Arab art is based on colour. Arab calligraphy and architecture are based on perception and inventiveness. When I portray Arab life I paint the designs with Arab colours. I express what I feel as an Arab, so that when someone sees the painting I'd like him to say: 'This is an Arab painting.'

In Arab countries such as Qatar, Kuwait and Saudi Arabia, the desert is a dominant feature of the landscape. Another feature is the scarcity of vegetation, of green colour. So our colours are light and very limited. We lack the different shades of green, red, rose, and so on. When an artist uses these you feel he is moving away from his environment and therefore does not reflect it. He is simply imitating foreign artists. I use blue and yellow. I grew up with these colours. I express a genuine feeling. We have white which moves on to yellow and blue which moves on to white. We have the white colour of our buildings, the earthy colour of the land and the blue of the sky. We have only two basic colours, and few trees.

Because of this limitation you find people themselves go for bright colours. People's clothes are white, blue and red. This is also evident in the colours of the tents and clothes of the bedouin. They use blazing colours. It is psychological. For this reason they try to bring out what they don't have. When a bedouin wanted to weave a carpet, the colours at his disposal were limited, so he turned to the natural colours of the animals he knew, like a black sheep, a russet-coloured sheep. So he began to combine the colours which don't clash. In recent years he discovered many different colours and used them only for rugs and saddle bags, but not for tents; because of the size of the tents it would be too costly to use many colours. The introduction of many colours to this region had an influence on everything. Now they paint houses completely white. For example the building of the girls' school is painted entirely in white. So is the museum. The new guest house, though the building is modern, is painted in white. The museum gave an impetus to the old tradition. When the effect of the discovery of the colours began to wear off, people turned back to their roots. It's psychological. People are conditioned by their environment and by what is available.

In the past we were influenced by Indian, Persian and Roman architecture. Islamic art has its own distinct character. The geometrical structure of Arab calligraphy, especially the Kufic script, has left a permanent mark on Arab art. It filled every available space with arabesques. This has a distinctly Arab-Islamic character. Islamic art was the first to fully exploit space. The Moslem artist used the decorative potential of the Kufic script to fill empty spaces. The structures are distinguished by repetitive and symmetrical decorative elements, for example a dome in the middle and two minarets on each side.

This influenced me very much. It influenced the form I follow. I think there is no other art which so much reduces details down to the essentials. I link minarets with everything and I use only one colour. The painting appears to me as a whole unit. Before I paint I try to study the elements in it, then I present them as a whole unit by means of colour, space and association.

It is difficult to present culture to the public in Qatar. First you must start with the traditional style. For example, I take to the exhibition a painting of a head of a gazelle. Then I exhibit modern paintings and explain to the public that the pictures have a meaning. Gradually the public shows some interest and appreciation.

The problem you face is lack of public response. It's difficult for the general public to appreciate modern art because it's not easy to understand it. It appeals only to intellectuals. But there is an engineer I know who, in spite of his qualifications—PhD in aviation—does not appreciate art. We can't say that his education has helped him to understand art. The artist feels this city is badly planned. If he were to replan it he would give it harmony and local colour.

The Arab Muslim artist was an abstract artist. We were back-

ward culturally because of colonisation. Suddenly we were introduced to a new world. So we took everything indiscriminately and
as a result we lost our roots. We took abstract art from Picasso.
Arab abstract art came before European abstract art, but, as I said
before, we lost touch with out roots. We took abstract art from the
West.

I never finished my schooling. I had to leave for family reasons
when I was in the second year of secondary school. I had to help
my father with his work. But this did not stop me from pursuing
my artistic inclinations. When my father's position improved, I
applied to the Department of the Arts of the Ministry of Information. Now I work in the Cultural section of the Ministry of
Information and I'm in charge of traditional crafts. Before the discovery of oil, people worked in crafts. Afterwards they gave up
crafts because they found working for oil companies was easier,
more secure and better paid. I'm trying to revive the crafts. I've
employed an artist to make a few samples of old crafts. I also try to
bring back the old arts. We have an artist we employ on a permanent basis. He makes incense holders like this white one which
they used to make in Qatar in the past.

When I finish school this year, I shall go to the Faculty of Arts
in Cairo, as soon as I possibly can. But I want to make a full study
of traditional Arab art before moving on to Western art.

Qatari art is recent. Since the return of our art students we've
managed to get somewhere. We hope one day to have our own
distinctive style so that when people come to Qatar they will want
to see our national gallery besides visiting our museum.

PART SIX

A Pioneering Television Programme

Television is new to Qatar; it is not much more than one decade old. And for the time being many of the programmes are imported from abroad, either from Egypt or from the West. There are some programmes which are produced locally and among those one stands out as being remarkable in a number of respects. It is entitled *which Path* and consists of dramatisations of social problems in Qatar. It ran for a long time, but has now come to an end.

Generally (but not always), the themes treated in the series were taken from letters sent by members of the public to the programme organiser. Each weekly episode centred on one particular issue and the dramatisation was followed by a discussion between a television announcer and a local notable specially invited for the occasion. Only a handful of the programmes have been summarised in this chapter, but they convey something of the flavour of the series.

The first remarkable thing about the programme is that it appeared at all. Few Western countries are notably frank about their important social problems on Government-controlled television channels. So one might expect a small, developing society to be even more sensitive to criticism, albeit self-criticism, and even more inclined to sweep problems under the carpet rather than to advertise them. In fact, the issues were handled with commendable honesty. Drinking alcohol, for instance, is forbidden by Islam and in the puritan societies of the Gulf, drink is something of a taboo subject; yet it came into a number of the programmes and was discussed quite openly.

The vast majority of the programmes in the series concern women in some way. It would have been surprising if it were not so, since womens' changing status is the central social issue in all the Gulf countries today.

When *Our Path* started, the response was not, initially, great. But gradually people grew interested and it became a very popular programme. After it was over, people used to often carry on the discussion among themselves. Since other public entertainment is almost non-existent, television plays an important role in Qatari society.

The series had one flaw which should be mentioned. Although the actors were Qatari, the producers were Egyptian and this fact accounts for some social incongruities and an occasional infelicity of tone. Obviously, Egyptians will tend to look at problems in the light of their own society and this led them to make occasional mistakes in both subject matter and production. In the first programme summarised here, *Times Are Changing*, a woman school teacher has a boy pupil almost her own age. If this might easily happen in Egypt, it would certainly not be acceptable in Qatar. But the rest of the tale rings true. One middle-aged Qatari lady, while she liked the series generally, complained that the tone was sometimes a bit 'hysterical'—as Egyptian films sometimes are.

This one reservation apart, the series, by and large, gives a very real picture of the problem areas of Qatari society.

TIMES ARE CHANGING

Two young Qatari friends are talking. Both of the women are teachers. Fatima describes to Suher the calamity that has befallen her. Her parents are forcing her to marry a schoolboy. The worst part of it is that he is her pupil and very lazy and stupid; he has spent three years in one class.

SUHER: So why do they want you to marry him?
FATIMA: Because his father left one million *riyals*. (*Speaks in vexed tone.*) When I remember how mad I used to get with him for not remembering his lessons! He's sure to take his revenge.
SUHER: (*Unsympathetically.*) You should thank God that the man has been to a primary school. At least he has some education.
FATIMA: (*Dismally.*) He's sure to take his revenge!

SUHER: (*Primly.*) You'll just have to accept him. Anyway, it's a good opportunity for you—you can wear him like a ring. Whether or not he's finished his studies, it's God's will.

FATIMA: Would *you* accept?

SUHER: Oh, yes.

FATIMA: What about your own fiancé?

SUHER: He is studying abroad. He has one more year to go before he finishes.

FATIMA: Why don't you join him?

SUHER: I prefer to wait. I can't stay in a country which has different customs to my own.

FATIMA: But you would be freer and able to lead a better life. It's because you're a teacher in Arabic that you don't like accepting changes in dress and life-style, that you stick to tradition.

SUHER: I was brought up to be a good housewife and think of my children. My fiancé will make an ideal husband. He's not like these other young men of today.

The phone rings. Suher's fiancé has just arrived back from the USA, and is already at the airport. She rushes to her wardrobe and tries on various different dresses. Eventually she chooses a long dress in sugar pink. The music rises to a crescendo as she advances demurely from her own room to the diwan where her father is talking to her fiancé. She appears to be staggered by what she sees and retreats in horror. The young man is not wearing Qatari dress but jeans, a check shirt and a medallion on a chain round his neck. He is bewildered by her reaction and follows her to her room.

SUHER: (*Turning on him viciously.*) What is this! I can't believe it! You have changed. You've become a heathen. So that's how living abroad makes you look! Who in the world wear shirts like *that*? And these trousers! You look like a woman!

FIANCÉ: And why shouldn't men wear coloured shirts may I ask?

SUHER: Get out!

FIANCÉ: Very well. But I am very angry with you.

Father goes to Suher's room.

SUHER: (*Apparently half demented.*) Haven't you noticed how he has changed?

FATHER: A man who lives for three years in the United States is bound to change. Times are changing, my daughter. What is it you want?

SUHER: I want him to be like he used to be. I should be ashamed to walk in the streets with him. I am a teacher. My job is to guide children. How can I go into the street with a man wearing a shirt like that?

FATHER: If he didn't love *you*, he would have brought home a wife from the United States.

SUHER: I will not marry him.

FATHER: Yes, you will.

SUHER: Father, this is the first time, but I must disobey you.

FATHER: If you don't marry him, then I'll divorce your mother.

Father and young man.

FATHER: How can you turn up looking like this!

FIANCÉ: Life is changing. We are leading a new way of life. Do you really think I can live in the States wearing clothes from the seventeenth century, uncle?

Suher and Fatima talking again. Fiancé is in the background. Pop music is playing.

SUHER: How can I face my pupils with a husband like this? (*Makes a grimace in the direction of her fiancé.*) What did I do to deserve this?

FATIMA: (*Looking severely practical in her turn.*) Because you are his cousin.

SUHER: I'll tell you another thing. There are times when I think I smell drink on him. Does your fiancé drink?

FATIMA: Apparently. Why don't you try talking to him.

SUHER: (*Bleakly.*) It's no use.

Commentary

The Commentator is the Headmaster at a secondary school.

COMMENTATOR: Fatima is afraid that her new husband will revenge himself because she used to get angry with him. But why should she look on the dark side? She only beat him out of zeal to teach him. This is how he will see it. When they marry both of them will change. She will make a new man of him.

ANNOUNCER: Women want to marry men they respect.

COMMENTATOR: I don't see why there should be any problem about her marrying him. She knows that her mission in life is to be a good wife and mother. As for Suher, it was a mistake to kick her fiancé out of her room. She knows, as traditional young women know, that her job is to look after her husband and children. Anyway, she said that her fiance was not like other young men; it seems he is made of good clay. If she married him, she can convince him to drop all these bad habits he learnt abroad, such as his dress and listening to foreign music. He must be sound because he's a good student. He will definitely change his habits.

ANNOUNCER: (*Less optimistically.*) The changes in him don't seem minor. He's gone too far—he even wears a chain.

COMMENTATOR: Yes. He should definitely remove that. When we sent our sons abroad we want them to acquire useful knowledge, not new customs that clash with our own. But he still passes his exams which means that he has not been entirely won over by the American way of life. When he settles back here I am sure that Suher is capable of convincing him by logical, rational argument.

ANNOUNCER: But the two girls say that their fiancés are drinking.

COMMENTATOR: I wish that our young men would give that up. Drink is harmful to the health and to the mind. One should be in full control of one's faculties. But every problem should be treated at the root. Why do the young men drink? Because they are living in a vacuum. It is the responsibility of Fatima and Suher to help them give up drink.

ANNOUNCER: Fatima is being forced into her marriage.

COMMENTATOR: Since the girl is the one who is getting married she should be allowed to express her opinion freely. The parents may guide, but they should never try to compel a girl to get married. She will only react against the marriage and the man.

THE DOWRY

Father and mother discussing a problem with their son. Khalid loves a girl and wants to marry her.

FATHER: Love is not everything. There has to be understanding.

The son convinces his mother who turns angrily on the father.

FATHER: (*Backing down.*) All I want is for our son's wife to be like you.

Family of girl arrive. Mother enters room last. Two fathers and Khalid stay alone. The formal greetings take some time. It transpires that Khalid has finished his studies and will be the Director of a government department.

GIRL'S FATHER: (*Meaningfully.*) You know that I have made a great effort to bring up my daughter well. We want to see her happy. (*The girl hands in the tea at the door.*)
I want 20,000 *riyals* as a dowry.

FATHER:⎫
KHALID:⎭ We don't have that amount of money.

GIRL'S FATHER: You can borrow it from the bank or anywhere you like. But you must pay it.

KHALID: This means you are trying to sell your daughter. I have only just graduated. And anyway all that I have will be spent on her.

GIRL'S FATHER: You are very young. And she is my daughter. Are you telling me what I should do with her? You are rude and have been badly brought up by your father. I shall marry her to anyone I like.

FATHER: You think only of money, but not of the happiness of your daughter.

Girl's mother comes in.

GIRL'S MOTHER: What you have done is not right.

GIRL'S FATHER: Don't interfere in my affairs. I am a man. I know what to do.

GIRL'S MOTHER: She is your daughter. You have to think what is best for her future.

GIRL'S FATHER: I am free to marry my daughter to any man I choose.

KHALID: I love her and nobody else. She will be a good wife to me. These fathers don't know what is in the interest of their daughters. They only think of money. To hell with money and whoever invented it!

Girl's father discusses marrying his daughter to another young man.

GIRL'S FATHER: I want 30,000 *riyals* and you'll have to pay everything else.

YOUNG MAN: That's alright. I have plenty of money. Agreed. When will the marriage be officially announced?

FATHER: Next Thursday.

Mother and father after the ceremony.
Mother complains bitterly that the daughter is sick and miserable.

MOTHER: Why did you agree to that marriage? She doesn't want to marry him.

FATHER: You will have to stop all this nonsense. You want to have her divorced so that she can marry Khalid. But this will never happen. I know that your daughter is not doing anything in her home and moving backwards between here and there—she is ignoring her duties as a wife.

MOTHER: You believe that because her husband told you? You are interested only in money.

FATHER: I have nothing to say. She has to go back to her husband's home.

MOTHER: Well, she's not going. You'll have to go yourself and explain why she is unhappy.

Young husband and wife.

HUSBAND: I have a job to do and have to go out for an hour.

WIFE: You have just arrived and yet you want to go immediately and leave me all alone. Every night you go out and come back at dawn.

HUSBAND: Why don't you bring a rope and tie me up? The world is surely coming to an end when women try to control men.

WIFE: I have my rights as a wife. But it's not your fault. It's my father's fault. He sold me to you.

HUSBAND: You are like everything in my house. I have bought it all with my money.

She is alone in bed. He arrives back drunk—hiccupping volubly.

HUSBAND: Good night.

WIFE: Why don't you say good morning?

HUSBAND: Then why not? Good morning.

WIFE: Every day you come back in the morning.

HUSBAND: Am I drunk? (*Hiccups. Talks to himself in the mirror.*) Do you think I have been drinking? But drink is only a medicine. It was the doctor who told me to have a drink every night.

Commentary

The Commentator is an assistant director of education.

COMMENTATOR: It is clear, of course, that Khalid is the man who would have made her happy. The father was an ignorant man, ignorant because he believes that money is the only source of happiness when it means nothing to the girl. Besides, it is irreligious to make money a criterion. Money should not be taken into consideration by Muslims.

ANNOUNCER: If only all the fathers who think of money had read the Prophet's sayings and would follow his example in marrying their daughters. He never thought of money.

COMMENTATOR: The Prophet said, if any man comes to marry your daughter, you must judge him by his moral worth. To impose a husband is irreligious because it is she who will live with him and not her family. We need campaigns to inform the people of religious teachings. We should also campaign to convince fathers not to exaggerate the amount of the dowry. I am confident that as a result this phenomenon would disappear from our society. In addition, the State should intervene in limiting dowries. Such legislation should be derived from religious teaching. Perhaps the State could even provide a subsidy.

ANNOUNCER: Perhaps the mother could have convinced the father?

COMMENTATOR: No. This is a problem which has to be solved not on a personal but rather on a collective basis. People should consult together and fix a maximum dowry. Fathers should be made aware of the religious rulings that apply to marrying their daughters. This would undoubtedly change some people's attitudes and in turn also affect others. Girls cannot be treated like chattels by their husbands. This is definitely a mistake. A wife has rights and she could, if she wanted, seek the intervention of the courts. I don't believe the law would allow the wife's husband to ruin her life like that. The solution is obviously that since the man treats his wife like a piece of furniture she should go to court and get a divorce.

ANNOUNCER: But why didn't the girl refuse to marry?

COMMENTATOR: The girl could have refused and taken up a firm stand. But the essence of the problem is financial and only legislation will solve it.

ANNOUNCER: Couldn't she improve her husband?

COMMENTATOR: I very much doubt it. The solution lies with the courts.

THE CHILDLESS COUPLE

FATHER: I want to see your children before I die. You know that your wife is barren and there is no hope for a cure. If there were any hope she would have given birth a long time ago.

SON: I do not understand you, father.

FATHER: I know you love your wife. But you should marry another wife.

SON: No. I couldn't hurt her.

FATHER: She wouldn't be hurt. All of us do that.

SON: I can't. I can't bring another woman to share her home.

FATHER: Who said they should share home? Put them each in separate homes. I'll pay all the expenses. What about Nasir's daughter? She is young, beautiful, wise. And don't forget that her father is my partner in our contracting business.

SON: No. Besides a matter of importance needs thinking about.

(*Wife looks miserable.*)

NURA: I am unable to give you a child. So why don't you get married so that you can have children?

SON: I have already married you. This is my fate. I accept it. How could I marry another woman?

NURA: I want you to be happy. You should have children to carry forward your name.

SON: Let's not discuss the matter any more. I don't want to talk about it further.

Romantic sequence as they watch children playing. Small child throws ball to the young husband, comes up and sits on his knee and cuddles him. They look gloomy.

At home.

NURA: Why don't you get married and have children?
YOUNG HUSBAND: (*Exasperated.*) Whenever I speak to you, all you ever say is get married, get married!
NURA: No, I mean it. What about your cousin? I know she loves you and longs to marry you.
HUSBAND: Whenever you say this I love you more and can't leave you or do without you.
NURA: Who said anything about doing without me? I want you to get married. There are men who married once, twice, three times. It's a law of life.

Wedding ceremony. The husband is marrying another woman. Both look pleased.

At home.

NURA: He married the girl I chose for him. To marry a cousin is natural. I was quite unaffected—until Badria became pregnant.

Husband comes in while the women are both doing the chores. The second wife is cooking.

HUSBAND: (*To Badria.*) No, don't do that. You must be tired. (*To Nura.*) She is tired today. Do you mind doing the cooking for her?
NURA: Willingly. If you say so.
BADRIA: I see that Nura is upset and pouting. The day I got pregnant she began to be jealous.
HUSBAND: I don't think she is jealous.
BADRIA: You are too good hearted. You don't know what she did

yesterday. She is so jealous that she left the soap on the ground in the bathroom for me to fall on.

HUSBAND: (*Angry. Wants to call Nura.*) I want to find out why she does things like that to you. She may have hurt you and your child.

BADRIA: We should be wiser than she is. Don't forget she is important to both of us. Why doesn't she go and stay with her father for some time? (*Nura comes in with a tray.*)

HUSBAND: Why don't you go and stay with your father for a few days.

NURA: Why?

HUSBAND: Just to have a rest, a change.

NURA: Whatever you say.

Later on.

BADRIA: (*To husband.*) Why are you so quiet?

HUSBAND: I am at a loss. I don't know what to do.

BADRIA: You must be sorry for Nura.

HUSBAND: I must ask her what she did to you.

BADRIA: You mean that you don't believe me? I can't live with a man who thinks I am a liar.

HUSBAND: What do you mean?

BADRIA: One of us only can stay in this house. Either she or me.

NURA: You stay, Badria. (*Asks husband to escort her to father's house.*)

At house. Nura gets out of car. Husband carries baggage. She asks him to divorce her.

HUSBAND: You want a divorce to get married to another man. Why divorce? You have everything you need. I don't know what to do. Because if Badria knows I come to you, she would stir up trouble. She might even leave the house. You don't want to deprive me of the child we have waited for, do you?

NURA: What sort of wife am I? I want to go my own way.

Commentary

The Commentator is a leading businessman.

COMMENTATOR: The young man yielded to massive persuasion from his father and Nura. Nura should not have insisted that her husband get remarried. Another point is that Nura's family did not participate in her decision. In my view it is normal for married sons and daughters to bring their families into important problems that arise. The husband was unfair because he believed Badria without trying to find out the truth. Besides which, it is a mistake to keep two wives in the same house.

PART SEVEN

Two Views of Arabs in the West

I. THE USUAL—WESTERNERS ON QATAR

The Football Coach

What brought me here was that the Minister of Education here, the late Sheikh Jassim, told the British Council, 'I want a British coach'. Because last March, March '75, was Qatar's turn to stage the fourth Gulf Games, and, of course, they wanted to do well. And he thought there was nothing like English football. He loved football. He spent some time in England watching English football, and he just wanted an English coach to take charge of his team. The British Council director then contacted the English Football Association and they asked me if I wanted to come out here, and I did. I arrived here in October 74.

Before I accepted the job, I had made it my business to try and contact one or two coaches that had been in this part of the world, and I asked them what the standard of football was like in comparison with England. They said it's a completely different game. Typical of the answers I got was—'You, Frank, have been connected all your life with professional football; out there in the Gulf they are amateur footballers, and this is one of the obstacles you have got to overcome'. But another answer I got from many people was,—'they are very charming people'. I have discovered they *are* very charming people. But I also realised when I arrived here that the football was of a very low standard. The kids could trap the ball, they could pass the ball, they could shoot the ball, they could head the ball, up to a certain level, but there was no tactical organisation or discipline on the field. I knew exactly the things that required to be done, but giving them the right priority was the main thing. When I first arrived, the team was involved in a world military games competition. I just had maybe thirty players and they said, 'There's your national team, you've got a match next week against Saudi Arabia, you've got a match in another ten days after that against Saudi Arabia.' The first match of course, was a disaster. You know, I had been given the team four or five days before, and I knew nothing at all about the opposition. They beat us five zero.

When we got beaten the boys were low—I was very low. When I arrived at my office the following morning, a guy I had never even spoken to before said, 'O, hullo, Frank—are you still employed here?' I felt they should be consoling me, saying 'Don't worry about it, it's your first game'. So I took a deep breath and I said, 'In two weeks time we'll have a return match in Riyadh, you just watch'.

In those two weeks we organised. When I announced the team, the day before the match, with all my strategies and plans worked out, I got this interference. I lay down in my bed the night before the match, and I was thinking 'Maybe they're right and maybe they're not right'—these people, who were interfering with my selection of the team. Then I said to myself 'You are the expert, Frank, that's what they are paying you to do'. So I said 'O blow the lot'. I just picked the team. We drew zero-zero, and we missed a penalty with the last kick of the match. We were the best team actually. And from then on, it's just snowballed. After that the boys started believing in themselves a little bit, because one of my jobs is to tell the players, whether I believe it or not, that they are good players. We try to build up their confidence—but not too much. These boys get enough praise. But there aren't enough people that tell them 'You had a bloody bad game'.

The boys start to play football at a very young age. They go to school till a very late age, they finish school at anything from nine-teen to twenty-five. They start school at maybe six-thirty in the morning and they finish at one o'clock in the afternoon, and then they come to practise football. This is true of the majority of my national team players. I've got a squad now of twenty-two players, and fourteen are schoolboys.

Getting the boys to come to practice regularly is a problem. You see we've got seven league clubs. The players are very loyal to their league clubs. They haven't had a national team long enough to feel anything very powerful about it. Then, too these clubs have very powerful people, very persuasive people, who say, 'If you come and play with my club, never mind about the national team, I'll give you this'. That sort of thing. But, we're winning.

They come regularly on time, because I found the best way to treat them was to ignore them, and they don't like being ignored, so they come. You know, if they come late to practice, I just leave them sitting on the grass—so the next time they say 'I'm sorry I was late, captain'. I say 'Get here at three o'clock and you can play football'. I joke with them, you know, If they say 'What time is practice tomorrow captain', I say 'Three o'clock English time'. They know that 'English time' means they've got to be on time.

I play here with the boys, and when it's hot—up to 150 degrees —we experience breathing difficulties. You never get anything in your legs but you get breathing difficulties. Most of the players train about four times a week, the best ones train every day, because there's not a lot they can do in the afternoons or evenings. And they are keen. They like playing football their own way. I might criticise them, I might call them names, I might swear at them, but on the match day those boys don't need telling from me 'Get to bed early, don't drink this, and don't have too much food'. They know what they've got to do, simply because we've taught them what to do. They abide by our rules. They are very sensitive. Whereas in Europe you can just yell at people, you've got to love these people a little more. I can yell at them and make it into a joke, it works sometimes, but most of the time—speak quietly and you get the best results. I think I saw this quite quickly. Going back to the first match again, the one against Saudi Arabia, the one where we got beat five zero, there was a young boy about seventeen years old, and he was having a terrible time. He was having a bad match but he was trying like bloody hell, you know, so I let him go on, and about half an hour from the end of the match I took him off and put someone else on. I think we were losing about three zero at this stage. I was sitting there and the boy came to me, and he knelt there in front of me, and wept. 'I am very, very sorry', he said, and there were tears running down his face, you know.

I still face one difficulty: the boys, if they know something, want to keep it to themselves. I find it hard, even after being here nearly two and a half years, to get the boys to open out, collectively. When I am there, I say 'What about this situation', and one of them will say, 'Well, I think this,' Then I'll catch two or three of them having a little chitchat and say 'Yes, have you got something to say about it?' They'll say 'Oh, no, no.' I'll say 'Come on, what were you talking about? Were you talking about what we were talking about over there?' and they'll say 'Yeah', and then within two or three minutes they're attacking each other like hell, you know. They can't compromise in their relations, they can't converse.

The Gulf Games was a tremendous success. We had an opening ceremony, which was the best thing I've ever seen in my life. First of all there was this new stadium that seated 45,000, and we had the opening ceremony. The schoolboys were doing flag displays, we had balloons going up in the air and exploding; gymnastics; a display from every country in the Games, Iraq, Kuwait, Bahrain, Saudi Arabia, Qatar, the Emirates and Oman. The opening ceremony lasted about four hours and was a tremendous success. I was sitting there watching these activities with my boys, and I thought, 'Well, you know, this is marvellous. We've got tomorrow, (the day after we were playing Saudi Arabia)—after all this we've got to win.' And we did win. One zero. So, from then on they thought they'd won the competition, not just the first match. We've eaten a few sheep since then. Sometimes we have a party, the sheikh'll say, 'Oh, you've played very well, give the boys a party'. We have a big spread of food and soft drinks, you know, a sheep on top of the rice. We played every country in turn. Actually we finished third behind Kuwait and Iraq. At the end of the league, Iraq and Kuwait had ten points each and Qatar had nine, and next after that I think was Bahrain which had about five. So it was a three-horse race, and I always say we finished second behind the joint leaders. We got the bronze medal.

Finance is one problem that you do not have in football here. If I wanted something and it was a reasonable request, for the benefit of the team, I will get it without a shadow of a doubt. And I can invite almost any team I want, and get them paid for. Last week we had Nancy Lorraine; we paid them £12,000 plus all expenses. League football in a small country like this is very important, because the national team depends on league players, we are limited a little as to how many international games we can play. So, apart from the competitions—we have the Asian Cup competition and there's the Military Cup competition, this next year there's the World Cup competition, and we have one or two other smaller competitions we participate in—we play maybe ten international matches a year. We work through the summer and we take the team away throughout the summer to Europe to give them a lot of experience. The players get rewards—watches, motor cars, money, from individuals connected with the various clubs.

I had a three-year contract when I first came here and I intended to leave after the three years. But now, I don't know. If they asked me to stay on with a better contract—I'd probably stay. My work's not finished here, by a long way. The team and myself have achieved a lot here together. The be-all and end-all of football in the Gulf is to win the Gulf Games. I'd like us to do that before I leave.

The Irishman

I remember the old *souk*. It was straw covered, now they've got a modern concrete *souk* with glass-fronted little shops. There's really no local craft. Everything they have here is imported. The only skills they had then were pearling and a little farming.

We were regarded with a certain amount of amusement and amazement by the locals. We came as technicians, bringing skilled techniques that were completely new and alien to them. We were the miracle workers—this is how it appeared to them. We found the Arabian Arab very polite and hospitable, a naive and simple person. Although they showed certain talents when it came to trading. I've been out in the desert with them. They are very unsophisticated people and laugh just like small boys. They will throw a pebble at their friends and hit them on the back of the head, or roll up bits of paper and toss them around, boyish things that you do in school. Of course they are very unsophisticated people. There's always been a language barrier—I can speak a fair amount of Arabic but it's not conversational Arabic.

At the Station we have a multi-national work force of Arabs, Indians, Pakistanis, Baluchis, Iranis. All the technical jargon that has developed in the course of our everyday operations is a mixture of all these languages, that we all speak between ourselves.

The first day I arrived here, I wondered what I had come to. There were no direct flights then from Britain and we had to go via Bahrain. We flew in from Bahrain in a De Haviland Heron, I think it had two engines. The planes coming from London at that time were DC 8's and Constellations and we used to stop at Frankfurt, Rome, Istanbul, Beirut. The journey took about nineteen hours. Of course, it was first class travel, which eased it a bit, we had larger, more comfortable seats. The airport then consisted of the tarmac and a couple of wooden buildings; there was no control tower. If there was anybody there to meet you they walked over to where the plane had come to a halt. There was little waiting. I believe there was a Customs officer down there; he put a chalk mark on your bag, that was all.

The community in Qatar then was very small, everybody knew each other. Going to the airport was a big occasion, everybody seemed to be there. We were always going to see somebody off or welcome somebody back. A friend would be met by about ten people, and then he'd invite us all back for a drink. Now it's becoming businesslike and commercialised. Everybody's becoming commercially motivated and more competitive. People are demanding their pound of flesh. Then it was the 'come day, go day, God send Sunday' attitude—as we say in Ireland. Now it's becoming like Europe.

There was a lot of party-going in the foreign community. There wasn't very much mixing of the communities. Of course, there was a certain amount of restriction because of the booze situation. You see, we had to get our booze from Bahrain, we didn't fly it in in those days. We had permits which lasted three months. It came in by *dhow*, and you could never be certain when it would arrive; for instance, adverse weather conditions could make the booze anything up to two months late. In winter time there were storms, rough seas. So we used to borrow booze from each other.

We used to get up to all sorts of childish wild pranks, probably out of boredom and frustration, and we kept to ourselves. One of the engineers was caught selling booze. It was a bit embarrassing for the community. The engineer and manager of the department called us all in and said 'It's a very sad day, to think that one of my engineers is in trouble for black-marketeering booze. Let nobody be under any illusion and claim that they aren't aware of the rules and regulations.' He then quoted a bit from one of those pamphlets you get from Her Majesty's Stationery Office, that it was forbidden to sell, trade, give booze in any shape or form to the locals, under penalty of six months imprisonment and a 3,000 rupee fine.

The sort of things we got up to! We all lived in identical houses in those days. If there was a party on at Shell Lodge, we would change everyone's furniture around. We'd do a complete change of furniture from one house to another. People would be very confused when they came home, especially if they'd had a few drinks.

I first came out here as a contractor to build this power station and it took about fifteen or sixteen months. I went back home with the intention of going out to Bermuda to do a similar job, but the Company said I'd got on well with the client, would I go back to Doha for another period? After coming out the second time, they said 'Would you like to take a job here for a few years?' as there was no-one else with my experience. So I said to my wife 'Come on'. I had been in the merchant service and had travelled before, and I told her it would be an opportunty to see around a little bit and get a bit of money. She came out here and she enjoyed it; she liked the people, liked the life. We had no school problems when the children started coming along. We used to go down to the beach. There were no hotels, no houses there then. Just up the road on the outskirts of town was the desert. Feriq Salata was only a small little place on the edge of the bay. Where the beach club is now and the Gulf Hotel, was just a great strip of virgin sand. None of the local population lived there. You could walk for miles along the beach. Where the sailing club now is, we used to put up a sheeting to give a bit of shade. And of course the leave was generous. We had two months' leave each year and it didn't cost us any more to stop off in the Middle East somewhere; we could stop off in Spain for a month or so, and then we'd go home and have a good time, spend our money. Then we had to come back here—we'd be skint! Or else we'd decide to sell the house we had and go for something better, now that we could afford it. Somebody said to me 'In twenty years time you'll still be here.' It seems so ridiculous. After all there's nothing in the place, why would anybody want to stay here? I don't know why I wanted to stay, whether I adopted the line of least resistance. I was, am, an easy person in that respect. I like the work that I'm doing, I have a lot of nice friends here, we have a lot of good times. I had knocked about quite a bit before that.

In those days, outside of working with the men, the work force, the whole of the government was run by expatriates. There was a British adviser here. He and his wife were great people. Everyone would be invited down to the advisorate. We'd have a couple of invitations down there to dinner and a couple of invitations to afternoon tea. These were known as Hancock's Half-Hour. There was also the State Engineer and a civil engineer, and in the government there were Europeans who were responsible for the allocation of houses. If we broke a teacup we just went down to the government furniture stores for a replacement.

I suppose things began to change in the 60s; it's hard to define. Things are changing, you are probably changing yourself, you are adapting and adjusting. I suppose when you spend a lot of time in a place you become emotionally involved with the country, with its development. There's always been a feeling of achievement. Very few people are actually in at the birth of a place, at the beginning. I've seen the place built, and pulled down, and built, and pulled down. You can see for yourself the terrible mistakes made because of lack of knowledge, lack of expertise. After all, they were then just starting a modern educational system, so at least eleven years had to pass for its effect to be felt. This modern educational system is completely the opposite of what they had before, education based on religious teaching. Now they have to be educated to go out into the modern, technically orientated world. So consequently the people who advised them on setting up the educational system had to allow a period to prove whether the system they had established was the right one. Taking 1955, or even 1950, as the starting point, it would be 1965 before the end-product of the system would come on to the labour market to start filling the role they had been trained for.

There is no work ethic here. I myself was born in 1924 and I can remember hard times. I knew how important it was to have a job. This seems to be the general consensus of opinion everywhere in the UK, that a person who was in work should be thankful. Also jobs weren't easy to come by in those days, so you had to look after your work. I remember when I was first working, we young fellers would be out playing football the evening before, and maybe going to a dance and fooling about half the night. We'd be heavy-headed the next morning. Our mothers would scream at us to 'get out of bed to go to work, otherwise you'll lose your job'. That doesn't happen here. There's no call for them to work. If they

feel hungry, they can just go in and sit at the sheikhs' table.
I think mention should be made of the part played in the building of this country by the Indians and the Pakistanis. After all,
they have been the work force and the builders of the towns. You
see the navvies, these fellows out on the streets working day after
day, even at the height of summer. They are Pathans from the
North-west frontier. They were the terror of the British Army.
They are ferocious, war-like and very proud and dignified people.
They have now—and this is a good thing—swapped their home-
made rifles for a pick and shovel. The Pathan is like the Irish
navvy was; you know how the Irish built the great American
railroads and one thing and another. They were the mainstay of
the workforce, hard, tough men, and the Pathans are the same.
You can see they are big, strapping, hard-working men.

There's something similar in the Irish and the Arab, you know.
We've both got this sort of wait-for-tomorrow attitude. Their
attitude is to relax and be at ease, though it may be a bit more
difficult for them in feminine than in masculine company. This
has been a male-orientated society. The women actually have a
tremendous amount of influence. The poor little woman isn't such
a docile little creature. I've heard them going off at quite a rate,
shouting and screaming; they can chase the old man completely
out of the house. I've seen it. Some of these Arabs are completely
dependent on their women. The women look after the children
and the home and the shopping, while their men are sitting around
in the *majlis* swopping yarns about falconing. The strength of the
woman's position here came as a surprise . . .

So did the position of the slaves. We'd been conditioned to
imagine a slave as somebody wearing a chain on his ankle, but
here it was just the opposite. The slaves were running round in
Cadillacs, flaunting great gold Rolex watches. The slaves were in
a privileged position in the households; they were more or less
responsible for the rearing and upbringing of the children, giving
personal supervision and protection. If you look at old Sheikh
Ali's Cadillacs up at the museum you will notice there are
chromium handles and runningboards where his bodyguards

used to stand on the side of the car. They had long flowing robes, crossed bandoliers and chromium-plated machineguns, and they were all slaves. They formed a special bodyguard, protecting the Ruler. I would say that the slaves were more arrogant and harder to live with than the ordinary people, because they were in a privileged position. The ordinary people here aren't arrogant. I like them. People are inclined to think of them all as Arabs, and they are lumped together with Palestinians, Egyptians, Syrians, Iraqis. But I'm talking about Arabians, and they're an entirely different type of Arab from the type you get in Port Said or Alexandria. They have a certain gentility, a certain simplicity. I always find them exceptionally generous, not avaricious or greedy. Probably it's part and parcel of their whole tradition. But you've got to be careful what you say to them because if you admire something, you'll probably find you have to take it when you go. They can be generous to a fault in this respect.

It used to be a regular thing at the Eids, at the end of Ramadan, to go visiting, to pay your salaams, to go *Eid Mubarak-ing*. The adviser's wife used to come and collect the ladies and they would go and visit the harems. This was a great occasion for the ladies. Our wives used to come home smelling like an old French whorehouse, drenched in scent. In some of the households it was literally Chanel No. 5 in gallon jars which was being splashed around. There'd be boxes of chocolates, boxes of sweetmeats and they'd be stinking to the high heavens of perfume, and they'd all complain of tummy ache for days afterwards. But they enjoyed it. Nowadays they don't go much anymore because the community has grown and the Arab women were being over-run by foreigners during Eid at one stage. So the visiting more or less stopped.

2. JUST FOR A CHANGE—WHAT QATARIS THINK OF THE WEST

The Officer at Sandhurst

Life at Sandhurst was odd. Every English cadet thought only of himself, never of other cadets. They treated us Arabs and other foreigners no differently from one of themselves; they respected nobody. They would pass you without saying 'Good morning' or 'Good evening'. They weren't even friendly to each other. But they understood each other; they knew each other's way.

For me it was different. I was brought up to be respectful and friendly to people, to make friends with them. But they didn't like this. On Saturdays I sometimes held a party in my room. Some- times they came and they said, 'You're crazy'. I was surprised. They said, 'Why are you wasting your money on this kind of thing?' I wanted to make friends, but they wouldn't be friends. They said, 'You must stand on your own feet'. I answered, 'Of course, I will stand on my own feet. But I also want to make friends with people as I do in my country.' But they only said, 'No, no. You're quite wrong. You should be spending your money for your own benefit, not on other people.' I got to the stage when I really wondered whether they might not be right.

Afterwards, after six months, I learnt their ways. I was as off- hand with them as they were with me. Sometimes I would simply pass someone by, pretending not to recognise them. When I saw them in Camberley—that was a town near Sandhurst—I just ignored them. I didn't like this, but I had to do it. They under- stand you better if you act like this, than if you are courteous to them. Believe me or not, this is the way it was at Sandhurst.

The course lasted for two years then, which was too long; it takes just six months now. I had friends from many other countries from Fiji, from Ghana. But in all that time the English never once invited me back to their houses.

Later they understood me better. At Sandhurst, you know, especially during exercises and things like that, you have to swear and be tough and rough. I didn't understand it, really. You can give an order and still be polite to people. It wasn't just the sergeant-majors who were rough like this, the other cadets were just as bad when it was their turn to be platoon commander. At the beginning I was civil. Not that you say 'please' in the army, no. I would simply say, 'Go there. Forward march. Move here.' But they would put it differently. 'Move, for God's sake!' I didn't think that was strictly necessary; I can move without being sworn at and screamed at. But in the end I just fell in with their way.

The officers training us were very good. They were chosen from different regiments so that only the best trained us. I learned a lot from them. After two years at Sandhurst I changed completely; my way of thinking was quite different.

But at the beginning I found it hard, very hard. The English cadets tried to force me out of the army; they really tried to make me leave Sandhurst. I don't know why—maybe because they thought I couldn't keep up with them. When I gave an order they laughed at my English amongst themselves. Sometimes I couldn't under-stand what was being said. The army has its own jargon—it takes time to know it. Then the whole way of life there was new to me. In those first three months everything was fast. They would give you about five minutes to finish your meal; you had virtually no sleep. You were always dirty—except at week-ends—because they never gave you time to wash. After three months, when you began the academic side of your training, you had more time. But in the first period, they taught you to be on your toes always. I lost my hair as a result: it all dropped out in the first fortnight. I was nervous and trying my best to hang on there.

There were so many difficulties. When you were given an exercise to do in your room, the English cadets would finish in two hours. But I had to translate it first into Arabic to make sure I understood the English, then I had to get to grips with the military language as well—all that used to take me six hours. In the mean-time, the others would be resting. At the beginning of the second year I caught up with the English. Sometimes I even beat them; sometimes I passed and they failed. I used to wonder about this

myself. I suppose it was because I was finally making headway
with my English.

But these first three months, my God! I had to drive myself,
force myself the whole time. I remember the first week I came to
Sandhurst. I had to learn the names of all the officers. The
English cadets learned faster than I did, of course, because the
names were English. But I had to *study* them! (*laughing*). I found
this very difficult. The senior cadet said to me, 'You are not to
sleep tonight. You must know all the names.' I studied very hard
and I forgot only one or two when he asked me them. He said,
'What's his name?' I said, 'I don't know'. He repeated the
question. I just stood. I couldn't say a word. Then I was able to
say: 'Do what you like, but I can't remember that name'. So he
said: 'OK. You can go to sleep now.' These senior cadets are
called 'the Government' because they rule the new cadets when
they come. My God, some of them are hard! There are some who
are helpful; but others, no, they drive you as hard as they can, no
matter what your nationality, whether foreign or English.

Our way of life here in Qatar—the way of life in Arab countries
generally—is completely different. When I went on a course to
Jordan, I found that people there were similar to people here: they
were keen to make friends, they held parties together, they helped
each other. If you needed something, somebody would come to
your aid at once. But in Sandhurst there was no help, no friendship. If someone passed while I was eating, drinking or smoking
in my room, I invited them to join me. It was automatic for me.
But when you went to their rooms, my God! They wouldn't even
say 'Hello' to you, or 'Good morning.' They didn't know such
words existed. Some of them put up a sign outside their room on
which was written: 'Go away'. Believe it or not: 'Go away!'

But, in the long run—as I said—Sandhurst taught me a lot. It
taught me leadership. There you are taught to make soldiers like
and respect you, not because you are an officer, no; but because you
are a good man. In Sandhurst the motto is: 'Serve to lead'. You
have to work in front of your men—you have to set the example in
everything.

When it comes to time and punctuality I think the British are the best in the world. Here in Qatar, a lesson starts one hour early sometimes, or one hour late: it means nothing. In my company, people have to come on time, exactly on time. I say to them, 'Time is very important. Suppose you are attacking and the artillery is two minutes late. The consequences could be serious. Two minutes could make all the difference.' We're OK on timing now. At the beginning I had to be tough with them to make them see it. In the end they got there because they know me and they know that what I tell them is right. Personally I don't believe in punishment. Of course, people are different. One man will respond to kindness, another you have to push a bit, the next you have to tell, 'For God's sake, will you pull your finger out!' Finally, there are some you just have to punish. Just as a last resort. They have to be discharged from the commandos and transferred to some other regiment. I have done this to about twenty of my men. I talked to them week after week and in the end I got fed up.

One of the English cadets I had known at Sandhurst came here two months ago. He was staying at the Gulf Hotel. He told friends of mine that he wanted to see me. I said I would think about it; I didn't like to say no. But I didn't go, because there was something about him that I remembered. We were in Germany and I was thirsty. It was really hot and I had no water with me. I asked him to give me just a drop of water. Believe it or not, he said 'No'.

Representative in U.S.

I have lived through two distinct periods in the United States: before 1973 and after 1973. After the 1973 Arab–Israeli war, everybody was talking about the Middle East. Before 1973 nobody knew what an Arab was—we were nothing. They really thought we lived in tents, that we didn't have cars and rode on camels. It was mainly the general public who thought like this: the businessmen who had visited the Middle East—Qatar, Bahrain, Egypt—

had a different idea. Because they have actually been here, they know we are a civilised people, have good hotels and so on.

Take American students, even they didn't know where Qatar is; they thought we were in Latin America, although some said Asia. The only country they knew in the area was Saudi Arabia because it has good relations with the States, because it is a large country, large enough for its name to be written on the map. They also had heard of Egypt and knew where it was.

New York is full of Puerto Ricans, Spanish etc. and when I first arrived they thought I was one of them. Sometimes they spoke Spanish to me. It was a big shock for me, this immense city where everything was fast, where people walk fast, eat fast, talk fast and nobody smiles and nobody welcomes you and nobody cares. To explain where Qatar is, where Bahrain is, was just too difficult. I thought the best thing was to say that I was from Saudi Arabia. What could I do?

Then the prejudices people had about Arabs created big problems for us. Take the movies. We saw in dozens of movies how Arabs—always in the olden days—chase after women, how they kill each other—in the Moroccan desert, collaborating with the French and the Americans against each other. We could never tell whether this was just prejudice or whether the Americans simply didn't know any better. There always seemed to be a bellydancer in a big tent, dancing and drinking, but never any-thing about Arab culture, except that they would sometimes show Arabs as brave and helpful to foreigners. Then they were always setting off the car against the camel—making the bedouin try to use a jeep as a great laugh. It annoys me because they don't know what they're talking about.

In the media, everything was dominated by politics and by Israel: 'Go to Israel, visit Israel for 800 dollars. Eat falafil, hum-mous.' They even claimed our food was Israeli food, though most Israelis came from Europe. Everything in Palestine changed to become Israeli. Nobody ever mentioned Palestine. I once saw a documentary on TV made entirely from the Israeli viewpoint: it showed Arabs killing Jews, but never the reverse.

All this was before 1973. Then came the October war. The day the war started, because New York is a Jewish city, all the media was entirely given over to the war. For three days we saw no movies, nothing but the war in the Middle East. For the first time I heard Qatar mentioned on TV. This was because they read all the telexes and telegrams connected with the war and with Arab countries.

After the war was over, we felt that they had started to know who is an Arab. They began to realise we could even use weapons. People began to speak of Arabs, discuss Arabs almost every day. As much as anything this was on account of the oil—when we started to use oil as a weapon. After the Arab oil embargo they saw that Arabs were a power in the world and since that time they have tried to find out about us. They tried to find out where Qatar was, where the Emirates were. We began to receive a pile of letters asking for information about Qatar. I remember we issued a book which nobody asked for in two years. But since that time we have had on average thirty letters a day. Lots of people want to go to Qatar. This is partly on account of unemployment, I think. Anyway we explain where and what Qatar is to them, who the Arabs are, it's a good opportunity. We have one man who is assigned to explain the position of Palestine. It's quite a surprise to them when they come to the Embassy and find that we speak English. We tell them about our free education, our free medicine and they ask, 'How come we don't have that?' When they inquire about the embargo we explain, 'This is our problem, our cause. We must help our brother Arabs.'

Can you imagine, we have had between one and two thousand letters from companies wanting to do business with us. They want to build houses, export cars. I once went to buy a car for the Embassy. 'Ah', said the man, 'you're the people with the oil. Now look, I've got seventy cars and I'll let you have them all with a good discount.' They think everybody here is rich. They ask me, 'Why do you work here? Why don't you have a business in Qatar?' —but I haven't. I want to do something for my country. Not every Qatari has a business.

During the embargo, we had a funny request: somebody trying to buy camels and to establish a company to do it. He was probably joking, but we're not sure because we get a lot of stupid questions.

In December 1976 when the OPEC conference was held in Doha we heard of Qatar from morning till night: Qatar on the radio; Qatar on TV, for three whole days, especially in New York. Now at least they know where it is.

We have 350 students in the US and they, too, are good ambassadors for their country. For instance when they have parties they call us to supply them with posters. During Eid they make a good meal, always lamb. They demonstrate Qatari dancing. Those Americans they invite often ask for *thaubs*, since they're more convenient than trousers. I took three or four back the last time for an American friend and his children. It makes us feel good when they want our national dress, because we feel that they like us.

Americans now generally know about the Middle East question and they want to know more. In the past there was more prejudice than interest, now it's the other way round and this is true even of Jews themselves—of those who want to do business with the Middle East at least! But these people want peace, and without a solution to the war there could well be a negative reaction. American businessmen want access to the Arabian market. America is business, and it is this fact that has so far turned the tables.

Student in England

If someone says to me, you're an Arab, I say, you're English: if they say, you're coloured, I say, you're pink. I don't take that kind of thing in. But one person can create a reputation for the rest. For example, I am a Qatari, right? They haven't seen any Qataris, they haven't seen any Arabs. If I make trouble at a dance then they assume that all Qataris are like that. I have met people who said, once they had got to know me, that they had never liked Arabs before, but now had a completely different idea of them; I had completely changed their mind.

While I was studying, I was sick and had to go to hospital for five months; it was my stomach and they couldn't find anything. I went in as a private patient because my Government pays. They look after you well. I was put in the Whitechapel Hospital but they couldn't get me a private room so they put me in a ward with six or eight people. I became friendly with them all. One day this man said to me, 'We're always talking and laughing and joking together.' And I said, 'Yes, why not? We're human. What's wrong with that?' He said, 'That's all very well, but if I were to tell you who I am, you might possibly not speak to me.' I said, 'Listen, you don't have to tell me. I know. But why is it that everybody thinks because I'm an Arab I'll kill a Jew if I meet him? That I'll refuse to speak to him?' He said: 'How did you know I was a Jew?' I said, 'We don't have anything against Jews personally. We're just against Israel—it's a political thing. I knew from the first day that you were a Jew. It doesn't make any difference to me.'

One day another boy came and sat by me. He said, 'I didn't know you were an Arab'. I said, 'What difference does that make? He said, 'I didn't want to stay here any longer because I had heard that Arabs catch Jews and kill them'. I said, 'Well, I knew you were a Jew, but did I do anything against you?' He said, 'No'. I said, 'Didn't I help you? You used to scream out at night, and I would come and help you out. I wouldn't do you any harm.' He said, 'Yes, sorry. I know. But when we see an Arab in the street we always keep away because they're dangerous.' It was really crazy.

Suppose I say to you, 'Do you know any Indians? What do you think of them?' You say, 'I've never met any.' If I then say, 'They make trouble, they're really bad. They're nice to you on the surface, but they speak about you behind your back,' you might possibly believe me—until you met some Indians. Then you would see that they were different and that what I said was wrong.

Old Man

I shall talk about our attitude to the West and the West's attitude to us. The Englishmen who came to Bahrain a century ago and took on the responsibility of protecting the sea, were very intelligent, farsighted, perceptive and realistic. Those who came fifty or so years ago were not up to the level of their predecessors. Nowadays, they are avaricious and look down on us. They envy us for our wealth and regard us as illiterates.

When oil was first discovered in this region, they should have cast off the mantle of greed and shown wisdom. They could have come to an agreement with us which guaranteed the interest of all, thereby doing themselves a good service. And everyone would be happy. There would be no need for threats and wars. But as the saying goes, 'Whoever wants something will want his whole dream'.

This is my opinion. The West could have put Israel aside. Israel is an obstacle between the Arabs and the West. The West gets no benefit from Israel. But the West, especially the Americans, created Israel so as to gain a foothold in the East and dominate it. If the East and West come to an agreement, it's God's will. When the Americans and the French sent their armies to Korea and Vietnam they undermined their moral and political argument. Korea will unite in any case in the future, either through peace or war.

We see the West as an advanced area which developed and exploited science. God has endowed the West with capability and strong will. They created a new world. They developed industries and invented planes, telephones, electricity, and so on. We established ourselves on the knowledge we got from the West. One cannot deny its contribution. Equally, the West admits that its civilisation was influenced by Arab culture. But the Arabs missed quite a lot because they neglected their own culture and relied mainly on Western culture. In the past the West learnt from the East. Now there is nothing the West can learn from us.

If Qatar were to adopt Western culture, I don't think it would be a good thing. Its culture must remain essentially Arab. Ideally it should be a mixture of what is best in the West and what is best in Arab culture. I would like us to preserve those Arab customs which do not clash with Islam. They should follow the teachings of the Koran. God says in the Koran, 'Everything is in the Book.' God says in the *Chapter of the Bees*, 'The horse, the mules and the donkeys are useful and they are also ornaments.' And he also says, 'And He creates what you do not know.' The Koran did not leave out anything. The Koran did not say, 'He created tanks, cars, airplanes and cables.' God did not say that because time was not yet ripe to produce such things. God was wise.

I don't like to see women going around without a veil. A woman's place is in the home. This does not mean she shouldn't go out to work. In the past women went to *Jihad* (Holy War) with the Companions of the Prophet. They took care of the wounded and buried the dead. There is no reason why women should not become doctors and work in hospitals; they can also work in business (buying and selling). Khadija, the wife of the Prophet, was a merchant.

In Europe, a man picks up a woman and goes to bed with her. In Europe couples walk about holding hands. If these Europeans are married then it's alright. If they are not, then it's disgusting. Married people can have all the fun they want in private, so there is no need for them to show affection in public.

What I also dislike is that everyone in Europe has a dog. Some women walk about with dogs as big as donkeys. Only twenty per cent of women don't go around with dogs. I don't know what makes them keep dogs. Dogs make their clothes dirty and every⁄thing else dirty. According to our tradition we must wash our hands seven times, if we touch a dog. First we wash with soil and then with water. If a dog eats from a bowl, the bowl must be washed seven times. The Prophet forbade us to eat pork and touch dogs. The other day, in Austria, an old woman came to us with a dog. I asked her why she kept that dog, and she told me that all her sons were killed in the war, so the dog had taken their place. I saw a dog in a hospital in Vienna. One of the children went to the bathroom and forgot a slipper there; the dog brought back the slipper. There is here an old blind woman who has a dog. It's alright to buy such useful dogs and also hounds for hunting. But those dogs who are as big as donkeys and eat a kilo of meat a day are obviously useless.

The first difficulty I had in Europe was when I went to Vienna during Ramadan. As Muslims, we have to fast until sundown and days are long there. I fasted only for nine days, then I broke the fast. It was too much for me: I'm seventy-five. Psychologically this was the most difficult thing I had to face. In all my life I had never broken the fast unless I was sick or travelling. In Europe people are honest. In shops they tell you which bread and fruit are fresh. If you don't speak their language and you give them a handful of coins, they only take what is due to them.

I like Western culture, their buildings and their electronic brains. I also like telephones, cables, radios and televisions. What they have created is fascinating. When you go to see somebody you press a button on the door. This button works with electricity; it takes a mind to invent it and make it work. But their ethics are peculiar.

Glossary

abbaya	thin black covering worn by women over their dresses
Alhamdillah	Thanks be to God
batula	beak-shaped face mask worn by Gulf women
bedu	wandering nomad of the Arabian desert
dhow	boat
diwan	reception room
egal	headdress worn by Arabian Arabs
Eid	religious feast
gheiss	diver's assistant who pulled him out of the water
Hadith	Muslim religious traditions said to originate from the Prophet
Haj	pilgrimage
Inshallah	If God wills
nokhatha	sea-captain
majlis	reception room (or receiving guests)
qadi	judge
Ramadan	the month of fasting, like Lent
riyal	local unit of currency. Present rate of exchange is between 5 and 6 to the £ sterling
seib	pearl diver
souk	market
tawash	small-scale pearl trader
thaub	long white dress worn only by Arabian Arabs

Index